Trevor F Vidic
1999

THE
URBAN
NATURALIST

Steven D. Garber

Illustrations by Jerome Lo

D1244964

DOVER PUBLICATIONS, INC.
Mineola, New York

Bibliographical Note

This Dover edition, first published in 1998, is a corrected, unabridged republication of the work originally published in 1987 by John Wiley & Sons, Inc., New York.

Library of Congress Cataloging-in-Publication Data

Garber, Steven D.
    The urban naturalist / Steven D. Garber ; illustrations by Jerome Lo.
        p.   cm.
    Originally published: New York : Wiley, 1987, in series: The Wiley science editions.
    Includes index.
    ISBN 0-486-40399-8 (pbk.)
    1. Urban ecology (Biology)   I. Title.
QH541.5.C6G37   1998
577.5'6—dc21   98-23990
                                                                              CIP

Manufactured in the United States of America
Dover Publications, Inc., 31 East 2nd Street, Mineola, N.Y. 11501

To Mom,
Pop's little boy

FOREWORD

Green spaces, trees, and places to walk around, drive by, and enjoy add pleasure to urban life. The highest level of commitment must be expended to maintain our natural areas because they are among our most valuable resources. Through parks we are able to learn about and respect the animals and plants that have every right to live alongside us. The learning that goes on in the parks is wonderful. We need to encourage all age groups to come and enjoy. Bird watching, plant identification, fishing (where permitted), learning about wild edibles (look but don't bite)—all are vital to the urban dweller. It is easy to lose sight of the larger picture when we become involved in our everyday activities. Cities have culture and excitement, but they also need nature. Our souls, too, need nourishment.

As commissioner of the New York City Department of Parks and Recreation, I oversee thousands of acres of natural habitat in the largest city in North America. My work has given me an opportunity to be a man for all species, to do things that will have a major, long-lasting, positive effect on our environment, that will benefit millions of people and even more plants and animals. Preserving and improving our wild areas in New York City will provide an uplift for all of us.

We've been neglecting the outdoor aspects of our sustenance. Enjoying fresh air and beautiful vistas, listening to the birds and feeling the breeze, watching the butterflies and appreciating the caterpillars—we should teach these pleasures to our children. Without nature we are deprived—and New Yorkers don't like being deprived of anything.

Reading this book provides an exciting and enjoyable experience. Steven Garber opens a window through which we can see our urban and suburban environments more clearly. He writes about the squirrels and the *Ailanthus* trees that we know so well, but he also discusses many less familiar species. In *The Urban Naturalist*, Garber reveals the landscape as a series of wildlife habitats, just as someone from another region might discuss the rain forests, grasslands, and tundra. He shows us that cities teem with plant and animal life and that new species continue to settle in our rich urban communities. If we can learn to understand, protect, and preserve what we already have, the benefits will fall to us. This book is an essential guide to the sources of those benefits.

Henry J. Stern
Commissioner, New York City
Department of Parks and Recreation

PREFACE

After years spent conducting biological research on remote islands, isolated mountaintops, and pristine forests, I returned to my home city and discovered that the urban environment, as an ecosystem with all its species and habitats, is every bit as interesting as any I had studied in the South Pacific or South America.

I found urban and suburban areas more compelling than I had imagined. Everything was new. The plant communities had never been carefully looked at, let alone studied scientifically. Most people thought that the urban animal communities comprised only rats, roaches, and pigeons. But many species live in cities, including some animals introduced from other regions of the world.

Why do these organisms live in cities? How did they get there? When were they introduced? Why do some species live in cities and suburbs while others do not? I needed to know the answers, and as I found them, I discovered a much more fascinating city environment in which to live.

But I found few readily available sources of information. Field guides for identifying organisms do not deal specifically with the urban environment. *The Urban Naturalist* is intended to fill the gap, to be informative and useful, to help identify species, and to provide background and ideas about each reader's urban habitat.

Steven D. Garber
New York City

ACKNOWLEDGMENTS

Many thanks go to Julie Cooper and David Sobel, who both made this project possible and enjoyable, and were supportive every step of the way. Susan Schwartz also helped significantly. Concerning nomenclatural anomalies as well as natural history notes, David Künstler was helpful throughout. John and Carin Winer greatly enhanced the value of my trip to the West Coast. And it was through Marion Winer that I met Claire Kire, who put me in touch with Jerome Lo, whose talent and demeanor made our collaboration pleasurable. Jen Kuo was a great help in that effort.

The particulars concerning getting bitten by poisonous spiders, and the relevant treatments, as well as other medical and biological insights were provided by Dr. John Scherr, a physician in Atlanta, Georgia. Rabbi Carol Glass elucidated early Hebrew and Aramaic writings with regard to the domestic cat, and Robert Musco and Pam Glassock's bedbug anecdotes helped enormously.

Gregory Pregill, the Curator of Herpetology at the San Diego Natural History Museum, shared his field observations about the African clawed frog and southern California lizards. Another colleague, Julian C. Lee, who is a professor at the University of Miami, in Miami, Florida, explained some of the subtler innuendos concerning southern Florida's introduced herpetofauna.

Information about marine turtles was graciously provided by Sam Sadove and Judy Raab of Okeanos Ocean Research Foundation. Matthew Lerman, the author of *Marine Biology*, supplied data about sea turtles that had washed up along the western end of Long Island, and Michael Klemens clarified a systematic question. Felippe De Jesus and Santa Alequin translated Spanish conversations and tracked down beekeepers.

Steve Brill was a constant source of wildmania, and Evelyn Dean provided much of his food for thought. I also greatly appreciated the advice of Dr. Edith Robbins and Dr. Lawrence Crockett, both of the City University of New York. Herbert Setlow, Carolyn Setlow, and Marcie Setlow were helpful as well.

Talking with Larry vanDruff of the New York State College of Environmental Science and Forestry at Syracuse University about his research with squirrels was extremely beneficial. And thanks also go to Charles Matson, who took the time to explain many of the nuances about dragonflies. A conversation about cicadas with Kathy Williams of the University of Arkansas was pertinent, and Ona Ryan of the City Health Commissioner's office in Danville, Illinois, answered questions about the crows in her city. James Quinn and Ted Stiles of Rutgers University offered their keen insights.

C. Lavett Smith, Sarfraz Lodhi, and Charles Griswold of the American Museum of Natural History helped verify and clarify nomenclatural difficulties. Marya Dalrymple was able to provide a photograph with a date showing an American kestrel eating a house sparrow on a Manhattan rooftop. Regarding Shakespeare, Chuck Boyce provided chapter and verse.

Richard Pouyat, Deputy Director of Technical Information for the Natural Resources Group of New York City's Department of Parks and Recreation, verified and corroborated material throughout the book. Ed Gill, John Feeley, Namshin Yoon, Josephine Scalia, Carol Davidson, Tom Pillar, Ralph Acompore, Julie Dorniak, Craig McKee, and Fred Lulka were all helpful in the field, as were Ethan Carr, Glen Nissan, Anne Farkas, and Susan Gottlieb. And Gordon Helman always did things few could ever think of.

Bob Cook, Clive Pinnock, Mary Hake, Don Riepe, John Tanacredi, and Bruce Lane, who are all with the National Park Service, provided data and background information. Hilary Lambert Renwick, previously with Rutgers University, the Center for Coastal and Environmental Studies, and the National Park Service, and now with Miami University in Oxford, Ohio, was exceptionally helpful.

I'd like to thank Bill Griner, who has few rivals botanically, and the Street Tree Consortium's Marianne Holden, who sent me a useful book. My thanks also go to Adam Brill, Casey French Alexander, and Wendy Grossman, as well as to Jennie Tichenor of the Radioactive Waste Campaign and Terry Keller of the Green Guerillas, along with Mary Leou and Peter Hearn of the Inwood Parks Alliance.

Comments concerning the care of street trees and related information from Geraldine Weinstein and Gregory Portley were appreciated. Donald Bruning, the Curator of Ornithology at the New York Zoological Society, offered his advice concerning urban crows. And John Behler, the Curator of Herpetology at the New York Zoological Society, explained a positive role that certain urban species provide. Jackie Brown and Dorothy Lewandowsky were both helpful, too.

Robert Timm, the Curator of Mammalogy at the University of Kansas Museum of Natural History, provided valuable comments on Old and New World rats and mice. And special thanks go to Lisa Joy Taranto for her synesthetics and syntactics.

Henry Stern, the Commissioner of the New York City Department of Parks and Recreation, Matthew Sanderson, Michael Feller, Sue Sisinni, Pamela Robbins, Therese Braddick, as well as Gary Zarr, Adrian Benepe, Fran Chan, Marianne O'Hea, and Elizabeth Crane were all good parkies. When it came to forestry, horticulture, and landscape architecture, Frank Serpe, Tony Emmerich, Harry Muller, and Vicki Moeser, the librarian at the Horticultural Society of New York, all had comments that added to the substance of this book.

Ruth Greif and Andrew Hoffer, of John Wiley & Sons, and Claire McKean and Joanne Davidson of G&H SOHO managed much of the production of this book, while Dawn Reitz helped with some of the logistical aspects.

Joanna Burger of Rutgers University was supportive throughout the entire project. Conversations with Lawrence Garber were always a source of new ideas, and Marcy Garber showed me the parks in Philadelphia, for which I am much obliged.

CONTENTS

INTRODUCTION

The Urban Naturalist discusses the most rapidly growing habitat in the world: the city. Urban ecosystems, new and expanding, are affecting the entire globe. What species live in cities and suburbs? Why are they there? How did they get there? Why are they able to do well despite the many obstacles that exclude other species?

Urban and suburban areas are biologically far more complex than most people realize. It is not only humans and a few related pets and pests that live in these densely populated regions.

The Urban Naturalist, after discussing the major transformations and colonizations of species that moved from sea to land, then inhabited all the major habitats of the world, will also consider the equally historic process that is occurring now.

Between 1985 and the year 2000, the world's population is expected by the United States Census Bureau to increase 27 percent, rising from 4.9 to 6.2 billion people. During that fifteen-year period, the number of cities with more than 2 million people will double to 170; nearly half the world's population will be living in urban areas.

Much current literature dwells on the negative aspects of human population growth, the destruction of habitat, and the extinction of species. In addition, scientists are monitoring nitrous oxide, sulfur dioxide, carbon dioxide, chlorofluorocarbons, methane, and ozone concentrations in the atmosphere. They are also studying acid rain, the greenhouse effect that is altering the earth's temperature, and the rise in sea level.

True, humans are affecting the world and are currently the cause of what may be one of the most dramatic, rapid transitions the earth's biota has ever endured. On a geologic time scale this period, from when humans began to markedly affect the earth until things eventually stabilize, will be categorized by changes as monumental as those that led to the extinction of the dinosaurs 65 million years ago.

In the meantime not all is negative, bleak, and dreary. While the tropical rain forests are being cut up into plywood and paneling, and while more species each day become extinct than used to become extinct in an entire year, we're finding that the rapid growth and development of our urban centers is having some positive impact. Although priceless habitat is being destroyed forever, habitat is also being produced. Nearly 60 percent of most urban areas could be classified as forest, according to Forest Service Unit Leader Rowan Rowntree. Richard Pouyat, the Deputy Director of Technical Services for the Natural Resources Group of New York City's Department of Parks and Recreation, estimates that 25 percent of New York City is parkland, much of it covered with trees, not counting the suburban trees in the residential areas and the 600,000 street trees, all within the 300 square miles that make up New York City. This adds up to a formidable tree cover. And most cities are far less built up than New York.

I am not saying that the new urban habitats are in any way equivalent to those being lost through logging, agriculture, erosion, and construction. However, although urban forests may not have the same qualities as more natural oak-hickory or beech-maple forests, by most standards, the species diversity and the quality of such urban habitats are astonishing. And urban habitats include far more than forests. The meadows normally associated with wild areas outside the city are not abundant in urban regions, but between the lawns, vacant lots, areas of landfill, and waste areas, there are thousands of urban acres that harbor wild communities.

These communities are still undergoing rapid change. James Bissell, the Curator of Botany at the Cleveland Museum of Natural History, states that there are already over 400 species of plants that have been identified in the inner city region of Cleveland, Ohio. In other cities where trains, trucks, boats, and planes continually carry in new cargoes, many inadvertent stowaways are establishing a foothold in new urban homes.

Cities are difficult places in which to identify species because it isn't always immediately apparent where the species came from or when they arrived. Grains, fruits, flowers, and vegetables flown in from all over the world arrive with a host of seeds and invertebrates from their native countries; eventually some of these species find the right conditions and establish urban colonies, either inside or outside.

We tend to think of wild areas as outside, but we have created so many stable environments indoors that these inside habitats now constitute a major area that species can colonize. Tropical plants and insects that otherwise could never extend their ranges into temperate regions are doing fine in people's homes, apartments, building lobbies, and corporate offices. Anyone who cares for these plants knows how many insects live on indoor plants and how their populations spread from one indoor region to another.

The warmer American ports are proving to be ideal havens for an ever-increasing number of new or exotic species. In these "boom towns," satellite populations are established that spread the range of these new plants and animals. People who live in or near an American city and who have an interest in observing something new or in studying something original are in the right place.

It's often at the expense of native species that introduced species thrive in this country. Our cities are living laboratories where anyone can become an urban naturalist par excellence. Processes similar to those that occurred eons ago when other habitats were initially opened up to colonization can be observed in cities. Waves of new species are spreading constantly through our densely populated urban habitats. We meet most of these colonizations complacently, though from time to time we try to fight some new pest or disease or aggressive invasive species that challenges our sensibilities.

Consider how much money is spent each year trying to fight dandelions, chickweed, Dutch elm disease, and gypsy moths. And who would have guessed how many common species, such as the house sparrow, pigeon, and starling, the cockroach, cricket, yellow jacket, and honey bee, are all imports, brought here within the past several hundred years? Even the stories of fish in city ponds are interesting—how they colonized and have survived in such seemingly polluted waters. There are intriguing stories behind every species in the city's environment.

Urban ecosystems, with their unique plant and animal communities, will be described in the chapters that follow. Included among chapter topics will be grasses and wildflowers, trees, insects and other invertebrates, fish, amphibians, reptiles, birds, and mammals. *The Urban Naturalist* is designed to help everyone view the urban landscape and its inhabitants as part of a vital, busy, intense, yet natural habitat.

1

URBAN ECOSYSTEMS

Just as oceans and forests and prairies are natural systems, cities and suburbs are also natural. While oceans have had hundreds of millions of years to evolve a network of interacting organisms, humans are relatively new to the planet. Cities are even more recent, the oldest having developed only about 5,000 years ago. We city inhabitants are animals who affect our surroundings in a natural manner, like any other creature. Other species have transformed the parts of the world in which they lived, but we have made by far the greatest impact.

When plants first moved from water and colonized the land, when the first vertebrates moved out of water and inhabited terrestrial environments, and when vertebrates evolved the capacity to lay shelled eggs on land, each innovation caused a major, irreversible revolution that transformed the world. The most recent transformation has resulted from the rapid growth of cities and suburbs, with entire regions greatly affected by humans.

Urban ecosystems are still in an early stage of development. For years our cities have been, and still are, built with only human needs in mind. Yet everywhere we go, we bring a similar set of variables, create a similar environment, plant the same trees, attract the same insects and rodents, and have many of the same birds. We take much of this for granted, without realizing that many of the species that live with us have not always been here. Starlings and house sparrows, for example, are abundant in every city in America, but they have been on this continent for only about 100 years.

New species continually move in, gain a foothold, and add to the diversity and complexity of the urban landscape. It is too early to predict with certainty which species will eventually adapt to, and thrive in, these new settings, but educated projections can be made. Opportunities exist for certain species in urban environments that do not exist in rural environments. Cities offer food sources, places to live, wide open spaces, species to parasitize, species to prey upon, trees to nest in, buildings to roost on, warm evening skies to catch insects in, warm polluted waters to seek refuge in, rich effluents that support aquatic ecosystems, under-ground sewers to breed in, and cavernous subway tunnels and hundreds of thousands of miles of pipes to move about in.

Cities have their own variables: buildings, pavement, scattered green areas, street trees, gardens, and house plants. These affect the ecosystem, as do the thousands of people who walk in the parks and compact the soil, making it difficult for rains to be absorbed, creating problems with runoff and erosion. Nutrients that flow into low areas and collect in city ponds feed the plankton and the algae so the water clarity decreases and blocks out sunlight. The plants die, fall to the bottom, and rot. The bacteria, while consuming the dead plants, also consume the oxygen, creating a deficit that is difficult for gill-breathing animals to tolerate. As a result, city ponds are generally inhabited only by species adapted to living in such an extreme environment. These aquatic ecosystems may exhibit less species diversity, that is, contain fewer numbers of species, than similar areas found outside the cities, but that's because it takes years for those species that can live in these new, isolated, metropolitan islands to arrive and become established. More often than not, they are brought here, sometimes unintentionally.

When natural areas are cleared to establish an urban landscape, most of the woodland, grassland, or desert species that once lived there will be unable to adapt to the changed environment. They must leave or die. Only a few remain and survive. One survivor may be the cicada. Years after a city has been built up in what was once a woodland, we still find cicadas each summer. These cicadas are probably descendants of popula-tions that lived there before the city was built. Their numbers may have diminished, but in some urban parks you'd never know it. In other parks, however, where the trees have been cut and the ground has been paved, the cicadas haven't had a chance.

Many populations of species continue to survive in cities after their natural environment has been radically altered. Some may even benefit from the changes because of reduced competition from other species. Painted turtles and snapping turtles survive in many freshwater environ-ments, sometimes even in brackish water, after other turtles are long gone. Pumpkinseeds and bluegills—two species of freshwater fish—actually experience population explosions after their habitat becomes urbanized. Some pioneer tree species, those that move into open areas, thrive in vacant lots after an area has been cleared. They would have

Cicada on empty nymphal sac

been significantly less numerous if the city had not been built because they do poorly among stands of mature trees. And many species of roadside plants, which never had roadsides to grow along before the people moved in, experience windfall increases in new places to live. Many of these plants thrive on alkaline soils, which are relatively scarce in the wild, while some are among the more successful species in cities because of the lime that leaches from the concrete, affecting the surrounding soil.

Other opportunities exist for species that can move in from surrounding areas and exploit the changed environment. For instance, chimney swifts and barn swallows, which nest in hollow trees, will sometimes nest in man-made structures instead. Because there are many more buildings than there ever were hollow trees, these species may actually increase in numbers as an area becomes more urban.

The changed microclimate of cities also affects plants and animals. Most cities are warmer than the surrounding regions because tar, concrete, and stone absorb heat and then slowly radiate that heat when the temperature drops. This allows some species to flower earlier, lay their eggs earlier, or store more food during the summer, changes so significant that some will do markedly better in cities than in the country. Other species will extend their ranges, moving from one city to another.

During recent years several southern birds and mammals, such as armadillos, opossums, mockingbirds, and cardinals, have been extending their ranges north in this way. The reasons aren't always clear, but the range extensions are well documented. Other species moved from the Great Plains into regions where forests have been logged. These include loggerhead shrikes, brown-headed cowbirds, cliff swallows, and dickcissels.

Some species accompany people wherever they go, arriving in a region once it has been greatly affected by humans. People bring along their pets such as dogs and cats, while many other species are brought along inadvertently, such as the book lice that live in old books and the silverfish and roaches that live in human dwellings. And of course rats and mice live in just about every city. Other species that commonly accompany people are the beetles that live in our stored grain, and the plants that have escaped from our gardens. Some insects from other countries come in on fruits and vegetables. Worms, centipedes, and millipedes may arrive in imported flowerpots. New species are constantly arriving; occasionally an alien becomes established in its new environment.

Some of these new species are seldom noticed; others become a tremendous problem. If a species has few competitors and predators, its numbers may increase dangerously. Or a plant disease may run rampant in a new area. For example, a disease that attacks chestnut trees did little damage in Europe where the trees had built up a resistance. When the disease traveled to the United States where the trees had no resistance, most of our chestnuts were dead in a matter of decades. A disease that attacks elms also managed to hop a ride to North America. It infected American elms, a favorite urban tree, and we lost hundreds of thousands of beautiful, mature trees.

American elm

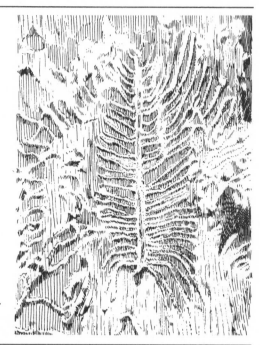

Pattern left from hatched-out elm bark beetle larvae, from under the bark

If a crate of parakeets breaks when being unloaded at an airport, all the birds may fly off, soon to become established in the surrounding region. Or rabbits from the West may escape and settle in the East. Fish may be released and survive in local waters. These things tend to happen with greater frequency in places where many people live; as a result, new species are introduced into urban areas all the time. Over the years, many of the same species repeatedly colonize other cities; thus urban ecosystems around the world slowly increase in complexity while their floras and faunas survive and even flourish.

In recent years, some cities and countries have begun to try to reverse the degradation of the urban environment. People are trying to clean the air and the water, create parks and improve those already in place, plant trees, and maintain green patches. It is possible to utilize natural processes and ecological principles to revitalize degraded habitats. Intervention can take the form of attracting, introducing, or re-introducing specific species that can add to the quality of an urban environment. More effort needs to be expended to make our cities more livable, for us as well as for other organisms. One way or another, species are going to move in and live by our sides. We can make it easier for them to survive and flourish, and in doing so, we will create a better environment for ourselves.

2

GRASSES AND WILDFLOWERS

Plants include fungi, algae, grasses, sedges, rushes, forbs, vines, shrubs, and trees. Since a full discussion of all plant forms that appear in cities would fill several volumes, I will deal only with those species of grasses, wildflowers, and trees that are very well represented in U.S. cities. In this chapter I'll discuss the most frequently seen urban grasses first, then talk about some important wildflowers in more detail. Trees are the subject of Chapter 3.

GRASSES

Of the 250,000 species of plants, over 10,000 are grasses. They include many of the economically most important plants. Species such as barley (*Hordeum vulgare*), bamboo (*Bambusa* spp., *Dendrocalamus* spp., and allied genera), corn (*Zea mays*), millet (*Setaria italica*), oats (*Avena sativa*), rice (*Oryza sativa*), rye (*Secale cereale*), sorghum (*Sorghum vulgare*), sugarcane (*Saccharum officinarum*), and wheat (*Triticum* spp.) are some of the most useful plants in the world. Once some 42 percent of the land area of the earth used to be grasses, that has now declined to about 25 percent. Grasses grow well in rich soils, but many species will thrive in less favorable locations. Some, in fact, flourish along roadsides or grow in the cracks in sidewalks and in other urban places where nothing else will grow.

Most of the prairie in much of the Midwest was once covered with grasses, legumes (plants in the pea family, Leguminosae), and forbs (flowering plants that aren't grasses, aren't grasslike, and aren't woody). In the East, the colonists cleared the forests and planted English grasses to feed their cattle, species such as timothy (*Phleum pratense*), a coarse grass with cylindrical spikes; Kentucky bluegrass (*Poa pratensis*); and fescue (*Festuca* spp.). These grasses still grow in cultivated hay meadows, but are a diminishing part of our landscape. When the settlers moved farther west, clearing the forest as they went, western prairie grasses and other associated species moved east, taking advantage of the new open habitat. In the East, where many of the meadows have been left un-mowed and where no cattle graze, the species composition seems to favor, along with many of the wildflowers, some of the coarser grasses, such as the little bluestem (*Andropogon scoparius*). The next step for these old fields would be the invasion of woody plants, but this can be averted by having controlled burns. The dried grass readily burns off, hardly singeing the soil, leaving the extensive root systems unharmed. The bark of the woody species burns, destroying the cambium layer or exposing it to insects and pathogens that kill the trees, allowing the grasses to grow back even more vigorously afterward.

In suburban areas, by far the most widespread grassland is the lawn. Left alone, lawns would become meadows, but social pressure keeps them carefully manicured. The social mores are sufficiently powerful to stimulate homeowners to spend more time, energy, and expense main-taining their lawns than it takes to maintain equal areas of corn or tobacco. The total acreage of American lawns amounts to 20 million acres, almost 2 percent of the entire country. In each part of the country these weed-free lawns usually harbor at least another 30 species of plants and 100 species of insects. As many as 10 to 15 species of birds often inhabit these communities, as well as several associated species of mam-mals. The importance of these habitats should not be underestimated.

Another grassland found near many coastal urban areas is the salt marsh. Only about one-half of America's original salt marshes survive. The others have been filled in and used for other purposes. However, the existing marshes are now recognized for their major ecological contribu-tions, and many of them are protected by law. Of course, developers will often try to circumvent the laws, but with the recent proliferation of grass-roots environmental organizations, it usually takes a consider-able fight to overtly destroy a salt marsh today. Many developers have learned that the occasional victory is rarely worth the expense and bad publicity.

The lush green salt marshes are flooded twice each day with the incoming tides. The salt-tolerant species of cordgrass in the genus *Spartina* tend to dominate these habitats.

Another well-known grass is *Phragmites*, the common reed, which is often found along the drier edges of the salt marshes. Until recently called *Phragmites communis* but now called *Phragmites australis*, this species is found around the world, in temperate climates. It grows in a wide range of habitats and is very much on the increase in urban environments. These reeds create a thick, tall mass of growth along the edges of marshes, especially those that have been disturbed. They often reach 6 to 9 feet (2 to 3 m) in height, creating a dense barrier that looks like a fence, which is what the Greek word *phragma* means.

Because this plant rapidly invades disturbed areas, doing especially well in low, wet regions, it finds many opportunities for growth in cities and suburbs, where the land is often disturbed. *Phragmites* moves in and outcompetes the other vegetation, creating what appears to be a monoculture, or a stand of just one species. Actually if you walk through a stand of *Phragmites* and carefully evaluate its value in terms of other species living there, you will find that the *Phragmites* may radically alter a habitat once it has moved in, but it doesn't totally destroy the habitat.

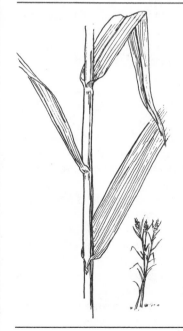

Phragmites

And in cities, where disturbed areas are often replaced by meadows of *Phragmites*, the beauty is unassailable. The cover for birds and other species is also valuable, and these meadows are better than no meadows. This species is not everyone's favorite. Some people consider *Phragmites* opportunistic, aggressive, invasive, and impossible to get rid of. But the grass is to be commended for its ability to move in and take advantage of the damage humans leave in their wake. If we don't want *Phragmites*, we should treat the soil with more care.

Once the land is disturbed, it's usually only a matter of time before *Phragmites* moves in to fill the void. Its large, feathery tops contain small, umbrellalike seeds that fill the air in the fall. Most people never notice the seeds, but on a good and windy day they are absolutely everywhere, millions blowing in from nearby *Phragmites* meadows, which may be miles away. Those that land on the water wash to shore where they germinate; those that land on suitable soil grow and in time make their presence known.

Some of the more remote, wild urban parks have large stands of *Phragmites*, and fires are common among the dead, dry standing canes. Most of these fires are thought to be a result of arson. Like it or not, arsonists may be as hard to control as *Phragmites*, so the frequent burns in urban stands of *Phragmites* might as well be viewed as a natural part of the ecosystem. Some of the fires can be traced to lightning; the dead vegetation seems to lend itself to ignition, as if waiting for lightning to strike. Some researchers have even suggested that the dead material may be capable of self-ignition, but that has never been shown. At any rate, these fires appear to be beneficial, as evidenced by the rapid increase in biomass (weight of living material, usually expressed as dry weight per unit area) after a fire. The fires seem to burn off the old, dead biomass, creating new hollows in the old wetlands and rejuvenating the habitat for the *Phragmites* and other wetland-dwelling species. Without such fires, the rapid buildup of dead canes would fill in the low areas, creating higher, drier ground where *Phragmites* would eventually be replaced by highland vegetation. So the fires tend to preserve the *Phragmites* populations.

Few people bother, but much of the *Phragmites* plant is fine to eat. Before trying it, be sure you have the right species. Look for the key characteristic—plumelike flower and, later, the puff of seeds at the top of the plant. The flower has a light purplish hue and is quite attractive. Another identifying feature is its extreme height: few grasses in North America get as tall as this species. The young shoots can be boiled, just like asparagus. They may be eaten warm, cooled, and served as a salad, or even pickled. Also, the young green stems can be taken while still fleshy. After they have been dried out, they can be pounded into a flour. Add water to this powder to form a dough. You can roast a wad of dough like a marshmallow, and it is quite good. The rhizome—the thick, horizontal, fleshy root—can be boiled and eaten like a potato. And the seeds can be ground into a flour, then mixed with water or milk and boiled to make a gruel.

Another grass that is easy to identify is one that grows along the shore in sandy areas. Known as beach grass, *Ammophila breviligulata* can survive drought, fire, and frequent burial by shifting sands. It can also tolerate being flooded with saltwater during storms. This grass holds the sand down with its roots, and the leaves and stems catch blowing sand and help build dunes. Where people and off-road vehicles are allowed to trample the beach grass, it may well be that the dunes will blow away.

You will find several other common species of grasses along the streets and sidewalks in urban and suburban areas. Few people ever learn to identify these plants, even though most are relatively easy to recognize. Part of the problem is that no adequate field guide has been available. Another part of the problem is that grasses do not have characteristics that attract people's attention. They do have flowers, but they rarely develop showy blossoms because they take advantage of the wind for pollination. This means that they don't have to attract insects with large, bright petals that would advertise the sugary nectar that they don't have, since the wind works for free, without being lured by sweet, colorful incentives.

One of the more common roadside grasses is crabgrass (*Digitaria sanguinalis*), a worldwide species that is quite familiar. It grows in lawns, usually in patches where nothing else grows. It is also seen among the weeds along sidewalks or under street trees. Crabgrass, which was introduced from Europe, does very well in lawns because its seeds are set very close to the ground, so lawnmowers are ineffective at controlling its growth. Keep in mind that crabgrass does very poorly in the shade. You can partially control it by allowing your grass to grow a little higher than usual until it shades the crabgrass out. Some weed-killers sold over-the-counter will kill crabgrass, but who knows what damage these products will do to other organisms?

Another roadside plant is yellow foxtail grass (*Setaria viridis*), which is widespread as a weed throughout North America. Sometimes called wild millet, this grass is in the same genus as millet and looks quite similar, though the seed heads are considerably smaller. All of the seeds, which are clustered at the end of the stems, have yellowish brown bristles; they look like a yellowish foxtail—thus the other common name.

Other common grass species include perennial ryegrass (*Lolium perenne*), goose grass (*Eleusine indica*), panic grass (*Panicum clandestinum*), switch grass (*Panicum virgatum*), barnyard grass (*Echinochloa crus-galli*), early chess (*Bromus tectorum*), and orchard grass (*Dactylis glomerata*). After you have learned these, you will find it easy to identify many other species. From there you can move on to rushes and sedges, which are grasslike herbs.

In addition to the numerous grasses that grow in urban and suburban areas, many species of wildflowers can be found growing in parks and woodlots, in empty lots, and along roadsides. A few urban wildflowers are valuable for their showy beauty. Many others have less spectacular blossoms, but are useful in some other way. And many others are just there, useful or not. In any case, they're all interesting.

CHICORY

Chicory (*Cichorium intybus*) tends to grow among weeds along roadsides and in areas with poor, sandy, disturbed soils. This plant would probably do much better on rich soils, but it doesn't always compete well with native species, and seed distribution may limit the places where it is found. It is amazingly widespread in this country, considering it isn't native. It was brought over from Europe, where it has a history going back to the times of the ancient Greeks and Romans, who found many uses for it.

Chicory

Chicory can be easily identified during the summer by its light blue, dandelion-like blossoms on either side of a long, stiff stalk that usually reaches a height of about 3 feet (90 cm). A member of the daisy family, Compositae, its flowers differ from other daisies in that they are composites of many ray flowers—the flat, long flowers usually thought of as the petals—and, also unlike other daisies, it does not have a tight center cluster of small, tubelike disk flowers.

Although its flowers are very pretty, chicory is a poor choice for bouquets. The flowers don't all open at the same time; the lower ones blossom before those higher up on the same stem. After each flower has opened, it will close while the seeds mature inside; these flowers aren't particularly attractive. An added disadvantage is that the blossoming of the flowers is staggered from June right through October, so there is no single time when you can go out and pick a stalk with many beautiful flowers on it. In addition, the flowers don't stay open all day. They tend to open very early in the morning on sunny days and somewhat later on cloudy days; most of the flowers are already shut by noon. This isn't a feature peculiar to chicory alone; many flowers open for a short time during the day, or even during the night, and then shut. The cycle seems to depend on their pollinating insects. Flowers that are pollinated by moths, for example, often open during the night. They have flowers that reflect as much light as possible, so they therefore tend to be white; or they have a powerful fragrance to pull in the pollinators that might otherwise have trouble finding the flowers. It seems to be more efficient for chicory to open during the early hours of the day, get pollinated, and then shut. Even if the flowers were not pollinated, they will shut anyway, and then open again the next day, thereby protecting their delicate structures from the hottest, most destructive part of the day.

Unlike dandelions, chicory seeds do not have little parachutes that carry them aloft, acting as a distribution mechanism. This makes it all the more amazing that this species has become so widespread since its introduction to this country. The chicory plant was probably brought here for its edible parts. The leaves taste best during the early spring when they haven't laid down the bitter chemicals that protect them against herbivorous insects. Again in the fall, after the weather gets cold, the raw leaves become quite mild and pleasant. In the spring, the toothed, elongated leaves, which are similar to those of the dandelion, grow in a tight circle, or rosette, close to the ground before the long stalk shoots up. No species with leaves like these are poisonous, so you shouldn't feel that foraging for chicory can prove dangerous. In Europe, especially in France, people dig up the long taproots, which resemble those of the dandelion, and plant them indoors. They pick off the young leaves during the winter for use as a vegetable.

A relative of chicory is *Cichorium endivia*, the cultivated endive, which is in the same genus. This, too, is picked when the leaves are young and is eaten raw in salads. Many consider it a delicacy. Some people, however, dislike the bitter taste of chicory, endive, and dandelion greens. These close relatives contain a chemical that is agreeable to some palates and offensive to others.

The roots of the chicory plant also have some uses. You can clean the taproots and then bake them in a 300° F (149° C) oven until they turn dark brown, dry out, and become crunchy and fragrant. Then you can grind them up and use the grinds just like regular coffee. They may be used alone to make a pure chicory brew, or added to coffee for a fuller, richer flavor. Unlike coffee, chicory contains no caffeine. It is also free from the many chemicals found in decaffeinated coffee, leftover residues from the decaffeination process. Next time there's a sharp rise in coffee prices, collect chicory roots. And if you need a reason to dig up the dandelions (*Taraxacum officinale*) in your yard, use their taproots, too. When prepared in the same manner, their flavor is similar to, though not quite as good as, chicory.

MUGWORT

There are about one hundred North American species in the genus *Artemisia*. Most are called mugwort, wormwood, or sage. Many of these were brought over from Europe where wormwood has been known and appreciated for years. In the United States, as an urban weed, mugwort has received little attention, but that does not mean it is insignificant. This is a major weed, and in many cities, it is to disturbed soils what goldenrod (*Solidago* spp.) is to old fields in the country. The major differences between mugwort and goldenrod are that mugwort isn't native, it thrives on disturbed soils, and it doesn't have a showy flower. Goldenrod, of course, has a lot of enemies because of the belief that its pollen causes hay fever. Actually, the pollen is quite harmless; it is the pollen of other, less conspicuous species, such as ragweed (*Ambrosia artemisiifolia*), that causes most allergy problems when the plants are blossoming in the late summer and fall.

Like ragweed, mugwort has inconspicuous flowers, which explains why it is not widely recognized. For the same reason, few people know the grasses, sedges, and rushes. People are more likely to notice showy flowers—the big pretties—and ignore the rest. Most observers don't even have the vocabulary to describe many of these species, and some of the popular field guides don't bother to include wildflowers having small greenish flowers.

Mugwort

Our urban mugwort (*Artemisia vulgaris*) is a relative of the native sagebrush (*Artemisia tridentata*), which is common throughout much of the arid West. Reaching heights of several feet (1 to 2 m), mugwort's alternate leaves are deeply cut and jagged. Every leaf is different, and adjacent plants also often look considerably different. Unlike sagebrush, which has silvery leaves, mugwort's leaves are usually dark green above and lighter, almost silvery, and slightly hairy beneath. The upper leaves usually sprout from the plant without much of a stem, while the lower leaves have longer petioles (the slender stems that support the leaves). Later on in the year, the tops of the branches develop heads of small, greenish yellow flowers that are either in rounded bunches or in spikelike heads. The flowers are disc-shaped, with a narrow base and a crown of tiny bristles at the tip. The stems are erect; the branches create a rather woody plant that stands during the entire winter.

A less common relative of mugwort that looks quite similar is the biennial wormwood (*Artemisia biennis*), another introduced species that does well in open, disturbed areas. Mugwort, however, has clusters of flowers toward the end of the stalk; biennial wormwood has leaves interspersed among the flowers, which are clustered next to the main stem.

The leaves of members of this genus have a powerful odor and a taste that is usually bitter and quite pungent. Some species that live in Israel are mentioned in the Bible. Solomon spoke to his son of "The lips of a strange woman as a honeycomb . . . but her end is as bitter as wormwood." The desert wormwood (*Artemisia herba-alba*) is very common on dry soils around Jerusalem. Its odor is strong, distinctive, and actually rather pleasant. The Judean wormwood (*Artemisia judaica*) has very bitter leaves and stalks, but the smell is even more pleasant than that of the desert wormwood. When a small amount of wormwood sap is added to wine, the bitter taste creates a new flavor, and this mixture is referred to in the Talmud as vermouth wine, or the "bitter absinthium wine."

Artemisia absinthium was used as a vermifuge, a medicine to kill intestinal worms, hence the name wormwood. Pieces of the dried plant were placed in cupboards to keep insects away. When tea made from the leaves is sprinkled on the ground during the spring and fall, it has been observed to reduce the number of slugs and beetles that might otherwise be there. Some of these uses were discovered in Europe hundreds of years ago, but they are just as valid today. Some people still crush the leaves and rub the juices on their clothes as an insect repellent. When you walk through a field of mugwort, you will notice that very few insect species live in it. This could be because the chemicals in the mugwort act as a natural repellent to many invertebrates, which may account for its bitter taste and odor. Or the fact that few species of insects live on mugwort could be because the plant tends to grow in urban areas where the insect fauna is generally sparse. Or, perhaps, in the short amount of time since mugwort was introduced to North America, very few native insects have had a chance to adapt to this peculiar plant.

Most stands of mugwort are rather uniform, composed primarily of this species. Other plants live among mugwort, but they are relatively insignificant in total ground cover. Because it competes so effectively against other species on dry, disturbed soils, mugwort is not popular with urban dwellers. This seems unfair, since mugwort is certainly preferable to many of the alternatives. It can even be mowed and kept short and neat. However, when kept short it looks ragged and uninteresting. But cutting a stand once a year, or once every other year, might allow other species to invade and compete effectively.

We do not completely understand why some plants thrive on disturbed soils when just a few miles out of town these species are virtually nonexistent. Factors such as the number of seeds, mode of seed dispersal, seed dormancy, time of germination, growth rates, energy allocated to reproductive effort, length of time from germination until flowering, mode of pollination, and when the plant sets its seeds may all be important. Species like mugwort, while phenomenally successful in the New

York metropolitan area, are almost unknown upstate. Today mugwort is found primarily in the Northeast, but it is spreading and now grows in many cities of the West.

PLANTAIN

The plantain family (Plantaginaceae) does not contain the bananalike plantains. This is a family of small plants that have leaves crowded into a tight rosette, and small flowers, which are characteristically located on the end of a long, erect stalk. The genus *Plantago* comprises more than 200 species. Two of them are very common, occurring on disturbed sites, especially roadsides, lawns, ball fields, and similar habitats throughout much of Asia, Europe, and North America. Having been introduced to North America during colonial times, probably with grains used for planting, both the English plantain, or the narrow-leaved plantain (*Plantago lanceolata*), and the common plantain, or broad-leaved plantain (*Plantago major*), are now found throughout the United States and Canada. These low plants are usually only about 6 inches (15 cm) tall, but

Plantain

they sometimes reach a height of 1 to 2 feet (30 to 60 cm) in unmowed areas.

The English plantain has narrow leaves containing three veins. When flowering, it sends out a long, grooved stalk with a bushy little flower head at the end. The common plantain has broad, more rounded leaves, all tightly clustered together near the ground. Its flowers blossom along much of the long, hairy stalk instead of in a tight cluster at the tip.

Plantain pollen has been found in archaeological digs at European sites dating from the Paleolithic period. This tells us that weeds moved in thousands of years ago when these areas were cleared for human habitation. Among those weeds were some of the same species still associated with human habitation, including plantain. It was noticed long ago that wherever people moved, plantain went with them. Native Americans noticed it when Europeans first came to America. The Indians, who had never seen *Plantago major* before the white men arrived, noticed that it grew only where Europeans had been, so they called the plant Englishman's foot, or white man's foot.

Throughout history, plantain has been used as a remedy for ailments. Shakespeare mentions it in *Love's Labour's Lost*: III. 1.71, where Costard says, "No salve, sir, but a plantain," and in *Romeo and Juliet*: I. 2.51, when Benvolio has a broken shin, Romeo says that "plantain leaf is excellent for that." It seems that the leaves were pounded into a paste and applied to open sores or to inflamed areas to help bring down the swelling. The juice from crushed leaves can still be applied to skin irritations and insect bites, but for anything more serious, see a doctor.

The leaves of both of these species taste fine in salads, as do those of the seaside plantain (*Plantago juncoides*). This plant is similar to the English plantain except that its leaves are fleshier, like those of many seaside plants. Also, instead of three veins, the leaves usually have only one vein. The flower stalk of the seaside plantain is generally shorter than that of the other plantains, and the flowering portion is usually longer. The smallest and youngest leaves taste best in salads; the veins in the older ones become tough and stringy.

The leaves of most plantain species can be cooked and eaten as a vegetable. People who want to eliminate plantains from their lawns can go out in the spring while the leaves are still soft and tasty, pull them up, and serve them for dinner. Plantain roots aren't very deep, and they aren't nearly as hard to pull up as species with deeper roots, like chicory and dandelion.

Several other common *Plantago* species grow in North American cities and suburbs, usually as weeds. *Plantago aristata*, known as bracted plantain or rat-tail plantain, is found in habitats similar to those where English and common plantains thrive. The leaves are much like those of the English plantain, except that they branch right off the stem instead of forming a rosette at the base of the plant. This species is native to the Midwest, where the plants grow on rather dry soils, in meadows, pastures, lawns, and waste areas. Populations are also found locally in eastern and western states.

Another *Plantago* found in lawns and waste places in the eastern United States, having been introduced from Eurasia, is the hoary plantain, *Plantago media*. This is similar to *Plantago lanceolata*, but its leaves are broader, more ovate, coarsely toothed, and whitish.

A few more species are found in urban areas around the country, but they are not included in most field guides. One of these is *Plantago purshii*, known as Pursh's or woolly plantain. Its leaves grow in a whorl at the base of the plant. They are narrow, with three veins, and have winged petioles; the main stems are woolly. This plantain is native to the Midwest, most common from Illinois to Ontario, but it has been introduced farther south and to the east.

Rugel's plantain (*Plantago rugelii*) is similar to the broad-leaved plantain, except that it's less hairy, the edges of the leaves have wavy teeth, and the petioles are purplish. This species is native to the East and has been introduced locally west of the Mississippi Valley.

The whorled plantain (*Plantago indica*), or sandwort plantain, has branched, linear, very slender leaves. This plantain was introduced from Europe and is now found in cities and towns in the eastern and northern states.

PURSLANE

The purslane family, Portulacaceae, has over 100 species in the genus *Portulaca*, of which only about a dozen are found in North America. The most common of these is a weed called purslane (*Portulaca oleracea*), an alien from Europe. Although purslane is cultivated in many parts of Europe and Asia, it grows wild throughout much of North America. It is found from Canada to the southern tip of South America. In the United States it can be found from coast to coast. American relatives in the genus *Claytonia* are the spring beauties. Unlike purslane, which has small yellow flowers, spring beauties have larger, more delicate pink or white flowers, and they grow on richer soils in the woods.

The small yellowish flowers have five petals; they bloom during mid- to late summer and will only open when the sun is out. The plants reproduce by seeds, and they are found growing in fields and waste places, though the soil they grow on is often quite good.

Like most members of the genus, purslane has thick, succulent leaves and stems. They often grow in large patches that lie close to the ground.

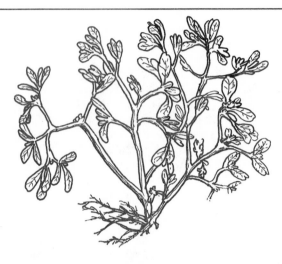

Purslane

The leaves are alternate, though they sometimes occur in bunches. Purslane leaves and stems can be eaten in salads or soups, or they can be served as a cooked vegetable. For thousands of years purslane has been consumed in India and Iran, and throughout Europe and Asia, where many different varieties have been developed. Purslane has a rather mild flavor; it lacks the bitterness of many other wild species. Some people dislike its mucilaginous, or gooey, texture, but this quality makes it valuable as a thickener in soups and stews, where it can be used in place of cornstarch or flour. Also, its thick leaves and stems can be pickled like cucumbers. In addition to these uses, you can collect the seeds and grind them into a flour to make gruel, bread, or pancakes. Or boil the plants briefly, pack them in plastic bags, and freeze them for future use.

Purslane is native to dry regions of India and Iran. The thick stems and leaves, which conserved water in those lands, have probably proved a worthwhile preadaptation for the urban environments. In arid areas where the sun and the wind can be fierce, plants tend to grow near the ground and have hairy or thick vegetation that protects them from evaporative water loss. As it turns out, water is scarce in many urban environments because of the heat as well as the run-off due to the soil compaction and concrete. Many weedy plants that thrive in arid places also show the capacity to survive and sometimes even thrive, in cities. Purslane is such a plant.

CLOVER

Clovers are members of a very large worldwide family, the Leguminosae, also known as the legume or pea family. All the peas and beans are cultivated varieties of plants in this family, having been selected for the taste of their seedpods or the value of the seeds within. The legume family has representatives ranging from small plants like the clover to shrubs, trees, and vines. The key characteristic that ties the entire family together is the distinctive five-petaled flower. The two lower petals are fused into a keel, which is bordered by two other petals forming wings, with a larger petal behind all of them like a backboard. The clovers usually have heads of small flowers, but when you look carefully you will see that each tiny flower has this general architecture. When most flowers in this family go to seed, they form a simple pea pod. The leaves are usually alternate, compound, and have stipules (leaflike appendages) at their base, although some species have tendrils or thorns instead of stipules.

There are almost 100 different species of clovers, and most live in

Red clover

western North America. Some clovers are very well known, being found in lawns everywhere. Their leaves are usually palmately compound, and most leaves have three leaflets. The flowers grow at the end of the stem, where they usually occur in clusters as a head or a spike. They may be white, pink, red, or yellow, depending on the species.

Of the three common white clovers, two are very similar. They are the low, white clovers that are found in lawns. Both of these species were introduced from Europe. They flower from late May until fall and are distinguished by their leaves. The white clover (*Trifolium repens*) has a light, triangular mark on each leaflet, which the alsike clover (*Trifolium hybridum*) lacks. The third common white clover is the white sweet clover (*Melilotus alba*), which is a member of another genus. It is a tall plant, growing several feet high, usually along roadsides and in fields. Its flowers grow in long spikes rather than in tight clusters like the members of the *Trifolium* genus. It, too, is an alien species.

Another common clover is yellow sweet clover (*Melilotus officialanis*), which is very similar to white sweet clover. The other yellow clovers have small, tight clusters of flowers. These are the hop clover (*Trifolium agrarium*); the smaller hop clover (*Trifolium procumbens*), which is distinguished by its stalked terminal, or middle leaflet, meaning it has a little stem; and the least hop clover (*Trifolium dubium*), which has a tiny flower head, much smaller than that of the other two hop clovers.

Red clover (*Trifolium pratense*) is also an introduced species that is now found throughout the country. This is the common pinkish clover found in fields, along roadsides, and on lawns everywhere. The leaves have pale triangles, similar to those on white clover.

The sweet white and sweet yellow clovers have a distinctive, rich, sweet smell, advertising their blossoms to pollinating insects. Clover nectar, in fact, contains approximately 40 percent sugar. Just to put this in proper perspective, the old Coca-Cola® (now called the Original Formula Classic Coca-Cola©) contains 10.9 percent sugar, and the new Coca-Cola®, which is sweeter, is 11.9 percent sugar.

As soon as the flowers are pollinated, they droop and turn brown. The young shoots of both the sweet white and sweet yellow clovers can be boiled and eaten like asparagus. The small pealike fruits can be added to soups and stews. Clover flowers and clover leaves, especially the young ones, may be put into salads. Some people dip the blossoms in batter and fry them, making clover fritters.

Most of these clover species can make a major contribution to the soil. Symbiotic bacteria live in small nodules in their roots. These bacteria are able to transform atmospheric nitrogen into a form that is useful and necessary to plants. Farmers have learned to plant clovers in their fields, reducing their need for expensive nitrogen fertilizers.

Besides the clovers, the legume family contains other well-known species and species groups. One such species is alfalfa (*Medicago sativa*), which has a purplish blue flower. It was introduced to this country from Eurasia and is now widespread everywhere except in the Southwest. It is planted as a forage species. The name comes from the Arabic, *al-fasfasah*, which means "the best kind of fodder."

Another member of this family that has been widely written about during recent years is kudzu (*Pueraria lobata*). This Asian species is well known in the southeastern United States. It has spread like wildfire and now extends as far west as Texas and as far north as Tennessee, though there are reports that populations survive even into Pennsylvania. This vine grows over everything. It is common along roadsides, where it climbs over the trees, growing as high as 100 feet (30 m), using all of the sunlight, and killing the trees. It hasn't been one of the most popular species in the Southeast, but people are learning to live with it. Acacia and mimosa trees are also members of this family.

PURPLE LOOSESTRIFE

When in bloom, purple loosestrife (*Lythrum salicaria*) is a beautiful plant that makes low, wet areas absolutely gorgeous. After a while, however, those who appreciate the subtle beauty of a wetland may miss the diversity that existed before the marsh was besieged with this alien.

Like many other species that have been naturalized from Europe, purple loosestrife is a plant about which little is known. It is thought to have arrived here during the early 19th century, when settlers probably brought it over to plant in gardens in the Northeast. As with most introduced weeds, little accurate information about its spread has been recorded, which is unfortunate. It appears that purple loosestrife rapidly colonized new areas, but this observation may have been made only because it is such an obvious plant. Its purple blaze is so overpowering that people can't help noticing it. Other weed species often grow in waste areas or on dry, trampled, urban patches, but this plant moves right into some of the best wetlands and takes over, outcompeting many native species. Because purple loosestrife grows in dense patches, choking out other vegetation, it can have a major impact on a habitat. There are some good qualities about this species, foremost of which may be its colorful beauty. Like it or not, purple loosestrife is here to stay.

Purple loosestrife reaches heights of several feet (1 to 2 m). The stems are stout, woody, and thick; on the larger specimens they will get as thick as ¼ to ½ inch (.5 to 1 cm). The leaves occur oppositely, on both sides of the stem, as well as in whorls of threes. They are sessile, that is, without stems, long and narrow, from 1 to 4 inches long (2.5 to 10 cm). The leaves are usually hairy. The flowers occur in a long terminal spike, each flower having six petals and twice as many stamens.

Naturalists don't know much about the movement of alien plant species after they have been introduced to this country, but we assume that different plants become established in different patterns. Purple loosestrife, for instance, seems to move rapidly along wet roadside ditches and into adjacent wetlands, where it takes over. Because new plants sometimes appear miles from the nearest established populations, it is likely that the seeds pass through waterfowl, then germinate elsewhere. It is also possible, of course, that some plants are transplanted by well-intentioned people. This may account for several plants that I saw flowering during the summer of 1986 in Central Park in Manhattan.

During the past fifteen years, purple loosestrife has expanded its range throughout the Northeast at a remarkable rate, but instead of starting in a city and then spreading out, like most weeds, this species started in rural communities and is spreading to urban areas. It is now found in all five boroughs of New York City—Staten Island, Brooklyn, Queens, Manhattan, and the Bronx—but so far it is common only in Staten Island. Presumably it is only a matter of time before its numbers increase in suitable habitats elsewhere. Its color will almost certainly be a worthwhile addition to the urban landscape.

Purple loosestrife, like *Phragmites*, is a plant that alters a habitat. Once it moves in and takes hold, a wetland may never be the same. Because wetlands attract a wide range of species, it is important that we preserve them. But we can go only so far as caretakers. We can prevent our ponds from filling in and keep our lawns from turning into fields, but we cannot control all the individual species. Such a task is impossible.

Currently, *Phragmites* is one of the most dominant plant species associated with disturbed urban freshwater wetlands, so any newcomer that increases the diversity should be welcome. People have been complaining for years that *Phragmites* doesn't supply enough food and worthwhile material to the wild communities. With a little bit of luck, purple loosestrife may change that in some areas. The drawback will be that shallow wetlands may be overrun by *Lythrum*. This will only increase the need to cut down old reeds, pull out the canes by the roots, increase the level of the water table, use chemicals to control the plants, or go in and dredge. All these options are expensive, and none offers a permanent solution.

Lythrum, a perennial herb, dies back each year, leaving tall hexagonal stems with a whorled branching pattern. Each node usually contains three or four smaller branches, along with small remnants from the tight

Purple loosestrife

clusters of dead flowers. *Lythrum* is still most common in the Northeast and the North Central states, but it has been found in the Northwest, and it is expected to continue its rapid advance right through the South and across the country, wherever available habitats permit. It is also found in most of Europe and central Asia, and it is spreading in Australia.

Another introduced loosestrife, *Lythrum virgatum*, also called purple loosestrife, doesn't have hairy leaves like *L. salicaria* and is still restricted to a relatively small area in New England.

Three native species in this genus are found on the East Coast. They aren't as aggressive as *L. salicaria*, and their flowers aren't nearly as showy. They are the winged, or wing-angled loosestrife (*Lythrum alatum*), which has a four-angled stem that is sometimes winged; hyssop-leaved loosestrife (*Lythrum hyssopifolia*), which has narrow, alternate leaves and grows in salt marshes; and narrow-leaved loosestrife (*Lythrum lineare*), which is similar to the hyssop-leaved loosestrife, except that its leaves are even narrower and have an opposite rather than alternate arrangement along the stem. The narrow-leaved loosestrife is also found in salt marshes in the East.

Another related species in the loosestrife family is swamp loosestrife, or water-willow, *Decodon verticillatus*, that, like the purple loosestrife, is tall, grows in wet areas, and has lavender flowers. The flowers have five petals, are bell-shaped, and occur in bunches in the upper leaf axils. The leaves aren't hairy.

Other loosestrifes in this country are members of the primrose family, Primulaceae, and of the genus *Lysimachia*. These species look something like *Lythrum*, but their flowers are usually yellow rather than pink or purple, and they grow on longer stems. Of these species, few ever occur in urban or suburban settings; they are more often restricted to places yet to be affected by people.

LAMB'S-QUARTERS

Beets (*Beta vulgaris*) and spinach (*Spinacia oleracea*) are both chenopodiaceous plants—that is, they are members of the goosefoot family, Chenopodiaceae.

This family contains some 550 species worldwide. One of the genera, *Chenopodium* (the pigweeds), has about 60 species, 20 of which are found in the United States. Goosefoot, pigweed, lamb's-quarters, and Mexican tea are the most common members of this group in North America. Probably the most widespread species is *Chenopodium album*, or lamb's-quarters. This plant grows as a weed along roadsides and in gardens, fields, disturbed sites, and waste places throughout the country. Small green flowers are common to all members of this genus. The flowers are crowded on spiked clusters originating from the leaf. The plants can attain a height of about 5 feet (almost 2 m) by late summer. The leaves are alternate, simple, and commonly vary slightly with respect to the pattern shown in the illustration.

Lamb's-quarters are edible. Pick only the young plants, found from mid-spring until autumn. The young shoots grow less than 1 foot (30 cm) high and taste fine raw. If cooked, they taste very similar to spinach. The foliage can be dried out and used in soups or stews. The seeds may be shaken off and fed to birds, along with the seeds of plantain (*Plantago* spp.), ragweed (*Ambrosia* spp.), smartweed and knotweed (*Polygonum* spp.). I've also heard that *Chenopodium* seeds are an antihelminthic, which means they expel intestinal worms, at least for some species of birds. As many as 75,000 seeds are produced by just one mature plant. Native Americans used the seeds extensively, boiling them to make gruel or grinding them into flour. It is interesting to note that when lamb's-quarters seeds were taken out from under old buildings in Europe, some still germinated, even after having been there for more than 1,500 years.

Lamb's-quarters came from Europe and rapidly spread across North America. Mexican tea (*Chenopodium ambrosioides*), introduced from

Lamb's-quarters

tropical America, was once confined to the southern states. It now has invaded the middle Atlantic states and is doing well in cities as far north as New York and beyond. Perennial goosefoot (*Chenopodium bonus-henricus*), originally brought to North America from Europe to be used as a potherb, has spread through many eastern cities and towns. Unlike the lanceolate shape of Mexican tea leaves, this species has triangular leaves. Another species brought over from Europe, now widespread across America, is Jerusalem oak (*Chenopodium botrys*). Its leaves are hairy and strongly scented. Strawberry pigweed (*Chenopodium capitatum*), a North American native, is found in the Northeast, the mountain states, Canada, and Alaska. Its leaves are triangular with wavy teeth. Oak-leaved goosefoot (*Chenopodium glaucum*) was introduced from Europe and now occurs in the northern United States and south and west to Virginia, Missouri, and Nebraska. The maple-leaved goosefoot (*Chenopodium hybridum*), nettle-leaved goosefoot (*Chenopodium murale*), pigweed (*Chenopodium paganum*), many-seeded goosefoot (*Chenopodium polyspermum*), red goosefoot (*Chenopodium rubrum*), and goosefoot (*Chenopodium urbicum*) are other closely allied representatives of this genus that are found in urban areas across America.

$\rightsquigarrow\!\!\!\rightarrow$ **3** $\twoheadleftarrow\!\!\!\leftsquigarrow$

TREES

Trees grow in cities all across this country. Street trees that are planted along sidewalks are carefully chosen for their urban-tolerant characteristics. Trees planted in lawns and parks are selected for their beautiful foliage or flowers. But in alleys and along the edges of parking lots, in waste areas and beside railroad tracks, in overgrown fields, woodlots, and the wild areas of larger parks, you will find trees that have seeded in on their own and have grown to maturity without any help from humans. It is interesting to observe these species. What kind of trees are they? How might they have been brought to the cities? What will their future be?

Cities have polluted air, so urban trees have to be ozone tolerant, capable of surviving air that has much more sulfur dioxide and carbon monoxide than would be found anywhere else, except perhaps next to a volcano. Northern cities have the added problem of salt, which is spread on the streets and sidewalks to melt snow during the winter. Salt-tolerant species are often among the trees found in these cities. Varieties, cultivars, and specific hybrids are constantly being developed for characteristics that make them more suitable to a particular aesthetic taste or environment. Rapid growth might be a desirable characteristic for street trees, for example, since a low tree is likely to have its branches knocked off or severely bruised by passing trucks. Early-blooming or disease-resistant trees might be suitable in some cities, perhaps a variety that never fruits and therefore doesn't drop anything that has to be cleaned up. Any of these characteristics bred into a specific strain might make it more likely to be widely used in urban areas.

It is especially important for a street tree to be able to survive periods of drought, because these trees seldom receive any care; their cramped conditions and overly packed soils mean that little water or nutrients ever reaches their roots.

Adaptations to dry conditions include anything that conserves water or increases the tree's chance of gathering as much water as possible when it is available. Taproots help when a plant needs to penetrate deep into the soil before it reaches water; thick fleshy roots that store water for future dry periods are common among plants adapted to arid climates. Thick hairy leaves or leaves with dense, waxy cuticles conserve water during the heat of the summer by reducing evaporative loss. It is interesting to note that many drought-tolerant species have compound leaves, and that several of the more popular street trees also have compound leaves.

Nowadays, tree species are being transplanted, propagated, and moved around the country, often the world. As a result, it can be difficult to identify certain species found in cities. In rural areas you can usually count on encountering species indigenous to that area, and only those species, but in urban areas you never know what to expect. Many forestry, highway, and parks departments restrict species that may be planted along streets, but restrictions are generally much looser in parks. Because there are parks that have existed for well over 100 years, generations of different administrations have planted species that are rarely documented in files. Since few of the people working for these cities know much about trees, you are usually on your own when trying to identify a species. Your best bet is to start with the most abundant species. Therefore, I will discuss only common species in this chapter—trees you will almost certainly encounter—rather than providing a long catalog of species you *might* encounter. By knowing a handful of species in each appropriate group, you can become quite well versed on the subject of urban trees.

LONDON PLANE

The London plane tree is a hybrid between two closely related plane trees, the American sycamore (*Platanus occidentalis*) and the Oriental plane tree (*Plantanus orientalis*). While both trees are prized for their beauty, neither does particularly well in the harsh urban environment. The hybrid between both species, however, possesses a vigor that surpasses that of the original plane trees. For genetic reasons, this is true of many hybrids; it is known as hybrid vigor. Because the *Platanus* hybrid was unknown during the lifetime of Frederick Law Olmsted, the designer of so many 19th-century American parks, those early parks were filled with American sycamores and Oriental plane trees, but neither species thrived. In cities, the American sycamore was prone to sycamore anthracnose, a disease that attacks the leaves and twigs. (A closely related fungus attacks many oak species in cities. It seems that the weakened trees in urban environments are subject to such diseases.)

The hybrid, or London plane tree, often designated *Platanus* x *acerifolia*, started to come into its own when Robert Moses, Commissioner of the New York City Department of Parks and Recreation, developed something of a love affair with the species and planted them throughout the city. Before long, the London plane had become virtually synonymous with crowded cities.

The trees have large, simple leaves that grow 6 to 10 inches (15 to 25 cm) wide, arranged alternatively on the stems. They are palmately lobed, which means they look very much like the typical maple leaf. In fact, the symbol used by the New York City Department of Parks and Recreation of a leaf in a circle, thought by most people to be a maple, similar to that on the Canadian flag, is actually a sycamore. I say sycamore; I'd be slightly dishonest if I said a London plane because the leaves are virtually identical. Their one characteristic that is unlike all other trees planted along sidewalks is the hollow petiole base that covers a bud. Underneath the point where the stem of the leaf attaches to the twig, you'll find the bud. I hate to put this in writing because I don't want to be responsible for tens of thousands of London plane leaves, as well as those of other trees with palmately lobed leaves, being periodically plucked in an attempt to expose the hollow petiole and bud beneath, but somehow I think I can live with that on my conscience. Pluck sparingly.

The distinctive bark of the London plane tree is smooth, with thin, brittle flakes exfoliating, exposing a greenish or brownish color underneath that creates a mottled effect. The seed heads, or seedballs, of the London plane occur singly and in doublets, triplets, and quadruplets. This tree grows rapidly, reaching heights of 80 to 100 feet (25 to 35 m). In fact, among those species that do well in cities, only the cottonwood (*Populus* spp.) and the silver maple (*Acer saccharinum*) seem to grow faster.

The wood of the London plane is relatively strong, hard, and heavy. Because it is hard to split, it has been used to make veneer, flooring, boxes, barrels, crates, and butcher blocks. When exposed to moisture and bacteria, however, it readily rots, which is why many of the older specimens are hollow inside.

The London plane has been planted along roads, highways, and city streets all across the country, and it has the capacity to grow almost anywhere. It is fairly tolerant of ozone and sulfur dioxide pollution, and it can survive considerable concentrations of salt. In addition, though this tree does best on moist, well-drained soils with a pH ranging from 6.5 to 7.5, it is adaptable and can withstand wet conditions, drought, and other pHs.

Although the London plane tree has been believed to be resistant to the anthracnose fungus (*Gnomonia platani*) that attacks the American sycamore, it has been losing its edge. In New York City an early leaf blight each spring can kill the young leaves and result in partial or even complete defoliation. Another type of damage can be seen in the small to large brown blotches that appear along the midribs and lateral veins of mature leaves; these can result in some defoliation. To control this disease, which weakens the trees but seldom kills them outright, it helps to prune the diseased leaves and to water the trees during droughts. It is also helpful to fertilize the trees properly, which is best left to a private arborist. Communities often raise money for professional tree care, with permission from the local parks department or the city agency that oversees street trees. The contractor fertilizes the trees with a very long injection needle, directing a water-soluble fertilizer about 8 inches (20 cm) deep to get below the compacted surface layer. The degree of reinfection can be reduced by thinning the dense canopies, pruning the deadwood, and removing leaves and twigs shortly after they fall. Local citizens often pressure their local parks department to use chemicals to control anthracnose, but there is no reason to believe that such care has any long-term benefits.

TREE OF HEAVEN

The unplanned and untended woodlands in and around cities are constantly regenerating themselves. Many of these woodlands have trees that seeded in on their own; when they die, they will be replaced by other trees that grow without human help. Here you will find some species of trees that would not have been found in such a region 100 or 200 years ago. Some of the newer species were brought in for planting; later they proved capable of moving into open areas, where they successfully competed with the local species, regenerated themselves, and have become a part of the urban landscape.

One of the most amazing self-regenerating species is the tree of heaven, or what some call the tree that grows in Brooklyn, *Ailanthus altissima*. This tree was transported from China to England in the 1750s, then introduced to the United States in 1784. Frederick Law Olmsted used it in New York City's Central Park because he liked the tree's tropical appearance. It is one of the last trees to sprout its leaves in the spring, but

Tree of heaven

finally its large buds swell, developing into long, pinnately compound leaves that often reach a foot or two or even three feet in length. At first the leaves are yellowish green, but in time they darken to a rich, dark green; by June the trees begin to blossom. These trees are dioecious—that is, the male and female reproductive organs are borne on different plants. The male trees grow foul-smelling, stamen-bearing flowers, while the female trees sprout greenish white pistil-bearing flowers. The pistillate flowers later develop into fruits, each bearing one seed, somewhat similar to those of the ash, elm, and maple. These reddish green and reddish brown seeds are called samaras, and they appear in clusters.

When in seed, some of these trees are absolutely stunning. Many people will strenuously disagree, of course, since it has become fashionable to grumble about this species, but that attitude is largely a response to the popular view that this tree has gotten out of control and now seems to be growing practically everywhere. Actually, the tree of heaven doesn't grow "practically everywhere." It doesn't compete at all well with native species on rich, undisturbed soils. But in cities, where rich, undisturbed soils are hard to come by, this tree does tend to crop up in unlikely places.

In the fall, when the thin, light, twisted samaras have dried out and turned brown, thousands are simultaneously picked up by big gusts of wind. Becoming lodged in cracks in the sidewalk, in crevices along the edge of a building, or in vacant lots or alleys, they set root. Indeed, these trees sprout up in cities like weeds, but what differentiates them from most herbaceous weeds is that they don't die back each year; in fact, they are next to impossible to kill. The more you cut them back, the better they seem to like it. As it turns out, while most plant species put a large portion of their effort into the part of the plant that extends above the ground's surface, *Ailanthus* invests a large percent of its resources in its roots. As a result, by the time you cut the tree down, it has so much energy stored underground that it will have no problem sprouting up again and again. Storing vast reserves appears to be a powerfully adaptive attribute for any plant that has to survive hard times, especially if these reserves are not vulnerable to herbivores. Cacti store most of their reserves above ground in their large, fleshy tissues: trees of heaven store much of their reserves underground, beyond the reach of virtually everything. This tree was the major symbol of life and survival in Betty Smith's 1943 novel, *A Tree Grows in Brooklyn*.

Ailanthus grows faster than almost any other city tree. But like many other rapidly growing species, it has weak, brittle wood that is easily damaged and broken by wind and ice. This causes a problem in cities, because no municipal government wants to be accused of planting dangerous trees that crack and fall on people. However, to my knowledge, no one has ever been killed by a tree of heaven, at least not intentionally.

The common name, tree of heaven, appears to be attributable to the fast growth and eventual heights reached. The average height is probably 40 to 60 feet (12 to 18 m), but many specimens, growing in favorable conditions, attain heights of 90 to 100 feet (27 to 30 m). The scientific name, *Ailanthus altissima*, means "tallest of the trees of heaven." It was probably chosen because this species is the largest in its genus.

This tree, as I indicated earlier, suffers from a bad public relations problem. Its human enemies regard it as a weed that will sprout up anywhere. But that seems to be a good thing, not something to complain about. Given half a chance, a few *Ailanthus* trees will transform a scruffy block into a classy area with shade trees that look as if they were planted long ago. And what if they are the much-maligned "trashy weed trees" that are practically impossible to kill? More power to them.

GINKGO

As a member of an ancient group, all of whose species except one are extinct, the ginkgo is credited with being a living fossil. This is one of the oldest of all living trees, with a fossil record that extends back 100 million years virtually unchanged. It has been said that city dwellers who walk by a ginkgo should be as surprised as if they were walking by a crocodile. I'm

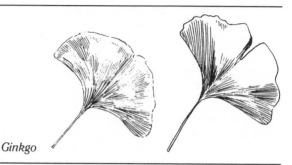

Ginkgo

not sure the analogy is valid, but I like it. The ginkgo came to this country from Japan, which imported it from China. It is widely planted as an ornamental and a street tree, but it is almost unknown in the wild. Other species have been bred in captivity when they became totally extirpated from their native region, but this is a unique situation. The ginkgo tree is now planted all over the world, but it does not seem to grow in China, Japan, Europe, or the United States beyond the spots where it has been planted. No one knows why.

This species, *Ginkgo biloba*, gets its name, ginkgo, from the Chinese gin-yo or gin-go, which means silver apricot, a fair description of the fruit, though it is smaller than an apricot. The ginkgo is also known as the maidenhair tree because its parallel-veined, fan-shaped leaves look like those of some maidenhair ferns. I don't find the name very helpful because, of the many species of maidenhair ferns, few look similar to the ginkgo. One species of maidenhair fern, however, that is currently very popular in plant stores in New York City has leaves that do look almost exactly like the ginkgo's.

Besides having fan-shaped, parallel-veined leaves with irregular lobes at the end and an indentation in the middle of the fan, the ginkgo's rather small leaves are usually only a few inches (5 to 8 cm) across, somewhat leathery in texture, and don't have a midrib.

There is a chance that the name maidenhair fern was adopted for this species when plant taxonomists thought the ginkgo was a close relative of the ferns. More recently though, rather than being grouped with the ferns, it has been ascertained that it should be assigned to its own class, Ginkgoae, even though other plant taxonomists only place it in its own order, Ginkgoales. Nevertheless, it is a member of the gymnosperms, which also include the cycads and the conifers. Unlike the ferns, these are all seed plants, or spermopsids. The gymnosperms are among the most successful plants in the world; pine, spruce, and fir trees constitute about one-third of all the existing forested areas of the world.

The seed plants, Spermopsida, represent one of the several subdivisions within the Tracheophyta, or vascular plants. More primitive vascular plants include the ferns, horsetails, and club mosses. The conifers and the flowering plants represent the more recent and currently most successful seed plants.

One of the main advances of the pines over the ferns was that they no longer had flagellated sperm cells. The pollen of the cycads and ginkgoes is carried by the wind to the ovules, but their pollen tubes still produce flagellated sperm cells that swim a short distance to reach the egg cells. This primitive characteristic is retained from their ancestors.

In 1900 the ginkgo was just becoming popular in Washington, D.C., and New York City, though it was still far from abundant. Because of the tree's beauty, as well as its ability to survive the gamma radiation, sulfur dioxide, and ozone pollution of the cities, it soon became one of the more widely planted trees in cities across the country. Given the right conditions, such as good soil in a city park, a ginkgo will grow as tall as 60 to 100 feet (18 to 30 m). As a street tree, though tolerant of dry conditions, it does better when the soil is kept moist rather than wet. Care should be taken not to let too much residue from winter saltings reach them, however, because these trees are not particularly salt tolerant. The soils in sidewalk tree pits often become compacted from foot traffic, but the ginkgo is able to tolerate this stress.

When the trees were first planted in American cities, males and females were used at random. In time, however, people tired of the odor and mess created by the ripe and overripe fruit of the female; today many parks departments avoid planting females. But in some older parks, where large female specimens still thrive, it is not unusual to find Chinese people collecting the fruit in the fall and early winter. The small, plumlike fruit is edible, but the flavor is both disgusting and pleasant, if that is possible. This is a bizarre fruit: you won't know what I mean until you taste one. It isn't the malodorous outer husk that the Chinese are after, however. Inside this covering is a silvery white kernel. People don't eat these kernels raw because they taste like rancid butter, but when boiled in a soup for a long time, they impart a rich flavor. The kernels are also roasted like nuts. Ginkgo fruits are sold at high prices in Chinatown in New York City. The Chinese also use the raw seeds to treat cancer, but great care is taken because the uncooked seeds can prove fatal.

In the autumn ginkgo leaves turn golden yellow and fall off. Because the trees can tolerate hot, dry summers as well as winter temperatures that drop as low as $-10°F$ ($-23°C$), they have been successfully grown throughout the United States, except in the coldest areas of New England, the Great Plains, and parts of the Great Lakes area. Ginkgoes do not suffer from any serious pest problems, perhaps because the waxy cuticular layer of the leaves is resistant to most common pathogens.

HONEY LOCUST

The honey locust (*Gleditsia triacanthos*) became popular in this country in the 1940s. At that time, American elms (*Ulmus americana*), which were very common street trees in the East, were hard hit by Dutch elm disease. Cities lost row upon row of beautiful old elms that had grown up along with the communities they adorned. The elms had to be cut down as soon as they showed signs of the disease; otherwise it would spread to the trees nearby. The honey locust became popular as a replacement.

Probably originally occurring along rivers and streams in the wild, the honey locust was the beneficiary of widespread agriculture. As areas were opened up for farming, cattle ate the sweet seedpods. When the seeds passed through the animals' digestive systems, gastric juices softened the hard outer seed coat, facilitating germination. As a result, honey locusts rapidly spread through pastures from central Pennsylvania, south to Alabama, west to Texas, and as far north as southeastern South Dakota.

When Frederick Law Olmsted was seeking tree species for the many city parks he designed, he would bring in new species to a city if he thought they would suit the area aesthetically, and could survive there.

Honey locust

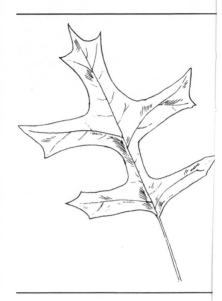

bright green. Pin oak acorns are only
inch (1.3 cm) in diameter. The shal
saucer-shaped with thin, small, redd
bark is grayish brown and slightly fu
parts of the tree is smooth, light gray
oak (*Quercus rubra*). Some of the
hybrids between pin oaks and red oa

The pin oak gets its name from
branchlets on the main branches.
mastlike trunk that ascends straigh
Many pin oaks turn a yellowish bro
reddish brown to purplish red, or ev

Recently the horned oak gall ha
are planted in large numbers, as in I
caused by a tiny black wasp, *Callirr*
pin oak twigs. These eggs slowly (
later, tiny, parthenogenic female wa
fly to the tree's foliage and, withou
their eggs in the leaf veins. The
midsummer both male and female
cycle is complete.

Horned oak gall quickly sprea(
trees in the area are infected. The u

He planted several clusters of honey locusts in Central Park, where they
quickly grew into fine specimens; after that, the tree was well on its way
to being planted elsewhere.

The honey locust has pinnately compound leaves, which means
there are leaflets arranged on both sides of the midrib. If you look closely,
however, you will see that it also has bipinnately compound leaves on the
same tree, usually on the same branch. Bipinnately compound leaves are
doubly or twice pinnate, meaning that the main axis is also branched, as
illustrated. The black locust (*Robinia pseudoacacia*) has pinnately compound leaves as well, but unlike the honey locust, *Robinia* has showy,
fragrant flowers. Another street tree with bipinnately compound leaves
that is popular in some cities is the Kentucky coffee tree (*Gymnocladus
dioica*).

The minute, hardly noticeable flowers of the honey locust rapidly
ripen into long pods, which you cannot miss. While the pods are still
young, they are soft and green, and their pulp is sugary sweet, which
accounts for the "honey" part of the tree's name. The name "locust" has a
more circuitous origin. According to the New Testament, when Saint
John went into the wilderness, he lived on "honey and locusts." The
locusts were actually the long, sweet pods from the carob tree, *Ceratonia
siliqua*. When ripe, the hard seeds inside the pods rattled like locusts, thus
the confusion in names. Even though the honey locust is unrelated to the
carob, because of its long, dark pods, it came to be called a locust, too.
Actually these trees have had many names, but honey locust is now by
far the most widely used. Some honey locust trees have thorns, and for a
brief period they were called Confederate pin trees, because the thorns
were used to pin together the torn uniforms of Confederate soldiers
during the Civil War. The long spines of these trees act as a deterrent to
any animal wishing to climb the tree to eat the young pods. Squirrels
never climb these thorned trees. The pods develop their sweet taste so
that when they ripen and fall to the ground, they will be eaten. This
effective dispersal mechanism is used by many pod-bearing trees,
however for the honey locusts, it did not take effect until they became a
popular replacement for elms. Their widespread use led to the development of a thornless variety (*Gleditsia triacanthos inermis*), which is
rapidly becoming predominant in urban areas in the East.

The honey locust is popular in eastern cities, probably for several
reasons. For one, it tolerates a wide range of climate conditions, very wet
to very dry. Its popularity may also be related to the way light filters
through the compound leaves, creating a pleasant mottled effect on city
streets. This tree's spreading branches and open, rounded crown also
make it look attractive along city streets. Remember, too, that street trees
are sometimes damaged by trucks pulling up to the curb or by kids
locking their bicycles to the trunk. Such abuse can damage the way a tree

grows and the shape it develop
dom shape somehow allows it
ming from an injury, and to stil
be added that in the autumn, w
brown, honey locusts brighten
prefer, a honey color. When col
leaving the long, twisted, darl
branches; the pods then fall duri

In addition to the trees (
species with compound leaves
pennsylvanica), the Japanese p;
rain tree (*Koelreuteria panicula*
julibrissin). These trees may
resistant; they may have been (
them attractive or because thei
the autumn.

F

Another tree that has been
pin oak (*Quercus palustris*). Thi
restricted to an area ranging fi
Virginia and Tennessee, wes
Oklahoma. It was not a fashior
popular in Europe since the ea
finally began to catch on in the
Washington, D.C., and parts o
slowly became one of the most

Pin oaks grow relatively r;
of many of the other oaks, bu
conditions. The pin oak's ma
conifer's, almost to the top, wh
The wood is strong and resist
lower branches, instead of fall
downward. This deadwood se
wood borers and damages the
primarily planted for their to
drawback.

Pin oak leaves usually hav
or even nine. They are oblong
slender petioles that are 1½ to
bristle-tipped with rounded n

and the trees may die before their time. When the infestations aren't very bad, the diseased limbs can be pruned; this will reduce the wasp population, but it will not entirely eliminate them. Few city agencies concerned with trees bother to prune the galls off all the infected pin oaks. Instead, they recommend that infected trees be fertilized and, during droughts, watered. This strengthens the trees so they can tolerate the weakening effects of the gall.

The pin oak also is susceptible to iron chlorosis, characterized by leaves that turn yellow. This condition seems to be a result of the tree's inability to absorb iron from neutral or basic soils. Usually the chlorosis only detracts from the overall appearance, but it also weakens the tree and may eventually prove fatal. To counter the effects of chlorosis, you can spray the foliage with a soluble iron salt, such as iron sulfate, an iron solution can be injected into the tree, or, better yet, an iron chelate can be put into the soil around the tree.

Many other species of oaks are found in cities. One is the sawtooth oak (*Quercus acutissima*), an import from Asia. It is tolerant of warmer climates and does well in harsh sites, but has yet to be widely tested.

The white oak (*Quercus alba*), though beautiful, long-lived, and popular, is not used often in cities, mainly because it is difficult to transplant.

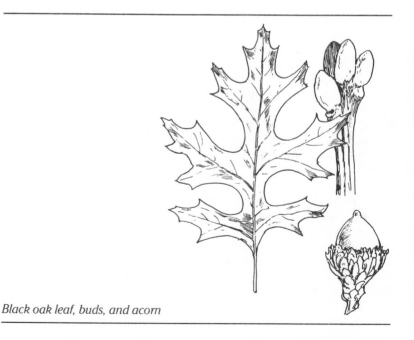

Black oak leaf, buds, and acorn

Because high success ratios are imperative when hefty fees are paid to have trees dug up and transplanted, any tree that does poorly rarely becomes a favorite. Where white oaks have survived transplantation, they usually do well. Generally they are confined to larger parks, however, rather than along city streets.

The swamp white oak (*Quercus bicolor*) isn't often found in cities, but it is seen in the wild, doing quite well under conditions that few other species could survive—including poorly aerated, compacted soils with high clay contents. With this in mind, it might be worth looking into this species as an urban candidate.

In the Midwest, the shingle oak (*Quercus imbricaria*) has been used extensively, but it is still largely restricted to this area.

A tree that was thought of as a southern species, the willow oak (*Quercus phellos*), has been widely used in southern cities as a street tree for years. More recently this oak has been found to do remarkably well also in northern cities. Because of its narrow, willowlike leaves, it adds variety to the urban landscape and should be used and appreciated. However, keep this important advice in mind if you plan to take seeds from any species for propagation: if the species has a southern range and you are interested in bringing it farther north, you should take seeds from the northernmost part of its range. Otherwise, the mix of genes that you get may not be able to tolerate the harsh northern winters. This advice also works in reverse, in case you plan to move a northern species to a location farther south.

The English oak (*Quercus robur*) is native to Europe, northern Africa, and western Asia. It has been successfully used as a street tree in Philadelphia, but there have been problems with it in the Boston area. Since there is wide variation among individuals of this species, it may be that the appropriate seeds were not used in Boston.

The scarlet oak (*Quercus coccinea*) is very similar in appearance to the pin oak, having a straight trunk and elliptical leaves, with five to nine narrow, toothed, pointed lobes. This tree can be counted on for excellent red foliage in the fall. Also, it appears to be less susceptible than the pin oak to iron chlorosis.

As you walk around wild, wooded areas in the larger city parks observing the species of trees that are regenerating, you will notice that while many of the older trees may be white oaks (*Quercus alba*), black oaks (*Quercus velutina*), or red oaks (*Quercus rubra*), which were often there before the city was built up around them, the most common oak species among the new trees that is replacing the old tends to be the pin oak. This is especially apparent in cities where pin oaks were never common until they were brought in and planted in the parks and on the streets.

WHITE MULBERRY

The mulberry was known thousands of years ago in China, where it was cultivated as a food source for silkworm caterpillars. In 1623, King James I had mulberry trees and silkworms' moth eggs sent to the Virginia colony in the hope that a silk industry would take hold there. Thirty years later, to provide a greater incentive to farmers, a law was enacted requiring every planter who hadn't raised at least 10 mulberry trees for every 100 acres to pay a fine of 10 pounds of tobacco. At the same time, 5,000 pounds of tobacco were promised to anyone who produced 1,000 pounds of silk in a single year. In response to this legislation, a member of the Virginia legislature planted 70,000 mulberry trees on his estate by 1664. In 1666 the law was repealed when it appeared that the silk industry had taken off, but the industry soon dissolved because new immigrants had considerable overhead and preferred to turn an immediate profit. So the culture of rice and indigo was introduced. Unlike silk culture, these crops did not require several years of start-up time; they brought in money almost from the beginning.

During the 1820s, the U.S. silk industry again showed signs of life. William Prince, who owned a nursery in Flushing, New York, was importing different varieties of mulberry trees from all over the world, but *multicaulis*, a cultivar of the white mulberry (*Morus alba*) brought over from the south of France, was one of the most sought-after breeds. The tree caught on rapidly among those attempting to get in on the ground floor of the revived silkworm industry. Prince plowed a substantial investment into propagating these trees, and while he was filling orders as fast

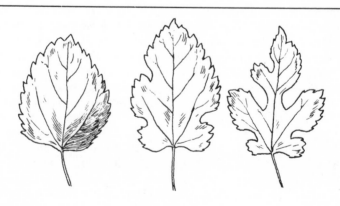

White mulberry

as he could get them out the door, he was also gambling much of his fortune on raising silkworms himself. Prince, as it turned out, was one of the few who succeeded in the venture. In spite of extensive efforts, all hope of establishing a silk industry in this country had been abandoned by 1900.

Although the American silk industry is now only a paragraph in the history books, it did serve to introduce a decorative and urban-tolerant tree to this country. That tree was the white mulberry. It was brought to the United States from Europe, but it is a native of China. Some 1,500 species of mulberries are found around the world, most of them in the tropics. Of those that will live in more temperate climates, the white mulberry was found to be a better host species than its American relatives, which include the red mulberry (*Morus rubra*), found from Massachusetts to southeastern Minnesota, south to southern Florida, and west to central Texas.

The leaves of the white mulberry can be either lobed or unlobed, as illustrated, with both types usually present on the same tree. White mulberry fruits look a bit like blackberries, but they vary in sweetness and in color, ranging from white to red or purple. The fruits are eagerly taken by birds and small animals. The seeds deposited in their feces have helped spread the trees through many habitats, and now the white mulberry tree is considered almost a weed species, sprouting up practically everywhere. It is a fast grower when young, and it can tolerate a wide range of conditions. This tree does well on a range of soils with different levels of compaction, in moist as well as dry conditions, and in the presence of salt. It does best on soils that vary in pH from 6.5 to 7.5. In spite of these advantages, the white mulberry is rarely planted along sidewalks because its fruit, when it drops, causes too much of a mess. There are, however, several nonfruiting cultivars, including the kingan, maple leaf, and stribling, which are often planted in public areas where the fruits would be an inconvenience.

The red mulberry tree is often confused with the white mulberry, but it is not difficult to distinguish between the two species. The leaves of the red mulberry are much larger, with hairy surfaces and long pointed tips. Do not count on being able to tell the two trees apart by the color of their fruit, however, since the white mulberry's fruit, as I said earlier, varies widely in color.

COTTONWOOD, POPLAR, AND ASPEN

The willow family contains both the poplar (*Populus*) and the willow (*Salix*) genera, which in turn contain about 350 species between them,

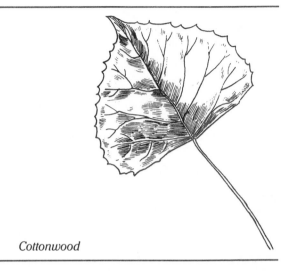

Cottonwood

though the willows are far more numerous than the poplars. Cotton-woods, poplars, and aspens are all in the genus *Populus*. These trees are found around the world, but are most common in northern temperate and arctic regions. The family has about 60 native shrubs in North America, about 35 native trees, and another 5 or so trees that have been introduced and are now reproducing on their own. By some counts, there are 15 native *Populus* species in North America.

All members of this family have alternate, simple leaves, which are usually toothed. Paired glands or stipules appear at the base of each leaf. The male staminate flowers and the female pistillate flowers appear on separate plants. The flowers are very small and are bunched together along narrow catkins. The members of the willow family are often associated with moist and wet soils because that is where the seeds germinate best. When they land on the water, they are blown or washed to the shore, often to moist, suitable soils. However, when they land on dry soils, the seeds rapidly dry up and are unable to germinate. Although they grow wild in wet areas, these trees usually do rather well when planted on drier soils.

The seeds are very small with long cottony hairs. The tree's common name is derived from the appearance of bunches of these seeds that look like cotton when they clump together.

The eastern cottonwood (*Populus deltoides*) is common in eastern cities and suburbs. Its large-toothed leaves are simple, alternate, and are shaped like triangles, with two corners rounded off and a third corner that comes to a long point. The shape is a cross between a triangle and a semicircle, with toothed edges. The leaves are thick and coarsely veined, 3 to 7 inches (7.5 to 18 cm) in length, often as broad as they are long. They are bright green and shiny above, paler below, with a light yellow midrib. The stalks are slightly flattened, often with a reddish tinge, and with small glands near the tip. The bark of the young trees is thin, smooth, and a greenish light gray color; it becomes more uniformly gray and deeply furrowed on the older specimens. Mature cottonwoods commonly reach heights of 80 to 100 feet (24 to 30 m), and can attain diameters of 3 to 4 feet (1 to 1.3 m). Most of the larger cottonwoods can live 75 years; on occasion, they even reach an age of 200 years. Early on, farmers began to plant cottonwoods widely because they grow very rapidly. Young specimens will grow from 2 to 5 feet (.6 to 1.5 m) a year on rich, moist, well-drained soils. Mature trees have a broad, spreading crown. This is one of the best shade trees when rapid growth is of primary importance.

Farther west, the plains cottonwood (*Populus sargentii*) is found in the prairie country of west central Canada and the United States. It has more ovate leaves. The narrowleaf cottonwood (*Populus angustifolia*) has narrow, willowlike leaves from 2 to 4 inches (5.2 to 10.4 cm) long, and from ½ to 1 inch (1.3 to 2.5 cm) wide. It is found most commonly through the western mountain states, usually along streams at altitudes of 5,000 to 10,000 feet (1,500 to 3,050 m). Narrowleaf cottonwoods are frequently planted as street trees in the Rocky Mountain region.

The Lombardy poplar (*Populus nigra* var. *italica*), a variety of black poplar (*Populus nigra*), is native to Europe and western Asia. Most people have seen this tall, spirelike tree. It, too, is planted for its rapid growth. Its compact crown makes it popular among those who wish to have a leafy border that blocks the view and breaks the wind. The Lombardy poplar seldom lives more than 50 years. These trees are often blown down during severe windstorms. The columnar look is so much admired that similar looking varieties of other species have been developed. They include varieties of crab apple, elm, ginkgo, locust, maple, mountain ash, oak, and pine. These varieties usually have such names as *columnaris, erecta, fastigiata,* or *pyramidalis*

Another closely related species—a native of Eurasia that was from Europe—is the white poplar (*Populus alba*). It has toothed leaves, usually with three to five lobes, which are dark green on one side and whitish and woolly on the reverse side. White poplars, unlike other trees in this family, often have several trunks. These trees have taken quite well to some of the wilder areas in urban parks, where their seeds have germinated, taken root, and grown, allowing the trees to become naturalized.

Quaking aspen (*Populus tremuloides*) is another species in this familiar genus. This tree's leaves quiver, shake, rustle, and quake almost all the time. It isn't the only *Populus* with trembling leaves, though. Cottonwood, bigtooth aspen (*Populus grandidentata*), and several others have leaf stalks that are long and flattened, especially at the base near the petiole, and this architecture is what perpetuates the leaves' constant motion. This peculiar adaptation may keep the contents of the leaves' cells moving around, increasing their photosynthetic efficiency, or it may give the trees a distinct appearance that attracts birds and insects which may benefit the tree in some way. The quaking motion may even shake eggs or insects off the foliage to prevent them from eating the leaves.

The quaking aspen's leaves flutter more easily and gracefully than those of the other quaking trees. This tree has a wider range than any other North American tree; it is native from New England and Labrador across to Alaska, and south along the Rocky Mountains to Mexico. But it is absent from most southern states east of the Rocky Mountains. The leaves are nearly round in outline, with 20 to 40 small teeth on each side. They are 1½ to 3 inches (3.8 to 7.6 cm) in diameter, thin, and firm, and they turn a distinctive golden yellow in autumn. This is a common roadside tree in disturbed areas. Quaking aspens are a little different in the West, where the leaves are thinner and rounder; these turn a paler lemon yellow in the fall.

The bigtooth aspen's leaves are slightly larger than those of the quaking aspen. These leaves also have fewer teeth, only about five to fifteen on each side. This species grows faster, gets a little larger, and appears to be more resistant to disease, but its range is more restricted; it is native from Nova Scotia south to North Carolina, west to Missouri, and north to Minnesota.

Many of the species in this genus, including both of these aspens and the eastern cottonwood, are thought of as pioneer species because their small seeds are easily blown by the wind to wide-open spaces where they will readily germinate and rapidly form large clones from shoots off the roots. After aspens move in, seedlings of conifers, hickories, maples, and oaks, all of which are more shade tolerant, readily grow beneath them. Within 100 years or less, only a few aspens will remain; the forest will be dominated by other species. However, in some environments other species do not displace the aspens. Several aspen clones have been aged, and one was believed to be approximately 10,000 years old.

In urban and suburban areas, land is constantly being disturbed, leaving open areas that are perfect for pioneer species to move into. Much work needs to be done to determine just what it takes for species to germinate in cracks in the pavement, along roadsides, in hot gravel, and so on. It would appear that the seeds and the seedlings need to be able to tolerate rapidly fluctuating temperatures, including the extreme heat of the summer. They also need to tolerate different moisture conditions, varying pH levels, and what for other species might be inadequate nutrients. Repeatedly we find the same characteristic species growing along roadsides and in abandoned parking lots and old fields; it shouldn't take too much work to find out what allows these species, to the exclusion of others, to move in and flourish, while most species are relegated to rural areas.

Hybrid poplars are very widespread in parts of Europe, where they are used in parks and lawns and along streets. They are favored for their beauty, their rapid growth, the relative ease with which they may be transplanted, and their hardiness in urban environments. Few can be seen in American cities, though, partly because they constantly drop dead twigs, which can become a maintenance problem, and because the females produce prodigious numbers of the cottonlike seeds, which blow everywhere. For these reasons, and because they are short-lived, they have yet to catch on as a street tree in many U.S. cities. However, advertisements appear regularly for these poplar hybrids, with accompanying promises of growth rates of 6 feet (1.8 m) a year. It's true that these trees grow rapidly, but they require optimal conditions and care, and as a result many who plant them never realize the advertised promises. One that has a narrow oval shape and grows fast is a hybrid between *Populus maximowiczii* and *Populus trichocarpa*. This hybrid is unusually tolerant to different soil conditions. Another fast-growing hybrid with a columnar shape is a blend of *Populus charkoviensis* and *Populus incrassata*. One columnar hybrid, which has small leaves and many small branches, is a mixture of *Populus deltoides* and *Populus caudina*.

Because so many different species and hybrids have been planted in cities and suburbs, it is not at all unusual to find poplars hybridizing on their own. Hybrids have been found in Central Park, where both Lombardy poplars and eastern cottonwoods were planted. The cross between these two species is known as *Populus* x *canadensis*.

WILLOWS

Although poplars, cottonwoods, and aspens, all in the genus *Populus*, are members of the willow family, the willows in the genus *Salix* are far more numerous. There may, in fact, be as many as 70 to 100 different willow species in North America.

Most willows are found in low, wet areas in rural regions. Those species that grow in built-up areas are sometimes difficult to identify because of the readiness with which they hybridize with one another. This problem is compounded by the similarity of so many of the species to begin with. Most have long, narrow, finely toothed leaves. The buds, arranged alternately and often right next to the twig, are usually small and single-scaled. The twigs tend to be long and thin and are often brightly colored.

The most familiar tree in this genus is the weeping willow, but this common name actually refers to a group of closely related species and hybrids, all of which have narrow, lance-shaped leaves, and long, thin, hanging branches. The most common is *Salix babylonica*, which is native to China. Because it doesn't do very well in the northern United States, it has been crossed with the crack willow (*Salix fragilis*) to produce a cold-tolerant hybrid.

The crack willow was initially brought over from Eurasia during colonial times and is now widely distributed from Newfoundland south to Virginia, west to Kansas, and north to North Dakota. Its wood was used to make the charcoal used in gunpowder. The tree spread rapidly, being planted for its shade and beauty. One of its problems, however, is that the brittle branches crack off during high winds, strong rain, heavy snow, or ice. This is a problem to varying degrees with most members of the willow family, and because the twigs tend to clog sewers, causing a significant maintenance problem, city officials usually avoid planting them along streets and highways.

One of the more widely planted hybrids of crack willow and weeping willow is the Wisconsin, or Niobe weeping willow (*Salix x blanda*), which is especially popular in the Midwest. Another popular hybrid is the golden weeping willow (*Salix alba* var. *tristis* [var. *vitellina pendula*]). This is a variety of the white willow (*Salix alba*), a Eurasian species that is easily recognized by its bright yellow twigs, but its leaves are very shiny, and the twigs are much longer. It is thought to have been derived from another cross between *Salix fragilis* and *Salix babylonica*. Weeping willows and the black willow (*Salix nigra*), a native of the eastern United States, are commonly planted in low, wet areas in city parks and back-yards.

The pussy willow (*Salix discolor*) is known by many for its fuzzy catkins, which appear during the spring. With the warmer weather they expand, revealing the tiny flowers that were concealed in the buds located underneath all the fuzz throughout the winter. Usually found in wet areas, they seldom exceed a height of 25 feet (7.6 m), and are most often only 10 to 20 feet (3 to 6 m) tall. The pussy willow belongs to a group of shrubby willows that are highly variable and very difficult to identify. Although few of these willows have wood that is useful, they are appreciated for their rapid growth and their ability to sop up water and thrive in areas few other trees could tolerate.

The bitter bark of the willows contains salicin, which was used during the 18th century to treat rheumatism and diseases of a periodic nature, such as malaria. Salicin is a bitter phenolic glycoside that is distasteful to many insects. While it protects willows from insect attack, it has beneficial physiological effects on humans, which explains its use in acetylsalicylic acid, or aspirin. The drug is now manufactured synthetically.

4

INSECTS AND OTHER INVERTEBRATES

Insects are the most widespread, diverse, and incredibly successful animals to ever live. They are among the most common organisms found in cities and suburbs. On the decorative plants found in corporate lobbies, for example, you'll find mealybugs, aphids, scale, and a host of other pests that are perhaps too well known to horticulturists. Many of the species of insects living in downtown lobbies were brought to this country from the tropics and cannot live outdoors in our more northern climates, but they thrive in such well-protected microclimates.

Every urban home has a wastebasket, stove, sink, toilet, and refrigerator, and many have cases of books and stacks of papers. All these objects attract insects. Most homes have a few species. Houses with basements may have more than a few. Apartment dwellers may occasionally have to deal with a horde of immigrant insects escaping from a neighboring flat.

Many other species of insects live in urban centers, parks, streets, and riverfront areas. Most of these species are adapted to living just about anywhere. I shall not list every insect species you may find in your urban environment. Instead, as in the other chapters, I shall discuss some of the more prevalent groups and some specific species.

SPIDERS

The phylum Arthropoda contains more species than any other phylum. Probably on the order of 80 percent of all animals are members of this group. Insects are arthropods, as are the crustaceans, which include crabs, lobsters, shrimp, and their relatives. The other major class in this phylum is Arachnida, which includes the spiders, scorpions, ticks, and mites. People regularly encounter some of these species in cities. This section concerns those arachnids that people tend to find in and around their homes.

Probably the best-known spider is the daddy-long-legs, which looks like a spider with elongate, stiltlike, spindly legs. Some of these are true spiders in the family Pholcidae, while others are harvestmen, members of the family Phalangiidae. Both harvestmen and daddy-long-legs have small, rounded, compact bodies surrounded by extremely long, thin legs. Don't worry if you have trouble distinguishing between these look-alikes. Few people can tell them apart. Generally, daddy-long-legs aren't nearly as abundant indoors as they are outside, but because they are so distinctive, people notice them and know their name. More than 100 of these very similar species are found across North America.

Another group of spiders that urban dwellers all know is the family of comb-footed spiders, also called cobweb weavers, members of the family Theridiidae. This is a large, varied group with more than 1,500 described species, more than 200 of them found in North America north of Mexico. One of these species, the American house spider (*Achaearanea tepidariorum*), is often responsible for spinning the silky cobwebs people are accustomed to finding in their homes. This spider is only about 1/3 inch (8 mm) in length, and is distinguished by streaks and patches of tan and darker brown on the sides of its spherical abdomen. Members of the cobweb weaver family are often found hanging upside down in their irregularly shaped webs. Two other genera in this family, *Theridion* and *Steatoda*, have members that cohabit with their human hosts. These spiders are called comb-footed because the last segment of their fourth leg is equipped with fine comblike bristles, used to draw silk from their spinnerets when encasing their prey.

Among the many groups with a spherical abdomen is the genus *Latrodectus*, or the widows. Of the cobweb weavers, these are the largest and probably the best known. All the widows are poisonous, although only the females bite. They are distinguished by an orange or reddish hourglass shape under their otherwise dark abdomen. The black widow (*Latrodectus mactans*) is found in warmer areas all around the world, but populations extend much farther north than most people realize. One congener—or species in the same genus—*Latrodectus curacaviensis*, the northern black widow, is found all the way from southern Argentina to southern Canada. Another similar species, the northern widow (*Latrodectus variolus*), ranges from northern Florida to southern Canada. This spider has the distinct hourglass, but it is usually broken into two parts. The northern black widow is often confused with the common black widow. Male common black widows are much smaller than the females, which are readily distinguished by that unmistakable hourglass marking underneath the abdomen. Of these species, the venom of the black widow is believed to be the most virulent. However, testing the virulence of any of the lesser known species is a task for which few people volunteer.

In North America the black widow spider ranges from Florida to Massachusetts, and west to Texas, Oklahoma, and Kansas. Because they are most common in the South, that's where most of the bites are reported. But in spite of its reputation, this is not a very bold spider. They usually retreat rather than stand their ground, unless guarding an egg mass. This is the job of the female, since after mating she usually eats the male, ergo the name "widow."

The greatest number of black widows I ever saw in one place was in an otherwise fine restaurant in downtown Veracruz, Mexico. While waiting for my meal to be served, I got up to look at the view out over the water, where several people had been eaten by sharks, and I noticed cobwebs in the windows. Looking more closely I found a female black widow guarding an egg mass in each of the many corners.

Several similar species of brown spiders (family Loxoscelidae) in the genus *Loxosceles* are found throughout the southern United States. Many of these spiders may be poisonous, but few live in close contact with people, except for the brown recluse (*Loxosceles reclusa*). Most of these spiders are only about ½ inch (12 mm) long. Their coloration is dull, and their web is a nondescript sheet of sticky silk that doesn't have any distinguishing characteristics. The brown recluse is found all through the south central United States, where it commonly lives in houses and comes out after dark. People rarely know they have them in their homes until someone is bitten. Dr. John Scherr, a physician in Atlanta, Georgia, reports that the majority of brown recluse bites occur in the garage or basement, areas that are usually dark, where there are spider webs. He says that the venom of the brown recluse is quite virulent to some people, and the painful bite can inflict a wound that sometimes stays open for weeks, occasionally even months.

The family Argiopidae, also known as the Araneidae, or orb weavers, range in size from ⅕ inch to larger than 2 inches (5 mm to 52 mm). They have a large abdomen in relation to their overall size, and their legs are strongly curved. The orb weaver constructs a vertical orb web with many concentric rings and a series of radii. In the center of the web is usually a series of zigzags, and the spider is generally nearby, waiting motionlessly, in a head-down position. Spiders in this family typically weave their vertical webs outdoors in vegetation, which is why some are known as garden spiders. Another genus in this family, *Araneus*, has more than 1,500 described species, and they occur all over the world.

CENTIPEDES

Another class of invertebrates, the Chilopoda, or centipedes, are distinguished by flat, long, wormlike bodies with fifteen or more pairs of legs. Each body segment has just one pair of legs, unlike the millipedes (class Diplopoda), which have two pairs of legs per body segment. (All the members of the class Insecta have three body segments and a total of six legs.)

Centipedes are usually found in soil and debris, as well as under rocks and logs. There are many additional species that live in a wide range of habitats. On the first body segment just behind the head they all have appendages that look like little pincers. With these organs they insert a poison when piercing their prey. The bite of some species of centipedes can be extremely painful to humans. The house centipede (*Scutigera coleoptrata*) that commonly occurs in homes and apartments in the eastern United States and Canada, however, is harmless, or usually harmless. The house centipede is a member of the family Scutigeridae. Unlike most other centipede families, this has long legs and a very distinctive movement.

There are no records of scutigerids ever having bitten anyone when not provoked. The only records of bites come from people who were handling them, which is neither easy nor pleasant. You have only to touch these centipedes and their legs start to fall off. We do not know whether this is an evolutionary strategy that has helped protect them, similar to the slippery scales or hairs covering silverfish, or the tails of some species of salamanders and lizards that break off when you grab them. It could just be that these animals are amazingly fragile. Since they live in dark places where they are seldom seen, their fragility may not matter very often.

Centipedes are more common in the southern parts of the country, but with central heating, populations have been known to thrive farther north, and they are now found in buildings everywhere, usually in damp areas like bathrooms and basements. Their numbers never reach the point where they pose much of a problem. Their diet consists of small insects, such as flies and moths, so if you find any in your home, it is probably best to leave them alone. An older, well-fed centipede may reach a length ranging from 1 to 3 inches (2.5 to 7.6 cm); at that size they will even eat large roaches.

SILVERFISH

Some of today's insects are thought to be early, primitive offshoots from the main stock. One such group is known as the Thysanura, or bristletails. Members of this wingless order of insects are somewhat different from most other wingless insects in that their lack of wings is thought to be primitive. They aren't insects that previously had wings and lost them due to evolutionary changes. Rather they evolved and became established before any predecessors had wings—in other words, during a time when insect wings did not yet exist. This group is even more ancient than the cockroaches, with a fossil record dating back well over 300 million years.

Another characteristic that sets this group apart from most other insects is that the adults look like the young. They are known as bristletails because most have two or three long, thin, jointed appendages, like bristles, at the rear of the body. Their antennae are long, and some species have leglike structures on segments of the abdomen, which is unique among living groups of insects.

There are not many species in this group, and the entire order contains only four families. One family, Lepismatidae, is the best known because it includes some domestic species that live in buildings throughout the United States. The most widely recognized species are probably the silverfish (*Lepisma saccharina*) and the firebrat (*Thermobia domestica*). These two insects feed on all types of starchy substances and can become pests. They have been known to damage libraries, being attracted to the starch in the book bindings and labels. Starched clothing, linens, curtains, silk, and the starch in wallpaper glue all provide nourishment to these organisms. In grocery stores they will prey on any foods that contain starch.

The name silverfish was undoubtedly suggested by the tiny scales or hairs that cover the body of this insect, giving it a shiny, fishlike appearance. Silverfish are silvery white with a yellowish sheen around the antennae and legs. Lengths may vary, but they are usually less than ½ inch long (8 to 12 mm).

Firebrats resemble silverfish except that they have darker markings on the upper surface, and they are more common in warm spots around the home, especially near stoves, fireplaces, and furnaces. The firebrat has also been called the asbestos bug because it feeds on the sizing in asbestos insulation, which was used to insulate hot water and steam pipes before it was learned that asbestos is carcinogenic.

Both the silverfish and the firebrat move around in the dark and, when startled, can move very rapidly. Because of the scales on their soft bodies, when you attempt to catch them, it's not at all unusual for them to slide right under your fingers, leaving a film of scales behind.

Should either of these species become a problem, methoxychlor, propoxur, Diazinon®, or Malathion® can be applied to cracks or places where the animals go. Since such pesticides aren't always as safe as the labels claim, they should not be used unless your silverfish or firebrats have become really destructive.

DRAGONFLIES

The dragonflies and damselflies are insects in the order Odonata. There are thousands of species worldwide. They have two pairs of long, thin, membranous, many-veined wings. Their relatively large heads easily pivot in all directions, being flexibly connected to their long, slender bodies. With their large eyes and rotary head movement, they seem to be constantly aware of everything going on around them. Most are rather large, usually 1 to 5 inches (2.5 to 12.7 cm) long. Their antennae are very short and inconspicuous.

Dragonfly flight is currently being studied by aeronautical engineers at the University of Colorado, where it has been learned that a dragonfly generates lift amounting to seven times its body weight. Airplanes at their best generate only 1.3 times their weight in lift.

Among the superfamily Aeshnoidea, the family of darners, Aeshnidae includes some species found around ponds and lakes in urban areas. The darners are the largest dragonflies in North America; most are 2¼ to 3¼ inches long (6.4 to 8.3 cm). They are strong and fast in flight, and are almost impossible to catch—unless you know that a startled dragonfly almost always shoots forward, up and away at a 45° angle. All one needs to do is hold a butterfly net in front of the insect, startle it, and it will fly into the net.

One relatively common dragonfly is the green darner (*Anax junius*). The males have a blue abdomen and no markings on the wings, with a greenish thorax. The females differ slightly; their abdomens are greenish violet and, when in a certain light, their wings are a faint golden color.

Dragonfly

These dragonflies are migratory and at times during the late summer and early autumn are seen congregating in large numbers.

Species of dragonflies that migrate are known around the world, though where they're migrating isn't always clear. One common species regularly migrates up and down the Nile. Some species have been observed grouping together by the millions, and certain species travel as much as several hundred miles. Most of the well-documented migrations have been recorded in Europe and Africa.

In the superfamily Libelluloidea, or the skimmers, is the family Libellulidae, the common skimmers. This family includes several of the brightly colored and distinctly marked dragonflies commonly found near urban ponds. Many of these skimmers are fast and strong in flight and like other dragonflies, they are often seen stopping in midflight to hover momentarily. The eastern United States has four especially common species in this family. All are found near ponds in urban, suburban, and rural areas.

One widely recognized species is the white-tailed dragonfly (*Plathemis lydia*). They measure from 1⅝ to 2 inches (4 to 5.2 cm) from the head to the end of the abdomen, with a wingspan of 2½ to 3 inches (3.8 to 7.6 cm). The males have a striking white abdomen, with a broad dark band toward the end of each of the four wings with four smaller markings closer to the abdomen, on each of the wings. The female doesn't have any white on the abdomen. Of all the dragonflies studied, this one copulates the fastest, usually lasting 30 seconds, while 5 minutes is more common for other species.

A smaller species that is frequently encountered in urban parks is the common amberwing (*Perithemis tenera*). It is a little more than an inch (about 3 cm) long from the head to the end of its abdomen, with a wingspan of about 1½ inches (3.8 cm). The wings are amber in the male while they are clear with brown spots in the female.

Another common species found around ponds throughout the eastern, central, and southern states is the blue pirate (*Pachydiplax longipennis*). The wings are often tinged with a light brown, and the female's body is usually brown with yellow markings, while the males develop a blue body after emerging. This developmental color change observed among the males of some species is known as pruinosity. The same process is involved with male white-tailed dragonflies when they develop their white abdomen. As the males of some species get their full colors, a substance emerges through the integument, which accounts for the whitish or bluish markings that appear. The substance looks powdery and feels greasy, and will come off if you rub it. Little is known about either the process or the structure. Recently it has been suggested that the function of the pruinosed colors could be related to vision in the ultraviolet spectrum, because most pruinosity is quite distinct in the ultraviolet.

The green-jacket skimmer (*Erythemis simplicicollis*) is another common species that is often found near ponds in urban parks. These dragonflies have a green face, and the females have a black and green body. The males are only black and green when young, and later pruinose to a blue or green that is significantly different from the green color of the female. The wings don't have any markings. The reason most of these dragonflies are found near ponds is because the males select a site where they wait for a female to come in. After mating, the female lays eggs, and then she leaves. Because the males stay and wait while the females come in, accomplish their reproductive functions, and leave to feed elsewhere, 95 percent of the dragonflies found near ponds are usually males.

Another family well represented in urban environments is the Coenagrionidae, or the narrow-winged damselflies, which includes many genera and species that live in a variety of habitats. Most are weak fliers and, unlike the other families already mentioned, when damselflies land on something, they usually hold their wings up over the body rather than out flat. The sexes are differently colored among most of the species, the males being brighter. The family comprises the bluets, which are usually light blue with some black markings, though some are bright orange or bright red. *Enallagma* is the largest genus in the family, with 38 species in the United States. They are usually found around ponds, with several species occurring in suburbs as well as cities. An abundant form in the eastern United States is the common forktail (*Ischnura verticalis*). The males are dark with green stripes on the thorax and blue at the rear tip of the abdomen. Most of the females are bluish green, though some are brownish orange, and still others look more like the males.

Next to mosquitoes, dragonflies and damselflies are probably the best-known insects having aquatic larval stages. Their nymphs, or naiads, known to some as perch bugs, are drab colored, usually brown, and somewhat bizarre looking. They live on the bottom of ponds, lakes, streams, or rivers, usually among the muck and vegetation. They are not common in fast-moving or polluted waters. Many city parks have ponds, and these habitats have proved suitable for several species.

Odonate nymphs are carnivorous, eating aquatic insects, annelids, small crustacea, and mollusks. The very small nymphs eat protozoa. The entire life cycle takes about one year in most species, though many have aquatic stages that overwinter, extending the life cycle to two years. When the nymphs are ready to be transformed into adults, they crawl out of the water, usually onto some vegetation or onto the shore. Their exoskeleton, the supporting structure covering the outside of the body, then splits down the back, and the adult slowly works its way out. Before it can fly off, it has to remain still for about an hour until the wings dry and stiffen.

The adults are often seen mating, and the females may be seen flying near the surface of the water, touching it with her abdomen periodically as she scatters her eggs. Some species deposit their eggs on the surface of the water; others put them in floating mats of algae or in the sand, mud, or vegetation along the water's edge. All damselflies and some true dragonflies cut holes in submerged plant stems with their specialized egg-laying apparatus, their ovipositor, and then insert their eggs. If you watch carefully, you can see these insects catching smaller insects with their feet while in flight and then transferring the prey to their mouths. To see this the light has to be perfect.

Fossils show there were dragonflies with wingspans of several feet, but the evolution of avian predators that were able to chase them down may have eliminated opportunities for all the larger odonates, forcing them to survive in the niches available for smaller odonates, where they continue to do remarkably well.

Dragonflies and damselflies recently were the center of a controversy in New York City. The New York City Department of Parks and Recreation planned to drain Belvedere Lake in Central Park, dredge the bottom, and rebuild much of the shoreline. What hadn't been considered was the effect this would have on the nineteen species of dragonflies known to occur there. There are many species of damselflies at Belvedere Lake, too, but they have yet to be properly identifed. While there are hundreds of odonate species across the country, to find this many doing well in the middle of Manhattan is significant. In response to pressures from conservationists, environmentalists, and organizations like the Audubon Society, the Parks Department is assessing its options with regard to potential alternatives without adversely affecting the dragonflies there.

CRICKETS

The cricket family, Gryllidae, is a member of the insect order Orthoptera, which also contains the grasshoppers, walking sticks, mantids, cockroaches, and katydids. Worldwide there are over 900 described species of crickets. Their hind legs, like the grasshopper's, are built for jumping. The antennae are long and thin; most forms are winged. The front wings are usually long, narrow, and somewhat thickened, while the hind wings are membranous, broad, and have many veins. When the cricket is not flying, its hind wings are usually folded like a fan underneath the front wings.

Crickets are probably best known for the sounds they produce, primarily by rubbing one part of their body against another. This process is called stridulation. Gryllids rub the sharp edge at one end of a front wing along a filelike ridge underneath the other front wing. Both front

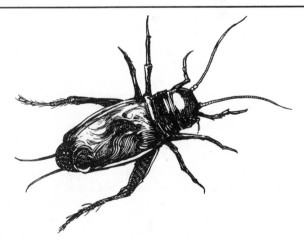

Cricket

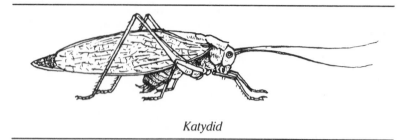

Katydid

wings have a file and a scraper. When the song is produced, the front wings are elevated and can be seen moving back and forth. The sounds made are usually species-specific—that is, each species produces a distinctive sound. Recently it has been shown that some species, which were previously thought to be undifferentiated, actually differ with regard to when they make their sounds rather than by what the call sounds like. The calls are usually delivered as pulses, often produced at a regular rate. They sound like a trill, a buzz, or a chirp. Some female Orthopterans make sounds, but sound production is primarily a function of the males, who do it to attract females.

A gryllid subfamily known as the Gryllinae contains the house and field crickets. They are usually over ½ inch (1.3 cm) in length, and they vary in color from brown to black. These crickets are common in fields, along roadsides, in lawns, and sometimes in homes. One of the most abundant species in the East is the northern field cricket (*Gryllus pennsylvanicus*). The house cricket (*Acheta domesticus*), an Old World species that was introduced into this country from Europe, was initially reported in New York State during the first quarter of the 19th century, and it subsequently spread rapidly. It could be that people helped move these crickets around because when they first arrived they were something of a novelty; their chirping was thought to be cheerful. They are now widely distributed throughout the United States.

Each year from mid-September to early October, a species of cricket becomes quite a nuisance in Austin, Texas, where the insects gather in hordes. Each morning masses of crickets are found next to the state capitol, where they seem to be attracted to the illuminated dome. They enter the building through any hole and can be found everywhere. When they die, their smell is awful, and they create a considerable maintenance problem; spraying apparently has no effect on these insects. The solution to Austin's cricket problem seems simple: turn off the dome lights in September.

COCKROACHES

The insect order Orthoptera includes cockroaches in addition to grasshoppers, crickets, mantids, and walking sticks. Some taxonomists—scientists who classify organisms into groups and categories—place all the cockroaches in the suborder Blattaria, which other taxonomists call Blattodea, or Blattoidea. The most widely recognized family in this suborder is Blattidae.

Worldwide there may be about 3,500 species, most of them found in the tropics. It is now believed by most experts that all cockroaches are native to Africa, and have been inadvertently introduced around the world. In the United States, at last count there were 56 species, most of which are found in the South. Several species represent those that most people see, the ones that are household pests. Cockroaches carry some pathogens, and it has been demonstrated that they can transmit food poisoning, but for the most part they do not spread much disease.

As a group, the cockroaches are identified by their flattened, oval shape and downturned, concealed head, which is usually underneath the large front section known as the pronotum. These insects have long, thin antennae, and some species have well-developed wings. They eat a wide range of food, including dead animals, and the more domestic species eat food left around the kitchen. Their eggs are enclosed in a capsule.

Cockroaches prefer to come out in the dark, so when you walk into the kitchen at night and turn on the lights, you find out how much of a roach problem you have. These insects breed quickly and do well where they can scavenge the small amounts of food left around the stove, kitchen table, floor, sink, and waste basket.

The smallest of the household species is the German cockroach

American cockroach

(*Blatella germanica*), which is ½ to ¾ inch (13 to 20 mm) long. Actually a native of northwest Africa, it is also found throughout Europe and parts of Asia. This roach is light brown with two darker longitudinal stripes on the pronotum. The female carries her egg case until the eggs are almost ready to hatch. If you kill a roach carrying an egg case, make sure you squash the egg case as well. German cockroaches are commonly found in kitchens. In the North, they appear to pass through about three generations a year.

In the eastern United States, some people still refer to the German cockroach as the Croton bug, or water bug. These names were coined during the 1840s when huge water pipes were constructed to bring water from the Croton reservoir to New York City. The pipes served as a route of dispersal for the roaches. Croton was the first town in America where these insects were found, and they rapidly spread when the Croton aqueduct was completed in 1842. In Germany these insects are called Russian cockroaches, but in the Soviet Union they are called South European roaches. No one seems to want to accept responsibility for the origin of this invertebrate.

The larger American cockroach (*Periplaneta americana*) is 1¼ to 1½ inches (32 to 38 mm) long. Adults are darker and more reddish than the smaller German cockroach, with a yellowish band around the margin of the pronotum. They are more often found in warm basements of city buildings than in kitchens. It is widely believed that this cockroach originally came to North America from tropical Africa with the slave trade.

The Oriental roach (*Blatta orientalis*) is a relatively large, dark brown roach, normally about ¾ inch (20 to 25 mm) long. For many years people thought it was native to North America. Early writings were interpreted to mean that this insect was already a problem shortly after the Pilgrims arrived on the Mayflower. Actually, without precise descriptions, it is impossible to be sure what insects were encountered. It is more likely that this roach traveled from Africa to Asia to Europe and then to North America, arriving after the Pilgrims came here. The Oriental cockroach is now found in many of our northern cities, though it is most abundant in central and southern cities.

The brown-banded cockroach (*Supella longipalpa*), also known as the tropical cockroach, is light brown with mottling. The females have reddish brown wings, while the males' wings are lighter. The adults are only about ½ inch (13 mm) long. Though more common in the South, they are found in the northern regions of the country as well, surviving in heated buildings where they usually live near kitchens and bathrooms.

There are many other cockroach species in the country, though none as widespread as the species mentioned above. Most of the species that have become household pests are found almost exclusively in densely populated areas. What may be the most recent roach arrival to join North America's growing cockroach fauna is the flying Asian cockroach (*Blatella asiana*). Though currently restricted to the Tampa, Florida, area, there are fears that within a matter of years, they may spread throughout much of the East Coast and, with few restrictions, they could continue their city hopping aboard trucks and cars right across the continent.

One way to control cockroaches is to eliminate most of their food supply. Without food, they will move elsewhere. If you kill every roach you see, over time you can amount to a formidable predator. But this method will work only if your population is small enough to deal with. Centipedes, mice, rats, and cats will also prey on your roaches. If, however, your population is so large that you and your household pests and pets cannot put a dent in the overall numbers, you can use chemicals. One of the least expensive and most effective is boric acid, which can be bought as a powder in most drug stores. Boric acid is toxic and it should be used appropriately. Sprinkle the white powder in places where the insects are likely to walk—behind the sink, for example, because they go there to get water, under the waste basket, along the floor against the wall, near holes in the floor and wall, behind the stove, and along the base of the refrigerator. The roaches will walk through the boric acid and get it on their bodies. Later, when grooming themselves, they will ingest the powder, which will kill them. Many commercial roach traps and poisons are available. The insecticides Baygon®, chlorpyrifos, Diazinon®, malathion, and resmethrin are also effective. Spray the chemical along baseboards, under cupboards, under the kitchen sink, in the bathroom, and in other warm, moist places. Don't apply these chemicals everywhere, only in places where you know the roaches hide.

No matter how many chemicals you use, if you don't cut off the roaches' food supply, you may be in for a long fight. Some people go so far as to rinse out cans and bottles before throwing them in the trash, and they carefully wrap all edible garbage before throwing it out in order to reduce the amount of food available to cockroaches. I even know a woman who puts her garbage in the refrigerator to keep it away from the roaches. I'd say she's taken the fight a step too far. In the aggregate, these techniques will keep your roach problem down to a minimum. But if your neighbors harbor large roach populations, you will always have the insects migrating into your apartment, so constant vigilance will be necessary.

TERMITES

Termites feed on organic matter and sometimes completely destroy wood and books. These colonial insects—insects that live together in colonies—are in the order Isoptera. Termite colonies contain both winged and wingless forms. Their bodies are usually whitish, but the winged adults are sometimes brown or black. This order has about 2,000 described species, most of which are tropical. About 40 species occur in the United States.

Termites, sometimes called white ants, look something like ants, though the two groups are not closely related. They differ in that termites are soft-bodied and usually light-colored. In the winged forms, the front and hind wings of termites are the same size and with the same venation—that is, the same pattern of veins—while the front wings of ants are larger and have more veins than the hind wings. The termite's abdomen broadly meets the thorax, whereas the ant's abdomen is constructed at the base and is joined to the thorax by a narrow petiole, or stem. Many other characteristics differentiate the two groups, including differences in the antennae and the caste systems.

Some termites live in dry areas above ground, and others live in moist, underground habitats. The termites that live in moist areas eat wood that is buried or in contact with the soil. In San Francisco, where the climate is humid and temperate for much of the year, a considerable termite problem has resulted in a building code that does not allow any new buildings to be constructed with wood touching the ground.

In the United States, most termite species eat dead wood. This is largely composed of the complex carbohydrate, cellulose, which becomes nutritious when broken down in the termite's gut. With the aid of single-celled, flagellated protozoans in the order Hypermastigida, which live in the termite's digestive tract, these insects are able to digest wood. Some termites have bacteria, rather than protozoa, that break down cellulose. Without either of these symbiotic microorganisms, termites would starve to death.

In the tropics, many species of termites build large, exposed nests constructed from termite excrement, soil, and chewed-up wood. American species, however, build small, narrow tunnels right through wood and construct covered passages that protect them from light and the desiccating effects of the air. The most common termite species in the United States, the one that causes the greatest amount of damage, is *Reticulitermes flavipes*.

The best way to avoid a termite problem is to be sure that your building has no wood that comes in contact with the ground. All wood should be at least 18 inches (45 cm) above the ground. Foundations should be sealed, and any cracks that form over the years should be patched. Expansion joints used to be filled with coal-tar pitch, and the wood was treated with coal-tar creosote, the same material that was used to treat telephone poles, for the same reason. But now many of the more susceptible construction materials are pretreated with termiticides as a preventive measure.

Once termites have infested a building, controlling them can be a long, expensive battle. When possible, the colony should be located and dug up, and all the adults, larvae, and eggs should be killed or removed. It used to be that the walls containing the termites' tunnels and the covered passages were scraped and treated with creosote. The wood containing the termites was removed and replaced with metal or cement, even if this meant replacing timbers in the main frame. The remaining, unaffected wood was treated with creosote, and, when possible, cement or metal was inserted between the ground and any wooden parts of the structure.

Such measures were complicated and expensive, and this was not a do-it-yourself job. Now, exterminators use strong insecticides that are not available to consumers because they are so dangerous. When you discover a termite problem, it is always prudent to hire an exterminator; waiting can only prove more costly. Hiring a reputable exterminator can also be important because when certain insecticides are applied incorrectly, the fumes may persist for years, creating a potentially hazardous situation.

Termite infestation occurs most often in humid, temperate areas that do not generally have severe winters, but the drier, more northern cities are not immune to such damage. Just recently, for example, in New York City, I inspected a brownstone that was being renovated. Its main beams revealed considerable termite damage, so they were all removed and replaced with metal beams.

BOOK LICE

Psocoptera represent an order of more than 1,000 species of small, soft-bodied insects. The United States has some 40 genera and nearly 150 species. Virtually no one has heard of any of them, and fewer people have ever seen any. Many species in this group live outdoors and have well-developed wings. Those that live indoors are usually wingless and are found in association with old papers and books—ergo, their name, book lice. Despite the name, however, they aren't related to the true lice, which are all members of Anoplura, another order of insects. Unlike true lice, book lice aren't parasitic, and few look louselike.

Trogiidae and Liposcelidae are families of book lice most commonly found indoors. The two groups are differentiated by the thickness of the femora in their hind legs; the trogiids' hind femora are more slender than those of the liposcelids. Psocopterans feed on fungi, such as molds and mildew, as well as on starch granules, pollen, and dead insects. If book lice are present, you can see them when you open old books or papers, if you search carefully. Look for a tiny, translucent, creamy or yellowish insect rapidly moving across the page. These insects are only about a millimeter long, so you will need a magnifying glass to see that they have six legs, no wings, a well-developed head with chewing mouth parts, small compound eyes, and very thin antennae that are about one-half as long as the entire body.

Don't be fooled into believing that book lice won't cause much damage because they are so small. Part of my library was once damaged in a flood that left considerable fungal growth on the books. The growth of this mildew was arrested when the books were dried out, but it was at this point that I noticed all the book lice. They had probably been there all along, but the population increased considerably with the new availability of mildew, which they were feeding on. People who purchase a lot of old books have a good chance of bringing book lice into their home. The book lice eat the fungi in old books, and they probably feed on the sizing in the paper and on the paste that holds the bindings together as well, particularly older bindings. Although they do only a small amount of harm at one time, over the years they can damage an entire collection.

Book lice are difficult to eliminate. Prolonged heat and dry air will usually decrease the size of the population, but it isn't always easy to apply this type of treatment to an entire library. Dusting or spraying a library with pesticides such as pyrethrin or malathion can also be effective. When properly applied, fumigants penetrate all porous materials, including wood and books. The best advice I can give is to keep your books in a dry, well-ventilated area. If you have book lice that you find difficult to live with, spring for a proper fumigation.

There is one other elimination method available that has been used successfully with the next group of pests, that may work with book lice. Some libraries, particularly rare book libraries, have purchased special freezers in which books are placed and left until all the eggs and insects have died.

BOOKWORMS, GRAIN BEETLES, AND MEALWORMS

The insects that eat through books and can cause considerable damage to libraries are often known as bookworms. The species that actually eat right through the pages, leaving behind nasty little tunnels, represent any of several species of bread beetles or furniture beetles. The adult beetles are usually small and dark, reaching a length of less than a quarter of an inch (6 mm).

The bread beetle that has been called the bookworm was originally a grain feeder; it will eat ground grain anywhere it is available. Having invaded a place where grain is stored, such as a warehouse or bakery, the adult beetle will eventually lay its eggs on the premises. During earlier times, when people kept grain and flour in and near their homes, these beetles presented a serious problem. If they laid their eggs on old books, the larvae would hatch and then eat through the pages. Eventually the fat grub, which is also quite small, rarely larger than the adult beetle, would pupate, metamorphose into an adult beetle, eat its way out of the book, and continue its life cycle. Luckily bookworm tunnels are seldom seen anymore.

Occasionally people still find grubs or beetles in their flour, cereal, dried fruit or vegetables, shelled nuts, chocolate, spices, candies, pet food, or birdseed. Infestation can occur in a warehouse, in transit, on a grocer's shelf, or in your home. You may discover the insects when you open a package of flour or when you see small brown or black beetles, or their larvae or pupae, in a cupboard near stored grain products. But very few products are purchased containing beetles any longer because most grain is treated with chemicals that eliminate insect problems. Also, products are packaged so well that few can become contaminated with insects during transit or while sitting on the grocer's shelves. Although the tendency may still be to blame the store or the manufacturer, in most cases the source of the beetle infestation is the home.

Twenty-five or more different species of insects are found from time to time in grain products used in the home. I will describe several of the most common species. The smallest is the saw-toothed grain beetle (*Oryzaephilus surinamensis*), which is only about $1/10$ inch (2.5 mm) long. Its name comes from the ridges, or teeth, on either side of its thorax. This species is distributed worldwide. A very similar beetle in size, shape, and habits is the square-necked grain beetle (*Cathartus quadricollis*), which is found in the southern states.

Probably the most common flour beetle is the confused flour beetle (*Tribolium confusum*), generally known among millers as the bran bug; it is only $1/7$ to $1/5$ inch (3 to 5 mm) long. This small, hard-shelled, dark brown beetle is the most serious flour pest in North America. It is more abundant in the temperate regions. The red flour beetle (*Tribolium castaneum*) is similar in size and shape and is usually reddish brown. It is common in the southern states. The key to telling these two species apart is the arrangement of the antennal segments. The antennae of the confused flour beetle gradually increase in size until they are much thicker at the outer ends than at the roots. In the red flour beetle, however, the outer segments of the antennae abruptly become markedly thicker than the inner segments.

Two species of mealworms are found in grain products around the world. They are the yellow mealworm (*Tenebrio molitor*) and the dark mealworm (*Tenebrio obscurus*). Both are considerably larger than the grain beetles described above. Mealworm adults are usually slightly more than ½ inch (13 to 17 mm) long. Adult yellow mealworms are reddish brown, while adult dark mealworms tend to be black. The larvae of both species are raised as food for captive animals and can be purchased in pet shops. Both species do well in a box containing oatmeal and a potato, or some other source of moisture. The larvae of these species, when just hatched from the eggs, are barely visible to the naked eye. The tiny, creamy yellow worms feed on grain and flour for a week or two until they pupate, then the adults lay hundreds of eggs and live a few years.

The best way to eliminate grain beetles and mealworms is to destroy all infested products. Store uninfested products in glass jars with tight-fitting lids. There may be unhatched eggs in some fresh products, so check the jars later and throw the grain away if you find any larvae. Thoroughly clean the infested area of your cupboard, including cracks and corners where small amounts of flour tend to accumulate. Treat the cupboard with the household formulation of malathion, known as Cythion®, or with Diazinon® or pyrethrin and piperonyl butoxide, using a paintbrush or spray can. Do not allow any of these chemicals to touch your food or utensils. Once the chemicals have thoroughly dried, cover the area with clean shelf paper, and then put everything back on the shelf. If the beetles reappear, you'll know that either the last cleaning was inadequate or you have bought another infested package. To avoid infestations, purchase smaller amounts of meal and flour products in tightly wrapped packages.

WATER BUGS

Lay people use the word "bug" to denote many species of insects. Entomologists, however, use this word only for hemipterans, the true bugs. All members of the order Hemiptera have piercing-sucking mouthparts that form a narrow beak, and the various water bugs discussed in this chapter fall into this order. A reminder, however, at the outset: cockroaches are sometimes referred to as water bugs because they are found near pipes and faucets, but they are unrelated to the true water bugs and were discussed earlier in this chapter.

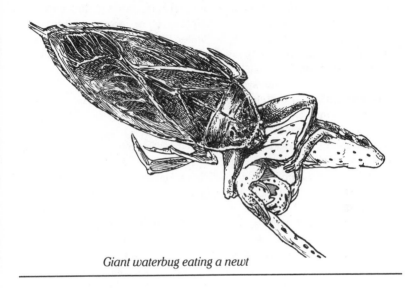

Giant waterbug eating a newt

Water boatmen, like all water bugs, are aquatic insects. These members of the Corixidae family have small, elongate, oval bodies with long hind legs that are oarlike. It takes an expert to distinguish the genera as well as the many very similar species. Most are only about ¼ to ½ inch (6 to 13 mm) long. They are grayish or brown; the upper surface usually has thin crossbands, and the two pairs of wings are concealed while the insect is in the water.

Most feed on algae and small aquatic invertebrates. Like other aquatic bugs, they don't have gills and must come to the surface for air, though they will often take a bubble of air underwater and carry it under their wings or on the surface of the body. Water boatmen can be found in city ponds. Many other aquatic bugs bite when handled; this one cannot.

Another group of true bugs, the back swimmers, are members of the Notonectidae family. These bugs look very similar to the water boatmen except that they swim upside down—but, of course, *they* don't think it's upside down. Back swimmers feed on insects, tadpoles, and small fish. They will often attack prey considerably larger than themselves, from which they will suck the bodily juices with their sucking mouthparts. When handled, they can inflict a rather painful bite that feels like a bee sting. It seems that the pain is caused by the juices in their saliva, injected under the skin. There are two genera of back swimmers in the United

States. The larger, more common species belongs to the genus *Notonecta*. *Notonecta undulata* is the species most often encountered.

The family of giant water bugs, the Belostomatidae, includes some of the largest members in the order Hemiptera. These insects reach a length of over 4 inches (10 cm), but in the United States few exceed 2½ inches (6.4 cm). They are brown, oval, and flattened; their wings are always tightly folded over their back when they are not flying. They readily leave the water and fly around, especially at night, when they are sometimes attracted to lights. Giant water bugs are frequently found in freshwater ponds and lakes where they feed on a wide range of insects, snails, tadpoles, small fish, and occasionally on salamanders, frogs, and even hatchling turtles. Be careful with these insects because they can inflict a painful bite. Three genera occur in the United States: *Abedus*, *Belostoma*, and *Lethocerus*, of which the latter two are more widely distributed. A giant water bug in the genus *Lethocerus* is illustrated on the previous page.

Of all the water bugs, water striders are probably encountered most frequently. The family of water striders, Gerridae, consists of a group of slender-bodied, long-legged insects that skate about on the water's surface where they feed on small insects, especially those that fall or get washed into the water and struggle at the surface to escape. Water striders have a dark brown body that is only about ⅜ to 1 inch (1.0 to 2.5

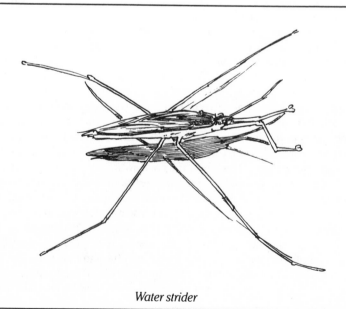

Water strider

cm) long. Although they have three pairs of legs, because their front pair is short and the two succeeding pairs considerably longer, one might think they have only four legs. Water striders are usually found on calm waters, in coves, and protected areas where they are most likely to find struggling insects. Apparently responding to the ripples created by any small floating animal, they orient themselves and move toward their potential quarry. Water striders frequently are seen in city ponds. Winged and wingless forms occur in many species; the wings enable them to move from one isolated body of water to another. All the genera are restricted to fresh water, except one; its species all live on saltwater.

BEDBUGS

Bedbugs are also true bugs in the order Hemiptera. They represent a relatively small family comprising only about 30 species worldwide, of which 8 species have been recorded in North America. They all feed by sucking the blood from birds and mammals. These flat, oval insects have tiny vestigial remnants of wings; they lost most of the structures after they took up a parasitic way of life. They are large enough to be seen quite easily, though when full-grown most are only $\frac{1}{5}$ to $\frac{1}{4}$ inch (5 to 6 mm) long and about $\frac{1}{8}$ inch (3 mm) wide. Their color is usually a reddish brown.

Some bedbugs feed only on the blood of bats. One such species is *Cimex pilosellus*. Other species (*Oeciacus* spp.) are found only on swallows and martins. Another species (*Cimexopsis nyctalus*) is restricted to chimney swifts. This is interesting, considering that although bats, swallows, martins, and chimney swifts are not related, most of them nest communally in dark, protected places, and all feed on aerial plankton or on insects in midair. In North and Central America, another species, *Haematosiphon inodorus*, is usually associated with chickens. One of the forms that feeds on humans is *Cimex hemipterus*, but this is a tropical species that is abundant chiefly in Africa and Asia.

The primary species that attacks humans in Europe and North America is *Cimex lectularius*, which is found around the world in temperate regions, having been carried everywhere that people have gone. Though it has long been well known in London and other major European seaports, the bedbug was not found in North America until the middle of the 17th century, when it was brought to New England by ship.

The thick, flat bodies of bedbugs allow them to hide deep in the cracks in wood, which was once used to make bed frames. It is here that they lay clusters of 50 to 200 small white eggs, which hatch about eight

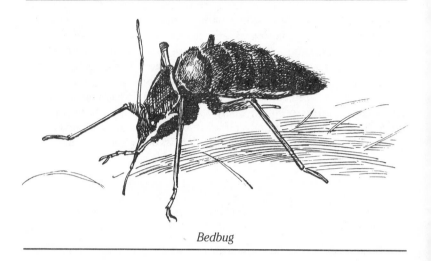

Bedbug

days later. The young are almost transparent, with a slightly yellowish tone. They moult, or shed their skin, five times before they reach adulthood. To grow they require warm blood, usually one meal between each moult. They are often found living in sleeping areas, typically in hiding places in the bed frames. They may also be found in other furniture, under loose wallpaper, or just about anywhere that they can hide. They feed only at night; each bug may feed only once a week or so, and they can live from four months to a whole year without ever having a meal. As a result, unoccupied houses and apartments can remain infested for long periods. When no people are around, bedbugs have been known to feed on mice or any other available mammals, which they seem to find, at least in part, by homing in on their warmth. Having once found an animal's nest or place that it sleeps, bedbugs will continue to return each time they are hungry.

It takes a bedbug five to ten minutes to complete a meal. But since they suck blood during the night, usually shortly before dawn when people are in a deep sleep, their presence often goes unnoticed. They do not inject any irritating blood thinners like some other sanguivores, and many people are never aware that they have been bitten by bedbugs. On some people, however, the bitten area becomes itchy and inflamed. It is common for the large, red bedbug welts to last for days before going away. People who have been bitten by most household pests usually feel that bedbug bites are more irritating than those of fleas or lice. Unlike fleas and lice, bedbugs have never been shown to transmit diseases.

Bedbugs are thought to have originated in the Mediterranean region and subsequently to have spread their range. Some researchers suggest that bedbugs originally fed on bats, but turned to humans when they lived in caves.

For years people fought bedbugs by catching and killing them and by painting the bed frame, especially the joints and the cracks, with a mixture of oil and candleberry wax, or with bitterwood. Actually, just painting over all the cracks with turpentine or an oily substance will kill most of the bugs present. Usually a dusting with malathion or pyrethrum is quite effective, but be careful when using these substances because they are quite dangerous. Not everyone is so patient. The New Yorkers I have known who had bedbugs dealt with the problem by throwing out the furniture that was thought to be harboring the insects.

Bedbugs do not seem to be nearly as prevalent in the United States as they once were, which may be due to a combination of factors. Bed-frames are rarely made of wood anymore, so there are fewer cracks in which the bedbugs can hide, insecticides have proved quite effective in eliminating infestations, and it may be that the heat generated by radiators has proved far too confusing for the heat-seeking sensors that enable these insects to find their warm-blooded meals. Nevertheless, bedbugs are still found in most major cities, where people bring them home on old

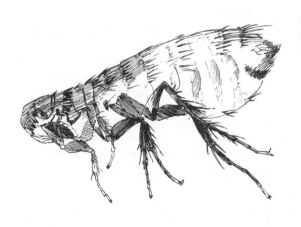

Flea

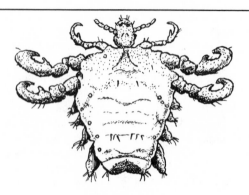

Crab louse

furniture and secondhand clothing. Many exterminators still advertise that they will kill termites, roaches, mice, rats, and bedbugs.

MONARCH BUTTERFLY

Because the unique life history of the monarch butterfly (*Danaus plexippus*) includes remarkable migrations, it passes through and settles in some urban areas. These large orange and black butterflies have a wingspan of 3.5 to 4 inches (8.9 to 10.2 cm). Monarchs are a member of the family Danaidae, and are known as the milkweed butterflies because each member of the family lays its eggs on milkweed plants (Asclepiadaceae), though some also lay their eggs on nightshade plants (Solanaceae). Monarch caterpillars feed on several species of milkweed (*Asclepias* spp.) and sometimes on dogbane (*Apocynum* spp.) and green milkweed (*Acerates* sp.). Danaids are distributed throughout the tropics and North America, where there is a vast supply of milkweeds. The monarch butterflies, like all danaids, evolved in the tropics, but they have developed a complex migratory behavior that brings them north in the spring through successive generations. Monarchs breed in the north, increasing their numbers throughout the summer, until the last generation begins to congregate toward the end of the summer. By mid-September their southern migration is well under way.

When fall approaches, the monarchs living east of the Rocky Mountains respond to the shorter, cooler days by flying south. When migration is in full swing, they can be seen gently wafting their way right through the cities that lie in their path, including midtown Manhattan. Once you become aware of their presence, you will notice monarchs floating

Monarch butterfly

Milkweed

Monarch butterfly drying its wings shortly after emerging from its chrysalis

through the air all during the autumn migration. Although several other butterflies, some moths, and numerous other insects also have mass migrations, nothing like the monarch's journey is known. What makes these insects different is the way they settle in one spot by the millions and remain there for months. Most other species could be so vulnerable in such a situation that predators would rapidly wipe out the entire species. Monarchs, however, are not attractive to most predators. The extremely bitter and poisonous chemicals that the monarch caterpillars ingest when feeding on milkweed plants are passed on to the adult butterflies, imparting a terrible-tasting poison that protects them. Some animals have learned to ingest only the safe parts while discarding the rest of the monarch, but despite these pressures, most overwintering monarchs survive.

On their route back to the tropics, once they reach Texas and northern Mexico, they start laying down reserves of fat so that by the time they arrive at their overwintering sites in mid-November, they are 50 percent fat. They stay relatively dormant throughout the winter, becoming active only on warmer days when they fly off looking for water. In mid-March they head north again.

Some monarchs overwinter along the Florida coast and on islands in the Gulf of Mexico, but during severe winters they are all killed by heavy frosts. In the West, the monarchs fly to the coast and to the south as the weather gets colder. Each year they return to the same overwintering grounds along the California coast from San Francisco to Los Angeles. These areas include the groves of eucalyptus trees north of San Francisco, which are far enough from the ocean to be protected from the winter winds. Although there are many overwintering sites up and down the West Coast, the best known are the moist pine groves in Monterey County. Thousands of monarchs overwinter in the "butterfly trees" in the town of Pacific Grove, where they are protected by law. Their bright colors that advertise the acrid, poisonous chemicals laid down in their tissues do not protect these butterflies from the onslaught of human encroachment. Seven of the forty-five known sites where about 10 million monarchs overwintered along the California coast were recently destroyed by developers in just two years. It is essential to preserve the remaining overwintering sites and also the patches of milkweed on which the larvae feed. The Monarch Project, organized by a conservation group on the West Coast, is attempting to increase public awareness of the precarious situation faced by the monarchs in the hope that builders will avoid developing any site that could endanger monarch populations.

GYPSY MOTH AND TENT CATERPILLAR MOTH

The gypsy moth (*Porthetria dispar*) isn't one of the major insects in urban areas, but it does have a significant impact on suburbs. Because of this, and also because the press periodically becomes obsessed with the species, it will be discussed here.

Gypsy moths weren't found in North America until the late 19th century when a Harvard University researcher, Leopold Trouvelot, received a number of gypsy moth cocoons from a friend who had sent them from Europe. Trouvelot, who lived in Medford, Massachusetts, may have been interested in raising them for silk production. The project never took off, but the moths did. When the adults emerged from their cocoons, Trouvelot mounted a few and allowed the rest to escape. Unchecked by natural parasites and predators, they reproduced, and their numbers increased.

At first, no one noticed that the moths had become established in the woodlands near Medford. About twenty years later, however, the caterpillars had begun to cause considerable damage to foliage in the Boston area. By the late 1920s, gypsy moths had spread throughout the New England states and southeastern Canada, and there was a population in New Jersey. They continued their spread toward eastern New York, through New Jersey, and into eastern Pennsylvania. Today gypsy moths are found all the way from Nova Scotia to North Carolina, and west to Michigan and Illinois. Occasional specimens have been collected as far south as Florida and as far west as Missouri. One hundred years after its introduction, the species is still alive and well and continuing its move across North America.

The male moths are dark brown with small bodies and strong wings. The females are light tan with darker, irregular markings across the wings. The males have a wingspan of a little more than 1 inch (3 to 4 cm), compared with the larger females whose wingspan is slightly more than 2 inches (5.5 to 6.5 cm).

The eggs are laid during the late summer in masses from 1 to 1½ inches (2.5 to 3.8 cm) in length. Each egg mass contains anywhere from only fifteen to hundreds of eggs. The masses are covered with protective, buffy, hairy scales that originate on the female's abdomen. They are usually laid on tree bark or stones, but can be found on any type of debris. They hatch in late April and May when the warm weather arrives. The larvae then climb up a tree, leaving a trail of silken thread. Once they reach the end of a twig, they walk off the tip and get picked up by a breeze. The thread and the long hairs on the caterpillar act as a sail, and the larvae are blown to other trees, where they climb to the top and get blown off once again. This ballooning behavior has proved to be an effective dispersal mechanism. After several trips from tree to tree, the caterpillars settle down to eating. Although they will eat the leaves from a wide range of different trees and shrubs, they seem to prefer oaks, willows, poplars, and birches. During years when there are major outbreaks of gypsy moth caterpillars and most of the preferred foliage is consumed, they will eat less favored species, such as pines, spruce, hemlock, and beech.

The older, hairy, brownish caterpillars are easily identified by the red and blue dots that appear in pairs on their back. In late June, they begin to pupate, emerging one and a half to two weeks later as moths. During the mating season that follows, the females emit a highly volatile chemical that acts as a powerful sex attractant. Downwind males detect the pheromone with their sensitive antennae, fly upwind until they find the larger females that are unable to fly, and they mate. The adult moths don't live long after completing their reproductive function.

Like many other insects, gypsy moths have population swings. Major increases in numbers are followed by years with considerably fewer moths. During the years with low densities, predators such as some wasps, birds, mice, and various parasites keep the gypsy moth populations in check. However, it takes time to develop the checks and balances that keep populations of most native species stable. To date, though the population swings aren't nearly as frequent as they once were, gypsy moths continue to have periodic outbreaks when their predators and parasites are unable to keep them under control; they end up eating virtually everything in sight.

After several years of declining numbers, gypsy moths again appear to be on the upswing. In 1985 about two million acres nationwide were defoliated, and twice as many acres were estimated to have been defoliated during 1986, according to John Neisess of the Department of Agriculture. Many types of control have been attempted, but all have been unsuccessful. New techniques are now being used to combat gypsy moths. One involves releasing the egg masses from specially bred gypsy moths into infested areas. The eggs hatch and grow into normal caterpillars, which then pupate and metamorphose into sterile adults. Eggs are produced as a result of matings between these moths and wild moths, but the eggs do not hatch. These carefully bred eggs can be produced in labs over a long period of time and stockpiled in cold storage until needed. The eggs are easier to handle and ship than the pupae or adults used in other sterility programs. It is hoped that this induced inherited sterility technique will suppress and contain low-density, expanding populations and thus protect highly sensitive natural areas, watersheds, and other high-risk areas. This method has been field-tested in several states, and larger applications are expected in the future.

Over the years we have learned much from the many different attempts to control the gypsy moth. One lesson is that it may not be worth the time or the expense to try to eradicate something that you haven't a prayer of controlling anyway. Another lesson is that it is dangerous to spray entire states with chemicals that cause lethal short- and long-term effects. Although the defoliation caused by gypsy moths during the bad years is startling, forests do survive and sprout new foliage. We hate to see trees being stripped of all their leaves, but the best approach may simply be to grit your teeth and bear it. Many of the weaker trees don't survive the defoliation, but they probably would have died anyway, though not quite so soon.

It may come as some consolation to know that many predators, competitors, and parasites are steadily incorporating these animals into their diets. Eventually the gypsy moths will be kept in check naturally.

Sometimes tent caterpillars are mistaken for gypsy moth caterpillars. The two larvae look quite similar, except that tent caterpillars have a white stripe down their back in addition to hairy bodies with blue dots. There are six species of tent caterpillar moths in the United States.

The eastern tent caterpillar moth (*Malacosoma americanum*) and the western tent caterpillar moth (*Malacosoma pluviale*) can both be identified by the white webs or tents that they spin from silk threads in the forks of trees and shrubs during the spring (see the illustration). These

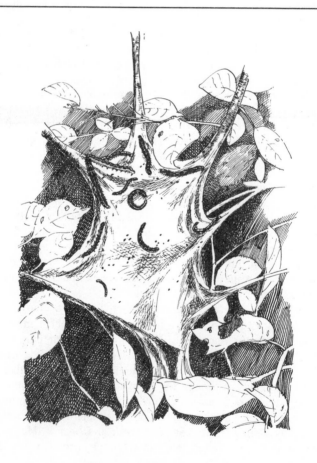

Tent caterpillars and "tent"

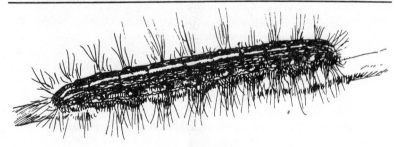

Tent caterpillar

caterpillars are most abundant in apple and cherry trees, to which they can do considerable damage. Tent caterpillars, native to this country, are social in nature, returning to the tents at night for protection. It has been found that the western tent caterpillars have a division of labor. Some of their larvae are leaders, moving out onto branches to look for the best areas in which to feed; others will go only where silken trails have been laid down, following the paths to active feeding areas.

Their tents have an added thermoregulatory function: they act like greenhouses, warming up when the sun comes out and retaining some of that heat when the surrounding air cools. As a result, on spring mornings and afternoons, when the air is too cool for other species, the tent caterpillars are warmed up and all set to eat. They may even shuttle between the feeding spot and their tents, in order to warm up. This increases the number of hours during which they can feed. The higher temperature inside the tents may also elevate their metabolic rates and their rate of digestion, making them more efficient feeding machines. This means that the caterpillars can emerge very early in the spring when the leaves are most tender and when few predators are present as they rapidly pass through their most vulnerable stages.

Those who have an isolated population of tent caterpillar moths may find them easier to eliminate than a colony of gypsy moths, because the tent caterpillars congregate at night in their tents, where they can be readily caught and then killed. For widespread infestations, however, it may be best to take the same resigned approach that I recommended for gypsy moths.

HOUSE FLY

The flies represent one of the largest groups of insects. All these members of the order Diptera have only one pair of wings; their hind wings have been reduced to little projections that are important in maintaining equilibrium during flight. Mayflies, caddisflies, dragonflies, and sawflies carry the name "fly," but they represent other orders, and they all have two pairs of wings instead of one. Most flies are small—some are incredibly small—and their bodies are soft and pliable. Black flies, horseflies, stable flies, punkies, and mosquitoes suck blood, and some of them are also scavengers. Of those that do not suck blood, many scavenge exclusively; these include blow flies, fruit flies, and house flies.

The house fly (*Musca domestica*) is now found all over the world and is one of the most common of the readily distinguishable urban flies. This fly multiplies rapidly, and populations, once established, tend to remain high. In 1911, C. F. Hodge calculated what would happen if a single pair of house flies continually bred from April to August, and all the offspring lived and reproduced, their offspring lived and reproduced, and so on. The number of flies that would exist at the end of the summer would be 191,010,000,000,000,000,000. He further calculated that these flies would cover the earth to a depth of 47 feet (14.3 m).

Obviously nature doesn't work that way because of factors like limited resource availability, competition, predation, starvation, disease, and the weather. But when a new species is introduced to a locality where it has no natural predators or parasites, without immediate checks and balances, the population can run rampant.

I saw this happen some years ago when I arrived on the small isolated island of Mokil in the South Pacific shortly after a typhoon had carried in a new species of fly. The entire life cycle from egg to adult was completed in a matter of weeks, and several batches of 100 to 500 eggs were laid in a female's lifetime. The island had a large supply of rotting breadfruit on which the flies could oviposit, or lay their eggs, and in a very short time the entire island was crawling and buzzing with flies.

The locals adapted with nonchalance; they didn't seem to mind having flies constantly crawling all over them. I wasn't nearly as complacent, being conscious that these creatures were probably carrying the pathogens of diseases to which I had built up little or no resistance. I had nicks and cuts all over my body from being knocked against a reef by the surf and from falling out of the trees I was climbing in search of eggs for use in taxonomic reseach at Yale University. Though the flies didn't bite, they were fond of crawling all over my open sores, which never seemed to heal. Since these flies did not discriminate about crawling over me, over dead fish, or over excrement, it wasn't long before my sores were harboring any number of staph infections.

I wouldn't be surprised to learn that the flies on Mokil, which is in the Eastern Caroline Islands in the Federated States of Micronesia, have long since come under check and are being controlled by predators and parasites. But considering how small that island is, it is difficult to say how long it could take for natural checks and balances to control this recently introduced fly.

The common house fly peaks in numbers during July and August. Another species, the lesser house fly (*Fannia canicularis*), which is slightly smaller and looks very similar, appears during May and June. Its larvae, known as maggots, differ from those of the common house fly in that they are flattened and have rows of spines. The flight pattern of the adult lesser house fly differs from that of the common house fly. Instead of buzzing around a room and landing on food, the lesser house flies are most often seen in the center of the room flying straight paths under a light fixture or dangling mobile. The flight is broken with erratic zigzags. Often several flies will fly together around the middle of the room. Most of these flies are males, and it is thought that the circling clusters are engaged in a behavior related to mating. Occasionally a male bolts off after a female that has been attracted to the cluster.

Another common fly is the face fly (*Musca autumnalis*), a new arrival to the United States. This fly is also similar to the common house fly, but it is slightly larger. It lives outdoors during most of the summer, coming inside when colder weather hits. Face flies will crawl into cracks and other small hiding places where they will overwinter, emerging on warm winter days or when spring arrives.

Other flies commonly seen in urban areas include bluebottle or greenbottle flies, which are blow flies, in the family Calliphoridae. They are distinguished by their shiny green or blue bodies, large size, and loud buzzing. It was a species of bottle fly that was blown into Mokil.

It has been shown that the common house fly is an important carrier and transmitter of over 100 disease-causing pathogens or the eggs of organisms that cause disease. These include amoebic dysentery, anthrax, cholera, gangrene, gonorrhea, salmonellosis, staphylococcus, and typhoid fever. Flies also carry the eggs of hookworm, pinworm, tapeworm, and whipworm.

Horse and human excrement are two of the preferred materials on which common house flies and lesser house flies breed. Since we now have flush toilets, and since horses are no longer common in urban areas, there are fewer flies in American cities than there were years ago. However, the eggs of house flies will hatch and the larvae will develop in many other types of organic matter, such as dead grass, rotting vegetables, and garbage. The recent advent of heavy plastic garbage bags has probably helped reduce urban fly populations. Of course, house flies are here to stay, but proper refuse disposal can substantially decrease the number of flies we have to contend with.

Horseflies, which are members of the family Tabanidae, are serious pests of humans and other animals because the females are bloodsuckers.

Since horses were replaced by cars, most of the urban horseflies that inflicted painful bites have disappeared. And nobody misses them. But in affluent suburban communities where horses are kept, as well as in those cities where the police use horses and where there is a carriage industry for the tourists, as in New York, horseflies still persist, though in substantially reduced numbers.

MOSQUITO

Another family of flies is the Cuculicidae, more commonly known as the mosquitoes. There are about 3,000 species of these small, widely distributed insects that are so well known they need little introduction. The adults can be distinguished from other similar dipteran families by such characteristics as the scales along the wing veins, by the specific arrangement of these veins, and by the long proboscis.

Mosquitoes lay their eggs either on the water's surface or near the water, depending on the genus. The larvae, which are aquatic, swim by wriggling through the water, where they feed on different types of food, depending on the species. Most feed on algae and organic debris that are in suspension, floating on the surface, or lying at the bottom. Some larvae eat other mosquito larvae. Most species breathe air through a tube at the posterior end of the body, which they project through the water's surface.

The pupae don't eat, but continue to breathe through breathing tubes. However, the tubes are different during this stage in that they project from the thorax. After two or three days, the skin of the pupa splits down the back, and the adult works its way out. Using the cast-off skin as a raft, it remains on the water's surface until its wings have hardened enough to be able to fly.

Many mosquito species do not suck blood. Some suck blood from species other than humans. Of the bloodsucking species, only the females are equipped with mouthparts that can pierce the skin. Instead of blood, the males feed on sweet substances, such as flower nectar and the juices of fruits. Many females supplement their diets with some of these same foods. The best way to distinguish the sex of a mosquito is by the antennae. The males have plumose, or featherlike, antennae; the females have only a few short hairs.

Mosquitoes in the genus *Culex* are the ones most commonly found in and around our homes. Although they bother many people and are important vectors of diseases transmitted to birds and some mammals, they are not very important carriers of human diseases. *Anopheles* mosquitoes belong to the genus that carries malaria. Several species in this

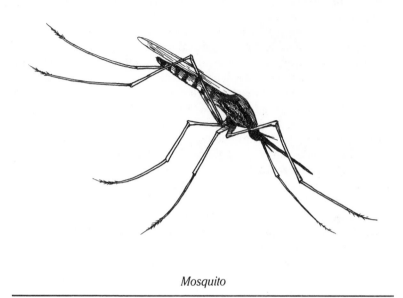

Mosquito

genus in the United States are known to carry the disease; most live in the South. Malaria is caused by a single-cell protozoan that feeds on red blood cells. More than one species of malarial parasite has been described, and each causes a distinct form of the disease.

Aedes is another important genus with a worldwide distribution; many of its species occur in North America. In this genus is the yellow fever mosquito found in all the tropical regions of the world. Its distribution cannot extend beyond areas where temperatures seasonally go below freezing, however, so outbreaks of yellow fever in the North are always cut back by the cold weather. Dengue, filariasis, and several forms of encephalitis are other important diseases that are spread by mosquitoes. Until recently there was no fear that dengue would become a problem in the United States, but that has changed since the Asian tiger mosquito (*Aedes albopictus*) became established in this country. These insects were first discovered in 1985 in the Houston area, and subsequently have become established in Dallas and in Anderson County. Outside of Texas, they have also become established around New Orleans and Baton Rouge, Louisiana; Jackson, Mississippi; and Memphis, Tennessee.

Dengue fever, a severe viral disease, has been increasing steadily during the last decade throughout the Caribbean, Mexico, and Central

America. It is the cause of painful aches and fever, and it can be fatal. In 1980 the first dengue cases in the United States in 35 years were reported from Texas. The Asian tiger mosquito carries dengue in Latin America, and there is concern that it will be only a matter of time before this mosquito carries it in the United States as well.

Asian tiger mosquitoes leave an itchy welt after taking blood. They could become a serious problem because they are efficient transmitters of so many diseases. In addition to dengue, they may transmit the La Crosse virus. This virus causes a form of California encephalitis that can paralyze and even kill. The danger is compounded by the fact that Asian tiger mosquitoes aggressively seek out humans. They also have the capacity to thrive in a wide range of climates. To date, no cases of California encephalitis have been positively linked to the Asian tiger mosquito, but the risks are increasing. In Asia this mosquito breeds in just about every area where there is standing fresh water. They are found in northern Japan, in the tropics, in forests, and in cities. There is every reason to believe this species is established and spreading in this country, and they may soon be found throughout much of North and South America.

Officials in the northeastern states have also been warned to look for this mosquito. Currently, the primary mosquito-borne disease in the Northeast is eastern equine encephalitis, which normally affects only horses. Occasionally, though, humans contract the disease and may suffer brain damage or die as a result. We do not yet know whether the Asian tiger mosquito can carry and spread eastern equine encephalitis.

Of the 3.2 million used automobile tires imported to this country in 1985, about 88 percent came from countries in Asia where tiger mosquitoes live. These imports are believed to account for the introduction of this species to the United States. Health inspectors checked 2,613 tires shipped from Japan to Seattle and found tiger mosquito larvae in 11 tires. The U.S. Public Health Service then ordered a hold on all shipments of imported used tires in the hope that they could curb the spread of this disease-carrying mosquito.

On both the East Coast and the West Coast there are species of mosquitoes that breed in saltwater marshes, as well as those that prefer freshwater wetlands. It was largely because of the numbers of *Aedes* mosquitoes that salt marshes came under attack for so many years. Since mosquitoes laid their eggs in the areas adjacent to and under the salt marsh vegetation, the marshes were burned over—until it was found that this had no appreciable effect on the number of mosquitoes.

Various other methods of mosquito control have been tried. One technique was to increase marsh drainage, which was accomplished by digging out rows of ditches. The idea was to eliminate any standing water in which the larvae could develop. A third method was to build dykes around the marshes, permitting the water behind the dykes to run out at low tide, but preventing water from returning during high tide. This dried out the marshes, many of which were then put to agricultural or industrial use.

Still another method of mosquito control was to keep a marsh flooded and well stocked with killifish (*Gambusia* spp.) or other larvicidal fish. Petroleum oils were also widely used to control mosquitoes. Oil was poured on the water to prevent the larvae from pushing their breathing tubes through the surface so that they would suffocate. Actually, the larvae survived for hours without pushing their tubes through the surface, but the poisonous nature of the lighter oils ended up killing many of them. This method and others that employ specifically targeted pesticides affect considerably more than the targeted mosquito larvae. New insecticides were developed, but the mosquitoes rapidly developed genetic resistance to them.

Biological control of mosquitoes with natural agents has been tried. Cannibalistic mosquitoes were used, as were minnows that feed on mosquito larvae, and a bacterium (*Bacillus thuringiensis israelensis*) that infects mosquito larvae with a deadly toxin. All have been less effective and more costly than initially hoped.

As with many other pests, the best solution may be simply to tolerate the mosquitoes and to use a repellent when you need to avoid being bitten. Scientists have yet to find a repellent any better than the compound they discovered more than 25 years ago: N, N-Diethyl-meta-toluamide, more commonly known as Deet®. This is the active ingredient in just about every mosquito repellent. The higher the concentration of Deet® listed on the label, the more effective that mosquito repellent will be.

In cities around the country mosquitoes find many suitable places in which to breed. Most cities have street vaults under the streets where telephone, gas, and electric lines run. The water company may also have underground vaults. Usually water stands in these concrete structures much of the year, and mosquitoes commonly breed there, too. They also use culverts, street gutters, broken and leaking plumbing, building sumps, wet basements, wet areas in abandoned buildings, discarded tires, pails, roof gutters, ponds, reservoirs, and sewage treatment plants.

YELLOW JACKETS

Yellow jackets, like all wasps, are members of the insect order Hymenoptera, which includes some of the most social insects ever to evolve. Included, in addition to the wasps, are the ants and the bees.

Other groups in this order include the sawflies, ichneumonflies, and the chalcids. When wings are present, hymenopterans have four, which are thin with relatively few veins. The hymenopterans' egg-laying apparatus has been modified into a stinger. Only the females can sting, but most colonies of ants, bees, and wasps consist almost entirely of females, so nearly all members of the colony have this capacity.

It is easy to distinguish any look-alike hymenopterans from other insect orders. The dipterans, or flies, have only two wings; lepidopterans, or butterflies and moths, have four wings that are covered with very small scales, and their mouthparts include a long, coiled proboscis. The ephemeropterans, or lacewings, and the odonates, or dragonflies and damselflies, have very short antennae and considerably more wing venation. If you are interested in the many other differences among these orders, you can consult a basic text such as Borror and DeLong, *An Introduction to the Study of Insects*.

Among the hymenopterans, in the family Vespidae, the typical wasps, is a subfamily known as the Vespinae, which includes the hornets and the yellow jackets. These wasps make their nests out of paper, which is actually composed of fragments of old or decaying wood. Some make their nests in holes in the ground, others attach conspicuous nests to branches or under the eaves of buildings, and some nest in holes in buildings.

Yellow jacket is a common name applied to several species that look quite similar. These small yellow and black wasps are all in the genus *Vespula*. Some of the species referred to as yellow jackets, particularly in the Northeast, are *Vespula arenaria*, *Vespula flavopilosa*, *Vespula maculifrons*, *Vespula vidua*, and *Vespula vulgaris*. Though most people fear being stung by these wasps—and the pain can be considerable—the wasps rarely bother anyone unless provoked.

Yellow jackets are occasionally seen flying around looking for insects, which they take back to their hives to feed their larvae. However, more often than not, they are usually seen collecting plant nectar and pollen, which is their mainstay. At least that's the way it used to be, until the early 1970s when people started noticing yellow jackets around picnic tables, barbecues, and trash cans, landing on hot dogs, hamburgers, soda, and beer. As it turned out, this didn't represent a change in the feeding habits of one of our native species. Rather, this yellow jacket was a new immigrant, *Vespula germanica*. Collectors are now finding them throughout New England, Quebec, Ontario, as far south as Maryland, and west to Indiana. It has been suggested that this yellow jacket be called the picnic wasp because of its habits. Garbage-can wasp would also be an appropriate name.

Picnic wasps are doing incredibly well in urban areas, probably resulting from the abundance of food, nest sites, places to overwinter, and because of the relative lack of predators and competitors. They are also abundant in European cities, but natural checks and balances, such as parasites and predators, keep them in control. In many towns they place their nests in cracks in and underneath the siding of houses. In Ithaca, New York, just one old city block was found to have at least one picnic wasp nest per home. In New York and other very large cities, most of the wooden buildings are in the outer boroughs and suburban areas, but the picnic wasps are also common in midtown, so suitable nest sites must be available.

Among all yellow jackets and paper nest wasps, the queens are produced in the fall. They mate shortly after emergence. The males soon die, and the fertilized queens then hide somewhere. Many go into cracks on the sides of houses or under clapboards, which isn't very different from going under tree bark except that the heat from a home may increase the queen's chances of surviving the winter. The following April or May the wasps resume activity, begin feeding, building a nest, and laying their eggs. Most of the broods develop into female workers and foragers, and by fall the nest may contain thousands of wasps. At this time the queens and the males are produced, and the cycle continues.

HONEY BEE

There is just one species of honey bee in this country, and it isn't native. Honey bees have many characteristics that distinguish them from other bees, but one of the more interesting differences is their hairy eyes. These small ($\frac{3}{8}$ to $\frac{5}{8}$ inch, or 1.0 to 1.6 cm, long), dark, reddish brown or black bees with orange-yellow rings on the abdomen are quite familiar to most people. To some, yellow jackets look similar, though they have black and yellow markings on their head, thorax, and abdomen. Unlike the yellow jacket's smooth thorax, that of the honey bee is very hairy.

Honey bees were introduced to America during colonial times, probably over 350 years ago. Most honey bees (*Apis mellifera*) live in artificial hives, but swarms regularly escape and establish wild hives, usually in hollow trees. American cities aren't regarded as the best places for profitable beekeeping ventures, and yet in the downtown area of any major American city during the summer, you are bound to see honey bees.

Where do these urban bees come from? Honey bees are colonial; hives usually have on the order of 60,000 bees. Most bees return to their hives occasionally during the day and then remain there during the night, so the honey bees seen in cities are probably not strays. Is it possible that

Honey bee

they shuttle from country to city and back again? Probably not. Bees generally fly only 10 to 100 yards (9 to 91 m) to forage.

The answer to this question is very simple: Many hives are kept in major cities, usually on rooftops. Given the large numbers of flowering street trees, curbside and windowbox flowers, plants growing wild in vacant lots, and flower beds in parks and gardens, there seems to be plenty of nectar to go around. In addition to the flowers, another source of food occurs in or around garbage cans and dumpsters in any city. Although honey bees feed exclusively on pollen and nectar, recently they found a man-made nectar equivalent in the soda and other sweet substances that people toss into trash cans on every street corner. It would be interesting to know whether they can distinguish between artificially sweetened soft drinks and the ones made with sugar.

Most commercial beekeepers maintain 40 to 50 hives in a single location. Urban beekeepers work on a much smaller scale since they cannot count on stands of flowering plants, such as alfalfa, clover, purple loosestrife, buckwheat, goldenrod, basswood, apple, and cherry. Most of these plants grow in cities, often in considerable numbers, but not in the densities found in more rural or agricultural communities.

There are even wild hives in urban areas, usually in hollow trees. When a honey bee colony reaches a large size, a group of bees will leave the hive together and look for a site to establish a new colony. From time to time such swarms are seen right in the middle of large cities. During the past several years I have seen honey bee swarms in midtown Manhattan, not far from Rockefeller Center. One was slowly moving across a playground, and another was attached to and buzzing about several garbage cans and plastic trash bags on the sidewalk.

These swarms were caught by Tony Crespo and Mario Cuevas, local building superintendents who recognized the opportunity and value of such a find. Subsequently they have increased their holdings to four hives, which are kept behind one of the buildings on Manhattan's West Side. During most summer days, Tony and Mario's bees buzz the neighborhood dumpsters, which contain many leftover Italian ices, basically frozen sugar water. Street vendors sell these ices from carts and later throw out their practically empty containers. The contents melt and attract the local bees. The bees are also seen regularly checking out the garbage cans and all the flowers in the area. It's interesting to watch them fly beelines from one potential food source to the next, then return around the corner to their hive. Four hives may not provide much additional income, but Tony and Mario supply several neighborhood families with honey all year round.

5

FISH

M any people fish for recreation at one time or another. Some go to a remote lake in the country and others go deep-sea fishing, but there's a good deal of excellent fishing going on in most urban areas, too. It is not always wise to eat the fish, but they're still fun to catch.

Some species of fish thrive in city ponds. Among them are pumpkin-seeds, bluegills, bullheads, carp, goldfish, and largemouth bass. Other species feed, spawn, or migrate through the brackish or salty waters that surround coastal cities. Still other fish can be found in urban rivers. For example, the striped bass (*Morone saxatilis*), which has been declining in numbers along the East Coast, is known to frequent the old pilings on the Manhattan side of the Hudson River. Or when specific species are running, you will see city people fishing off bridges, from docks, or in the surf.

In this chapter I shall describe the more common fresh water species, and explain why they do well in urban environments while other species can't compete. Some management problems are presented, along with solutions that have been tried with varying degrees of success.

COMMON CARP, GRASS CARP, AND GOLDFISH

City ponds are usually murky, turbid affairs, but they offer aesthetic appeal to city dwellers. They also provide valuable habitats to the species

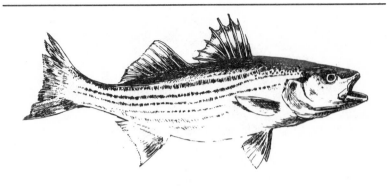

Striped bass

able to survive such conditions. We repeatedly find the same species turning up in these urban ponds.

One of the most widespread city fish is the common carp, also known as the German carp (*Cyprinus carpio*). This good-sized fish reaches lengths of 1 to 2 feet (30 to 61 cm). It has large, conspicuous scales, and two pairs of barbels—beardlike projections that hang from the sides of the mouth. The carp is brownish on the back and sides, grading to yellow on the lower sides and belly; the fins usually have a reddish tint.

The carp and minnow species represent a very large family of fishes that inhabit fresh waters of Europe and North America. The family Cyprinidae contains about 200 genera and more than 1,000 species, of which about 225 are found in North America. This family has more species of freshwater fishes than any other.

Some people regard the common carp as the fishy equivalent of a weed. Since most disturbed freshwater habitats have sizable carp populations, it has become one of the more abundant species in urban lakes, ponds, and rivers across the United States. The carp's tolerance of conditions that often accompany dense human populations has helped make it an urban success story, for fish. The fact that most other species cannot survive in urban waters partially explains why the carp has done so well.

The original range of the common carp encompassed the basins of the Black, Caspian, and Aral seas and may have included western Europe, the Volga River, the rivers flowing into the Pacific, and eastern Asia from the Amur River south to Burma. Carp were domesticated long ago in China, probably sometime between 800 and 300 B.C. They were an excellent choice for pond culture because they survived well under conditions that killed most other species, and they stayed alive when transported to market in tanks. Even now many fish markets carry live

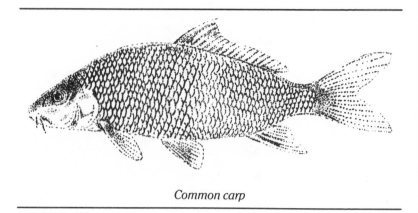

Common carp

carp in cramped tanks, where they are ready to be pulled out and prepared fresh to a customer's order.

Around the first century A.D., the Romans independently discovered the merits of carp culture, obtaining their stock from the westernmost border of the species' range, probably from the Danube River. Carp culture was primarily confined to monastery ponds at first; the escaped specimens helped increase their range during the Middle Ages. By the 16th century, carp were present almost everywhere on the European continent and were almost a staple in the diet of many Europeans. So it is not surprising to learn that they were brought to the United States and cultured in New York by the 1830s, when some were introduced into the Hudson River. In 1872, Julius Poppe, an early aquacultural entrepreneur, brought five carp from Reinfeldt, Germany, to the Sonoma Valley in northern California. From these original fish he bred enough to distribute their offspring through the western states, Hawaii, and Central America.

In 1876, a Professor S.F. Baird, U.S. Commissioner of Fisheries, hired a German fish culturist, Dr. Rudolph Hessel, to bring the best European fish to America. After several unsuccessful attempts, Dr. Hessel in 1877 introduced 345 young carp to ponds in Baltimore, Maryland. A year later, over 100 were removed and put into the ponds built at the base of the Washington Monument. In 1879, congressmen began sending carp home to their respective states. Demand for the fish peaked in 1883 when 260,000 carp were sent to 298 out of 301 congressional districts. The carp program ended in 1897. By then carp were so numerous that additional introductions were unnecessary, although they continued.

Since large females can lay up to two million eggs per season, the numbers of carp increased dramatically. In addition, carp often travel long distances and can survive an incredibly wide range of different conditions, including warm, shallow, muddy waters, clear mountain lakes, small streams, rivers, ponds, reservoirs, and even brackish estuaries. It has been estimated that carp may now be the most abundant fish species inhabiting the inland waters of North America.

As their numbers increased, the American public's respect for the species decreased. Things got so bad that in 1962, when state and federal biologists attempted to rid a 450-mile stretch of the Colorado and Green rivers in Utah and Wyoming of all nongame fish, carp were one of the primary fishes targeted. The waters were treated with the piscicide rotenone (a chemical that kills fish), and the rivers were restocked with the desired game fish. Despite such drastic—and environmentally unsound—measures, most of the nongame fish populations recovered. Three species that were targets of the poisoning are now on the federal list of endangered species and are currently being raised in a fish hatchery where there is hope of ultimately restocking the rivers with them. They are the bonytail (*Gila robusta jordani*), the Colorado squawfish (*Ptychocheilus lucius*), and the razorback sucker (*Xyrauchen texanus*). Meanwhile, the carp is as common as ever. In fact, the use of the piscicide seems to have given them an edge over other fish in becoming reestablished.

For hundreds of years the Japanese have been breeding the common carp, selecting for a wide range of exotic colors and patterns, which now include beautiful hues of red, orange, yellow, blue, white, and black. Many of these fish are very costly, sometimes bringing as much as $1,000. The popularity of these fish has extended beyond Japan, and the exports currently amount to over $100 million per year. These Koi carp, as they are called, are put into ponds, indoors or outdoors, and are usually given excellent care, including the best water filtration, purification, and special foods, including brine shrimp, daphnia, worms, and trout pellets. Some of these fish have escaped and are mixing with wild populations. Soon, it may not be unusual for the occasional angler to pull in a strikingly colored carp.

Another cyprinid has been recently introduced. This one is the grass carp, also known as the white amur (*Ctenopharyngodon idella*). Since it is primarily herbivorous, it was brought here in order to evaluate its potential as a biological control agent for rampant aquatic plants. These fish were credited with much success in Russia, where 246,000 grass carp were introduced into the Kara-Kum Canal. The waterway had become choked with freshwater plants that impeded the flow of water needed to irrigate the cotton fields. The grass carp efficiently cleared the canal, and test trials have begun in other countries.

The introduction of this fish to North America presents certain ecological dangers, however. Grass carp are large, fecund, and adaptable, much like common carp, and they possess the potential to destroy aquatic plant beds that now provide cover for native species. Since grass carp are already widespread in the Mississippi River and many of its tributaries and have been collected in 35 states, it is only a matter of time until we know more about their effects on native communities. At this time we still don't know whether they are breeding in the wild.

Recently I was asked to evaluate this species as a possible solution to the aquatic weed problems that New York City has in many of its park ponds. I recommended alternative solutions, such as erosion control to prevent runoff. It is runoff that fertilizes the water and causes the rich aquatic environments that feed large blooms of aquatic vegetation.

The goldfish (*Carassius auratus*) is a cyprinid that is native to the People's Republic of China, Taiwan, southern Manchuria, and Korea. It was known to range from the Lean River of eastern Europe to the Amur Basin and the Tym and Poronai rivers of Sakhalin. This was probably the first exotic fish species to be introduced into North America, brought here in the late 17th century. It has been collected in all of the 48 contiguous states, though there do not appear to be self-sustaining populations in Maine, Vermont, Florida, West Virginia, or Utah. This is one of the species found in most city ponds, released there by aquarists, ornamental pond fish hobbyists, and fishermen discarding excess live bait. Some goldfish may also have escaped from state and federal hatcheries where they are used to feed different species of game fish. Goldfish reach a length of about 1 foot (30 cm) and are as adept as the common carp at surviving in shallow, murky water, where both the goldfish and the carp will hybridize. Goldfish retain their bright orange color after being released into the wild, though they tend to revert to their natural brown or olive coloration after several generations.

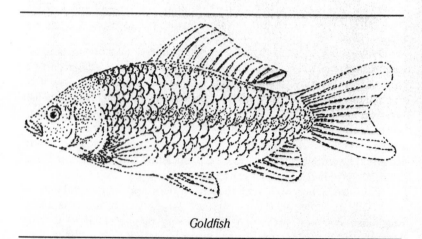

Goldfish

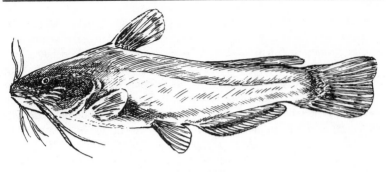

Bullhead

BULLHEAD AND CATFISH

The North American freshwater catfish are members of the family Ictaluridae. They are known as catfish because of their whiskers, or barbels, which are thin soft appendages extending from their lips (two nasal, two maxillary, four chin). Their skin is naked—that is, they have no scales—and all the species occurring in the United States and Canada have a spine on the leading edge of their dorsal (back) and pectoral (side) fins. There are several genera in the family. The members of one group of species in the genus *Ictalurus* are generally known as bullheads, but they are also called catfish and horned pout in different regions of the country.

Bullheads are rather stout in body shape, with a head that is large and wide. There are several species in the United States. Bullheads were once found in virtually every pond and slow stream in the eastern half of the country. Now, due to introductions, they are also abundant on the Pacific Coast. These species vary in appearance and are not easily differentiated. Distinguishing characteristics include the number and length of anal rays, whether or not the lower jaw protrudes, and the length of the pectoral spine. Bullhead species were hard to tell apart to begin with, but now that these fish have been introduced all over the country, the entire group is a mess. To add to the confusion, much of the older literature calls the bullheads *Ameiurus*, but that genus has recently been subsumed by the genus *Ictalurus*.

The common bullhead, or brown bullhead (*Ictalurus nebulosus*) ranges from Maine westward through the Great Lakes to North Dakota and south to Florida and Texas. It is also abundant in the West where it has been introduced and is now well established. Because this species naturally thrives in slow rivers and weedy ponds and lakes, they do well in city ponds, which are often murky and overgrown with algae and other aquatic plant life. Common bullheads will reach about a foot (30 cm) in length, though larger ones have been recorded. They are among the several species of fish that state fisheries usually dump into lakes and ponds when they stock an area. This accounts for the bullheads having been introduced everywhere. Sometimes a closely related species may be used in place of a fishery species that is in short supply. The result has been that yellow bullheads (*Ictalurus natalis*) and black bullheads (*Ictalurus melas*) are found in many places alongside the brown bullhead. While the yellow bullheads usually prefer clear, flowing streams, the black bullhead tolerates turbid backwaters as well as city ponds from New York to Tennessee, west to North Dakota, and south to Colorado.

Bullheads breed during mid- to late spring and early summer when the water temperature reaches about 70°F (21°C). The male selects and clears a shallow depression, usually sheltered by rocks, logs, or vegetation. The female then drops her eggs, which stick together in firm, cream-colored, jellylike clusters. The eggs, which are about ⅛ inch (3 mm) in diameter, are fertilized as they are laid. Afterward the male stays with the eggs to keep away predators and to fluff or fan the eggs, which he does with his pelvic fins. Sometimes the males are observed sucking the eggs in and out of their mouths. All this motion keeps the water in constant circulation over the eggs, which is important for their development.

The eggs hatch in about five days when the water is around 77°F (30.5°C). The jet black young are about ½ inch (13 mm) long when they hatch, and are attended by the adults until they reach twice that size. The young school together during the first summer, usually hidden in vegetation or under objects near shore. One reason they are sometimes found under floating boards or boats may be because the young and adults are largely nocturnal; they seek dark areas during the day. As it gets darker each evening, their activity increases. Fishermen report catching the adults at night, often in deep water, where the bullheads tend to spend much of their time right next to the bottom. Being bottom feeders, they eat a range of material including plants, worms, insects, mollusks, and occasionally even other fish.

The barbels appear to be useful when the fish feed in dark, murky waters. They are often thought of as feelers, but that does not appear to be their only purpose. It has been shown that each bullhead has tens of thousands of taste buds all over its body, and the tips of the barbels contain the greatest concentration of taste buds. Fish, like other vertebrates, smell and taste through two separate channels. Each channel responds to a different kind of stimulus, though there does tend to be some overlap. The fish's taste capabilities, like ours, are restricted to sweet, salty, sour, and bitter compounds.

The chemicals that fish smell belong to a variety of substances that are very volatile. It has been found that bullheads are able to recognize one another as individuals, and it is primarily the nose, and therefore the sense of smell, that mediates such recognition. Experiments have shown that bullheads smell the dilute concentrations of slime produced by the mucous glands in their skin. When this mucus is dissolved in the water to even very weak concentrations, it is still recognizable by other bullheads. It is interesting that each fish has its own chemical signature that is probably the result of a combination of several different chemicals. With such keen senses, bullheads are able to identify and locate food without having to see it. The more visually oriented species, such as bass, pickerel, and trout, do not have this ability.

The spines in the dorsal and pectoral fins appear to be formidable weapons when bullheads are dealing with predators. Any animal attempting to swallow a whole bullhead finds the painful spines sticking in its throat or gut a powerful incentive to disgorge the fish and avoid making a similar mistake in the future. Some catfish species have poison glands in their spines, but in the common bullhead such glands are either not present or are rudimentary.

Bullheads are able to survive for hours out of water without lasting detrimental effects. They have accessory breathing structures that allow them to use their air bladders as something akin to a lung, thereby breathing atmospheric air rather than just air that is dissolved in water. A few other American fish have such a capacity. They are the bowfin (*Amia calva*), the common carp (*Cyprinus carpio*), the common eel (*Anguilla rostrata*), and the tench (*Tinca tinca*). These breathing structures may be part of the reason bullheads and carp are able to survive the deoxygenated condition of many city ponds, particularly during late summer when bacteria, digesting the rotting plants and algae, consume much of the available dissolved oxygen. Conditions become very stressful then for many aquatic animals, including fish and tadpoles. This is when you see these species coming to the surface to take gulps of air. There are even reports that bullheads are able to survive for several weeks encased in mud when ponds dry up.

Some catfish, especially the channel catfish (*Ictalurus punctatus*) are kept in ponds where they are fed and grown as a valuable crop. Yields on such a project can be as high as 2,000 pounds per acre. The brown bullhead is also used in aquaculture. In 1984, some 470 million pounds of cultured fish and shellfish were raised in the United States—12 percent of the total fish and shellfish produced in this country. Of the catfish commercially sold annually, 95 percent are grown on fish farms.

Several years ago newspapers were full of reports about walking catfish (*Clarias batrachus*), which had been introduced to Florida and were taking to land, moving from one body of water to the next. This species, a member of the family of air-breathing catfish, Clariidae, is found in fresh and brackish waters in Sri Lanka, eastern India, Bangladesh, Burma, the Malay Archipelago, Syria, and much of Africa. Albino juveniles of this species were first imported to Florida during the early 1960s from Bangkok, Thailand, and were sold in pet shops. Later, adults were brought over for breeding. Some of these walking catfish escaped or were released from culture facilities. As of 1968 they were found in only three Florida counties, but by 1978 they had spread to twenty counties in the southern half of peninsular Florida, and their range is still expanding, though at present the cooler regions to the north are thought to be confining their population growth.

Aquarists may be interested to know that at least three species of suckermouth catfish, all in the genus *Hypostoma*, family Loricariidae, are now established in this country as well. The genus is native to South America, from the Río de la Plata system north to Panama and Costa Rica. One population has been reported in Six Mile Creek near Eureka Springs, Florida. Another species is established in Indian Spring, Nevada, and the third population is in the San Antonio River in Bexar County, Texas. The Florida population is probably the result of released aquarium fish; in Texas the population stems from the San Antonio Zoological Gardens.

PERCH

Another family, the Percidae, or perch, has members distributed through much of the northern hemisphere. These fish naturally occur in North America east of the Rocky Mountains, extend well into northern Canada, and have been introduced to the Pacific slope. Members are also found in England and most of Europe, and as far as western and northern Asia. The family contains 9 genera and 146 described species, though there are several others that have yet to be described. Most species are quite small, but some members of the family, such as the walleye (*Stizostedion vitreum*), will grow as long as 3 feet (91 cm).

The family, though diverse, is identified by two dorsal (back) fins, which are either separate or narrowly joined, one or two anal spines, five to eight branchiostegal rays (the long curved skull bones just below the operculum that support the gill membranes), and thirty-two to fifty vertebrae, as well as other characteristics. Only the yellow perch (*Perca flavescens*) commonly occurs in urban and suburban ponds and lakes in the United States; most of the other species are less well known or rarely live in heavily populated regions.

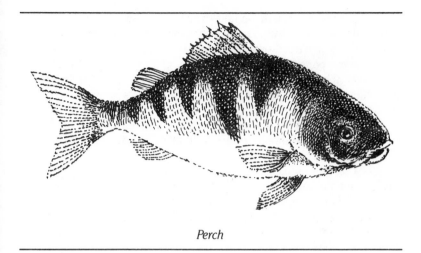

Perch

For comparative purposes, it's helpful to know that perch have two dorsal fins, whereas sunfish have just one. The dorsal fins of pike, salmon, and trout are short and lack the support of stiff, bony spines. While the anal fin—the fin on the underside of the body, toward the tail—of the perch contains one or two thin, weak spines, that of the sunfish has three or more obvious spines toward the front. The pike, salmon, and trout never have any spines in front of this fin. Also, no member of the perch family ever has a dark spot on the gill like the ear spots or ear flaps found among the sunfish. Some of the perch are nearly as flat and platelike as are many of the sunfish.

The yellow perch rarely gets more than 6 to 10 inches (15 to 25 cm) long. Its weight ranges from ¼ to ¾ pounds (114 to 341 gm), though larger specimens are caught from time to time. It has an olive back, yellowish sides with six or eight distinct, dark vertical bars interrupting the lighter colors. The lower fins are usually reddish orange, especially in the spring. Spawning takes place when the water reaches 45 to 50°F (7.2 to 10°C).

As many as a dozen males will follow the female, fertilizing the strings of eggs as they are laid. Each string of eggs may be several feet long and can contain 10,000 to 50,000 eggs. The eggs are laid in shallow water, either on submerged stones, branches, and roots, or on the dense growths of aquatic vegetation that often occur in city ponds. In these environments yellow perch often lay their eggs on plants such as elodea (*Anacharis* spp.), water milfoil (*Myriophyllum* spp.), water buttercup (*Ranunculus* spp.), water marigold (*Bidens* spp.), coontail (*Ceratophyllum* spp.), water nymph (*Najas* spp.), and fanwort (*Cabomba carolinia*). The adults do not guard the eggs, which will hatch in about three weeks.

The young feed mostly on microscopic organisms at first. As the fry increase in size, they eat aquatic insects and other invertebrates. When larger they will eat minnows and other fish.

Perch are popular among anglers, though they don't give much of a fight. Anyone can catch them anytime, since they strike all year long. Many feel that, among freshwater fish, this has the sweetest flesh and is the most delicious.

Perch can often be found in park ponds, but for some reason they are not nearly as common as sunfish, bullheads, and carp. It could be that yellow perch cannot stand up to the competition, or they may simply be unable to tolerate the conditions in these environments. Also, state fisheries historically have been disinclined to stock city ponds with perch, although they've been generous with bass, bullheads, and sunfish. Where perch have been introduced, they tend to reproduce in such numbers that they overpopulate the ponds, and their size becomes stunted. It would seem that they are not sufficiently cannibalistic to control their own numbers when stocked alone, and if they occur with other fish that aren't piscivorous, the competition may not be enough to control their numbers.

SUNFISH AND BASS

Sunfish are members of the largest vertebrate order of all, the Perciformes. This is the most diverse of the fish orders. It is the dominant group of oceangoing vertebrates as well as the dominant fish group in many tropical and subtropical fresh waters. The family Centrarchidae, or sunfish, is a freshwater group found in most of North America east of the Rocky Mountains. One species, the Sacramento perch (*Archoplites interruptus*), is native west of the Rocky Mountains.

Several characteristics identify the members of this family. These fish are unique in that they have three or more anal spines, a small, concealed pseudobranch, or false gill, and five to seven branchiostegal rays (the bones that support the gill membranes), as well as separate gill membranes. Most sunfish are nest builders, and they range in size from less than 2 inches (4 cm) to almost 3 feet (91 cm), the record for the largest largemouth bass (*Micropterus salmoides*).

Sunnies, bluegills, pumpkinseeds, sunfish, and crappies are all members of this group, which includes nine genera and thirty species. Other members of the family include largemouth and smallmouth bass and rock bass. One or more of these species live in almost every part of every state east of the Rockies.

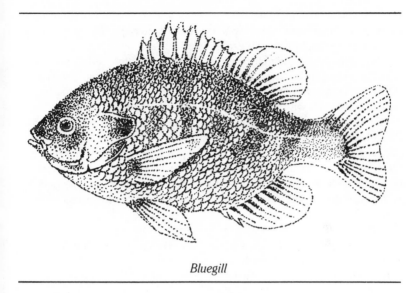

Bluegill

Sunfish are known to nearly everyone. They are the bold little fish that you see near the shores of streams, ponds, and lakes, in clear water as well as in most of the murkier city ponds. They are a beginner's fish; children fishing at the water's edge usually catch sunfish before catching anything else. And since sunfish are drawn to a wide variety of live bait and artificial lures they are also a good sports fish.

Sunfish are diurnal; that is, they are active during the day. They feed on insects, small crustaceans, snails, and sometimes on smaller fish. They find food primarily by sight. Their jawbones and muscles are extremely versatile, enabling them to inhale their food whole. Upon approaching prey, a sunfish thrusts its jaws forward and out, increasing the amount of space inside its mouth, which is then filled by water and whatever prey may be at hand. The size of a fish's mouth and stomach will limit the size of the prey it can take. Some of the largemouth bass and the green sunfish (*Lepomis cyanellus*) can take prey up to half their size.

In early spring, most members of this family leave the deeper, cooler water where they overwinter and move into shallow, warmer waters along the shore. The males select and clear the nest sites, using their fins to fan away the silt until the gravel, sand, or clay bottom is exposed. They usually make their nests out in the open without any overhanging logs or rocks and without any nearby aquatic vegetation. You can easily observe these cleared areas from shore. They look like circular, light-colored patches, usually with a male standing guard nearby. Bluegills (*Lepomis macrochirus*) and pumpkinseeds (*Lepomis gibbosus*) often prepare their nests close together in what appears to be a colony. Many city ponds support large populations of these species.

Bluegills are identified by their light blue to slightly reddish color, the bars that usually run down their sides, and the dark "ear spot" protruding from the back of their gills. Pumpkinseeds, or common sunfish, are brilliantly colored with tinges of yellow, orange, and brownish red. They have a distinctive dark ear spot or ear flap; in the adults, this protrusion has a bright orange, red, or scarlet tip. Other species recorded in city ponds include the black-banded sunfish (*Mesogonistius chaetodon*) and the long-eared sunfish (*Lepomis auritus*). These species do not appear to be as competitive and well suited to city park ponds as are the bluegill and the pumpkinseed. As a result, neither species has been recorded in Central Park in recent years.

At first the fry feed on microscopic organisms; later, they eat larger aquatic invertebrates. Only full-grown crappies and bass are known to eat other fish. The growth rates largely depend on food availability. In city ponds, which are often crowded, a large number of sunfish will be abnormally small. Part of this stunting may be a result of the species composition. In healthier, cleaner ponds and lakes, where a wide range of species exists, the larger, more predaceous species feed on the smaller fish. But in city ponds the number of species is often quite limited. As a result, the large numbers of each species may have the effect of reducing the overall size of the individuals. Also, since smaller individuals can survive and breed, the gene pool may actually shift to favor the smaller fish.

In North America, bass are among the best freshwater game fish. Only warm water species—those that do well in water that remains above 74°F (23°C) all summer—will be found in urban ponds and lakes. Small-mouth bass (*Micropterus dolomieui*) and spotted bass (*Micropterus punctulatus*), which naturally inhabit clear streams, have been introduced to some lakes and reservoirs, where they do pretty well. But only the largemouth bass has taken well to the shallower, warmer, and murkier urban and suburban lakes, ponds, and impoundments. However, like the other species in this family, bass locate their food visually, so the water cannot be too turbid. Largemouth bass are identified by a longitudinal stripe down each side, a greenish back, and a whitish belly. Unlike the smaller sunfish, some bass reach 5 to 10 pounds (2.3 to 4.5 kg), and occasionally even larger. The record bass, caught in Florida during the 1930s, weighed 22 pounds (10 kg).

In ponds that are overpopulated with stunted sunfish, the tiger muskellunge has been introduced. This fish, a cross between the northern pike (*Esox lucius*) and the muskellunge (*Esox masquinongy*), is sterile. When tiger muskellunges are stocked in a pond, they will thin out the stunted fish, providing a better fishery. The surviving sunfish grow larger, and the largemouth bass no longer have to contend with sunfish constantly raiding their nests. Since the tiger muskie does not breed, it never has a detrimental effect on the numbers of bass. Both the northern pike and the muskellunge are members of the pike family, Esocidae. These fish can be recognized by the duck-bill shape of the front of the head. Because they require clear, cool, weedy waters that don't fluctuate much in level, they have difficulty breeding in the warmer ponds typically found in urban and suburban areas.

6

AMPHIBIANS

Few amphibians have been able to survive the urban environment. Unlike plants, whose seeds are blown in the wind or deposited in bird droppings to grow wherever they land, or fish, which complete their entire life cycle in a pond, most amphibians are not well suited to living in densely populated human environments. Many salamanders live on land much of the year and then migrate to water to lay their eggs; most frogs spend part of their lives in the water and another part on land. Urban and suburban environments do not offer habitats suitable to this kind of movement. Although there are ponds and woods, the two are not always adjacent, forcing amphibians to be exposed part of the time. This exposure substantially increases their risk of predation, not only by animals but also by humans, who are among the most dangerous predators for small, harmless, fascinating vertebrates. For example, people who wouldn't dream of bringing a water bug home will eagerly catch a spotted salamander. A few people, over a period of several years, can extirpate an entire population of salamanders just by going out a few nights each spring when the salamanders gather to lay their eggs. Greed is one of the motivating factors in the extirpation of amphibians, since pet shops will buy anything that will sell. Most of the animals die in captivity without ever reproducing in the wild again.

Some amphibians, however, can still be found in urban areas, and these examples are discussed in this chapter. The ones that do best in towns tend to be those with the simplest life histories: species that don't migrate across roads, so they don't get run over; species that don't pass through an aquatic stage, so polluted waters are not an issue; and species that spend much of their lives underground, so people don't pick them up.

These are the animals that often do well in suburbs and cities. Other species have preadaptations that allow them to survive around people. Some toads will lay their eggs in just about any pool of standing water; since the tadpoles metamorphose so rapidly, the young toads often reproduce in an area where few other amphibians would have a chance. And frogs that spend almost all their lives in or next to the water, never venturing far from the safety of their pond, can escape danger and do just fine in an urban park.

SPOTTED SALAMANDER

The spotted salamander (*Ambystoma maculatum*) ranges throughout most of the eastern United States from Maine to northern Florida. These amphibians are heavy-bodied salamanders that are usually about 6 inches (15 cm) long, though specimens as long as 9 inches (almost 23 cm) have been recorded. They are generally jet black above, with a number of yellow-orange spots. Some specimens have very few spots, but 25 is about average. The venter, or belly, can be gray to almost black. In between the front and the hind legs, along each side, are from 11 to 13 costal grooves.

You will not see these large, attractive salamanders, though, unless you know when and where to look for them. The adults spend most of their lives moving about in underground tunnels and burrows where they feed on soft invertebrates that are narrow enough to fit into their relatively small mouths. In the early spring, they come out of the burrows to mate and lay their eggs in small freshwater pools and shallow, slow-water areas in rivers, ponds, and lakes. In the North, spotted salamanders appear when the spring thaw sets in, the ground becomes saturated, and the vernal ponds are full.

Natural selection has favored spotted salamanders that breed in temporary ponds, the small pools that dry up before the summer ends. Because fish do not live in these ponds, the larvae avoid these potent predators. But the larvae must hatch, develop, and leave before the ponds dry up, and this can create a race for time, since many of these ponds are gone by July. The spotted salamander is among the more highly adaptive amphibians in this respect. It has developed a rapid reproductive cycle that tends to accomplish all the necessary tasks before midsummer. It migrates during the first warm nights of early spring, when the temperatures are still too cold for most other amphibians. Movement starts after sundown when few bird and mammal predators are active.

This journey may last one to several nights, depending on the distance, terrain, and weather. Some salamanders travel as far as a mile (1.6 km) at a top speed of about 2 yards (1.82 m) per minute. When the temperature falls below freezing, they usually seek shelter until the weather warms up. A few salamanders arrive at the ponds during these cold nights, but warm rains are more suitable for mass migrations.

The females deposit masses of 15 to 250 eggs on submerged twigs and other plant material. Each egg is surrounded by gelatinous material that immediately swells when it hits the water. This substance attaches all the eggs to one another, as well as to the twig or plant material to which they are attached. The clump of eggs will remain in position for four to six weeks, at which time the partially developed larvae wriggle out of their protective sheaths.

As they grow, the larvae feed on small aquatic invertebrates ranging in size from daphnia to fairy shrimp to larger water bugs. Most spotted salamander larvae grow for three to four months, by which time they have resorbed their gills and begin to show faint markings where their yellow spots will appear. In time these young assume the more terrestrial appearance of the adults. The transformed juveniles leave the pond and water for the woods, where they will complete their maturation while feeding in the leaf litter and abandoned rodent tunnels. To avoid desiccation, an individual may spend the remaining summer months in a single tunnel, moving little more than six feet (1.8 m) a day.

While spotted salamanders still thrive in a vast portion of the country, the increased numbers of people have decimated many populations. When pet stores began to sell spotted salamanders, collectors in search of quick money reduced and even eliminated many of these amphibians' breeding populations. This practice is still going on, posing a serious threat to salamander populations.

It is important to spotted salamanders that large woodlots be left intact, without being crisscrossed by roads or disturbed by people. Suburbs and spotted salamanders can easily coexist, and do, as long as large tracts of valuable habitat are left intact. Some spotted salamanders still hang on in New York and other cities. While small patches of their habitat may be protected, in most urban areas they could still be wiped out as a result of relentless collecting.

Spotted salamanders are identified by their yellow spots, which may serve as a warning that there are toxins in their skin. Raccoons and opossums are known to prey on spotted salamanders. Some larger animals have learned to swallow the salamanders whole, rather than to chew on the unpleasant-tasting skin, which might make them sick. As far as I know, no one has ever adequately investigated the purpose and effectiveness of the spotted salamander's black and yellow markings.

Other amphibians on other continents, for example, the European fire salamander (*Salamandra salamandra*) have evolved a similar pattern so the markings are presumed to have some value.

RED-BACKED SALAMANDER

The red-backed salamander (*Plethodon cinereus*) ranges from southern Quebec and Nova Scotia south to North Carolina, west to Minnesota, and through the Great Lakes region, Indiana, Ohio, West Virginia, and Virginia. These salamanders vary in appearance from one individual to another. The two most common variants are called the red-backed and lead-backed phases. Salamanders in the red-backed phase have a reddish brown dorsal stripe extending down their back, from their head practically to the tip of their tail. In the lead-backed phase, the salamanders are uniformly grayish black all over. These phases may be related to the localities in which the salamanders live. Though the adults reach lengths of about 5 inches (12.7 cm), they are usually only 3 to 4 inches (7.6 to 10.1 cm) long, and because they are so thin, they look quite small. They are rarely seen out in the open, unless you go out at night with a bright light and look harder than is usually worth it. Instead, just lifting rocks and logs will be sufficient to turn up some red-backs if they're in the area, although if the soil is dried out, they may have gone down deeper. When looking for salamanders, it is important to return the stones and logs to their original position to avoid disrupting the microhabitat.

In many cities and suburbs, where much of the vertebrate fauna has been altered significantly and few reptiles and amphibians survive, the red-backed salamander is one of the last to persist. These amphibians need woodlands, but beyond that, their requirements are few. Unlike many other salamander species, the red-backed salamander lays eggs on land. These hatch directly into small terrestrial salamanders without gills, which means that their habitat requirements are less complex. In many suburbs, red-backed salamanders can live in small woodlots that remain relatively undisturbed.

Red-backs don't migrate to breeding pools in the spring, so they don't expose themselves to predators or collectors by gathering together each year. And the young aren't exposed to the risk of insufficient rainfall, which dries out many vernal ponds before salamander larvae of other species are able to leave the water. The red-backed salamanders spend their entire lives in the leaf litter and underground. In some healthy woodlands, calculations have shown that the total weight of the red-backed salamanders exceeds the total combined weight of all other vertebrates living in the same area. That's how numerous these animals are in undisturbed areas.

Once you understand how many red-backed salamanders can live in a healthy forest, you can't help but wonder what the effect is when salamanders no longer live there. It appears that woodlands in busy urban areas get trampled until the top layers of earth are so compressed that rain runs off instead of percolating through. The runoff causes erosion, and the compaction kills off species that normally burrow through the humus and lower levels. This process is accelerated by off-road vehicular traffic. Over the years, the wheels of lawnmowers and brush cutters can do considerable damage to an area. For most species, soil structure is far more important than many people realize.

COMMON TOAD, WOODHOUSE'S TOAD, AND FOWLER'S TOAD

The Fowler's toad is one of several subspecies of the common toad (*Bufo woodhousei*) that is distributed across the United States. *Bufo woodhousei fowleri* extends from southern New Hampshire west to southeastern Iowa, south to the Gulf Coast, and east through northern Georgia and South Carolina to the North Carolina coast. In these regions, it is probably the most common of the toads that are able to survive in city parks and in the more wild areas in the suburbs.

Although Fowler's toads previously lived in many coastal areas, including most islands near the mainland, insecticides—particularly DDT, which was sprayed from the late 1940s until the 1960s—decimated total populations of these animals. Often the insecticides were sprayed in an effort to control mosquitoes, but the toads died, too. In those days, all it took was a few suburbanites complaining to their local elected officials about mosquito bites; in no time a truck was dispatched and deadly chemicals were sprayed everywhere.

Attitudes toward insecticides have changed, and government workers are now less inclined to respond to complaints by spraying indiscriminately. Officials have learned that other taxpayers will strenuously object to chemicals being used to kill mosquitoes, which are a valuable asset to many ecosystems. Besides, no one ever told people to move in near marshes where mosquitoes are known to be numerous. An interesting twist to this problem took place in Breezy Point, a coastal community in Brooklyn. The residents wanted to do something about their mosquitoes, so Fowler's toads were introduced as a form of biolog-

Fowler's toad

ical control. Now Breezy Point has both, lots of mosquitoes and lots of toads.

The common toad breeds opportunistically in vernal, freshwater pools and marshes any time from spring to fall. The tadpoles rapidly metamorphose into small toads, which leave before the pools dry up; otherwise the tadpoles die. The dark tadpole coloration helps them blend in with the bottom, where they sit while filter-feeding shortly after hatching. When larger, they are often seen in clusters in shallow water near shore. This may be to avoid fish that can't pursue them into such shallow water, and it may also be because the shallow water is warmer. Another reason the tadpoles often swarm together is to stir up the bottom sediments, increasing the food in suspension that can be consumed by these filter-feeders. Another possible explanation for why they have such dark coloration may be to absorb the sun's radiation when in shallow water; this could help elevate their body temperature so they can feed and metamorphose as rapidly as possible.

Some of the larger toad tadpoles eat the smaller ones. Carnivory helps stagger the emergence of the metamorphosed toads. Those that consume the greatest percentage of the resources are the ones that grow the fastest and are the first to metamorphose and leave the pools. Unlike most frogs, these toads metamorphose and leave their breeding pools when they are still very small, which is another adaptation that helps get them out of the water before it dries up.

Adult toads have dry, warty skin, which helps conserve body fluids by reducing evaporative loss. This is valuable in coastal and arid environments where fresh water is in short supply much of the year and where the desiccating effects of the sun, salt, and breeze can prove deadly, especially to a terrestrial amphibian.

The large bumps behind the eyes are parotid glands, and are filled with a thick, milky, and poisonous solution. On common or Woodhouse's toads, these glands are about twice as long as they are wide; they just touch the cranial crests, which are the bony ridges on the head. Most common toads also have a light line going down the middle of their back.

The southern toad (*Bufo terrestris*), which is closely related to the common toad, is an ecological equivalent that replaces the Fowler's toad along the coastal plain in the South. Three subspecies of the common toad are distributed in the Midwest and in the West. Other common toads, such as the American toad (*Bufo americanus*), still persist in many suburban areas, but they don't seem to last in more built-up areas.

MARINE TOAD

The marine toad (*Bufo marinus*) is a tropical and semitropical species native to South America and Central America, as well as to the southernmost regions of the United States. This species has become established in many warm areas around the world where it was introduced to control snails, insects, and rats. It is now found in southern Texas, Jamaica, Puerto Rico and many other Caribbean islands, Bermuda, Hawaii, most of the larger islands of Micronesia, New Guinea, Fiji, Tonga, the Solomon Islands, the Philippines, and Australia.

These are the largest toads found in North America; they are usually 4 to 6 inches (10.1 to 15.2 cm) long, though they occasionally grow as long as 9 inches (22.8 cm). Besides their size, they are also identified by their enormous, pocked, parotid glands that extend back from their cranial crests to a level equal with their mouth. The poison from their parotid glands is purported to be able to blind a dog, though it almost never does.

Bufo marinus is remarkably well suited to breeding in temporary pools that form in suburban and urban areas any time of the year. Like other species, the toads have learned to take advantage of the "night light" that exists in urban and suburban areas. Street, building, and porch lights attract moths and other insects, which the toads have come to rely on as a food source.

AFRICAN CLAWED FROG

The African clawed frog (*Xenopus laevis*) was brought to this country for a variety of reasons. For many years it has been a useful laboratory animal because it does well in captivity and is easy to breed. During the 1960s this frog was used for pregnancy tests. Later on, some of them showed up in pet shops, and by 1974 African clawed frogs were found breeding in a reservoir in San Diego. In time they were found in several reservoirs in San Diego County. From there they moved into permanent ponds, and by 1980 they had spread throughout the county.

These frogs have voracious appetites and will eat almost anything that moves. Now turning up in backyard ponds, they are even eating goldfish. So far they are found only in Los Angeles and San Diego counties. Whether they will spread cannot be predicted. Since these cities are surrounded by arid areas, it will be difficult or perhaps impossible for the frogs to disperse on their own. However, humans have repeatedly shown that they are effective vectors of a wide range of species that otherwise would have never dispersed beyond their restricted range.

Of all the frogs now living in North America, this has to be one of the more peculiar looking. Its body is flattened, the head is much narrower than the rest of the body—not unlike the narrow-mouthed toad (family, Microhylidae). The little, round eyes, on the top of the head, have a staring gaze because they lack eyelids. The small forelimbs stick out from the front of the body, and the larger hindlimbs project from the back of the body, all in the same flattened plane. Their dorsal coloration ranges from a light to a dark olive gray, and there are dark blotches spread about at random. The venter, or belly, is white with a creamy or yellowish tinge on the arms and legs. The largest specimens reach a length of only about 4 inches (10.1 cm), while many of the smaller ones are about 1 inch (2.5 cm) in length.

CUBAN TREEFROG

The Cuban treefrog (*Osteopilus septentrionalis*), which is native to the Caribbean, has been introduced to northeastern Puerto Rico, St. Croix, and the Florida keys, as well as the U.S. mainland from Collier County to Highlands and Palm Beach counties.

It has been rapidly expanding its range in the urban areas of southern Florida, where it does well near swimming pools, in gardens, around exotic trees such as *Ficus* and *Casuarina*, and near rundown buildings, railroad trestles, and bridges. This frog seems to be associated with a wide range of vegetation growing on disturbed areas.

For a while it was feared that this frog was seriously decimating the native treefrog populations in southern Florida, but actually it hasn't been having such an effect. Although the Cuban treefrog does eat other frogs, even members of the same species, it doesn't seem to be totally displacing the native species. The green treefrog (*Hyla cinerea*) and the squirrel treefrog (*Hyla squirella*), two closely related frogs, still occur in adjacent natural areas, as well as in suburban areas. Most people in southern Florida who have been observing the expanding numbers of the Cuban treefrog feel that there is a chance it could eventually displace the native species, but at this point it still occurs primarily in disturbed areas where the native species are usually reduced in numbers anyway.

For identification purposes it should be helpful to know that the Cuban treefrog is by far the largest treefrog north of Mexico, some reaching a length of about 5 inches (12.7 cm). All the true treefrogs have an expanded pad at the tip of each toe that is used for climbing. The dorsal surface of the Cuban treefrog is all green or brown, or it may be irregularly mottled. The skin on the head is fused to the skull, giving this frog an unusual appearance.

BULLFROG

The bullfrog, the largest North American frog, ranges from southern Canada to central Florida, and west through Wisconsin, Nebraska, most of Texas, and northeastern Mexico. There are also many isolated populations farther west all the way to the coast, where they are widespread throughout western California. Many bullfrog populations in Mexico, Canada, and in the western states were introduced to those areas as an edible species.

Of all the frogs found in the United States, this one probably has had the most success in surviving the effects of human encroachment. The bullfrog (*Rana catesbeiana*) has gone right on living in aquatic habitats in many of the largest, most populated urban areas despite everything that's going on. In many cities, bullfrogs appear to be doing even better than their rural counterparts. This isn't to say that they can live anywhere, because they can't, but they are very tolerant and well adapted to some of the conditions that prevail in urban areas.

The bullfrog gets as large as 8 inches (20.3 cm). It's usually greenish or a greenish brown on the back, with distinct bands on the hind legs. The underparts are generally lighter, with some blotching. The throat of the male is yellowish, like that of the green frog. A ridge extends from behind the eye, back over the tympanum, the frog's equivalent of an eardrum. This ridge, unlike that of the green frog, does not extend the rest of the way along the back. The longest toe on the bullfrog's hind feet extends beyond the webbing. This is in contrast to the pig frog's (*Rana grylio*).

The bullfrog tadpole takes longer than most other species to meta-

Bullfrog

morphose. Two years seems to be typical, which means this species will not become established in areas where ponds regularly dry out completely. The extended larval stage allows the tadpoles to reach lengths of almost 4 inches (10.1 cm) before metamorphosing and emerging from an underwater, gilled lifestyle. This may be important for efficient utilization of the available resources in city ponds, and it may also be an important factor leading to the large size attained by the adults.

These frogs are abundant in relatively rich, shallow ponds that have gently sloping banks and never dry up. City ponds are almost always rich in nutrients, the result of erosion from runoff caused by soil compaction and exposed soils along paths where the turf gets trampled around urban ponds. In addition, fertilizers that are applied to lawns are often washed into the ponds. Resident waterfowl constantly stir the nutrients from the bottom of the pond, as well as adding their excrement to the water's richness. Sometimes effluents from local leaky sewers also drain into these bodies of water. Together, these sources of nutrients make the ponds very rich environments. The tadpoles eat the algae that thrive under these conditions. Because the water is often quite murky, avian predators have trouble preying on the amphibians, and the dense fish populations have poor species diversity, which leads to high numbers of stunted fish. As a result, the larger tadpoles and frogs are relatively immune from the predator pressures that they might normally face elsewhere. These factors all create an environment where the bullfrog thrives.

GREEN FROG

The green frog (*Rana clamitans*) closely resembles the bullfrog, but it is only half as big. It can also be identified by the distinguishing ridges that extend from its head back about two-thirds the length of its body before they reach the legs.

Two subspecies of green frogs have been described. The northern form is known as the green frog (*Rana clamitans melanota*). It ranges from southern Canada to North Carolina, west to Wisconsin, south to Oklahoma. The southern form is the bronze frog (*Rana clamitans clamitans*), which ranges from eastern Texas to southern North Carolina, and south to northern Florida.

Courtship among these frogs extends through the warmer months. In the northern part of their range they lay their eggs during May, June, and July. This species is closely associated with permanent water and is never

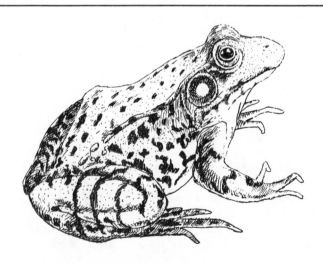

Green frog

as terrestrial as either the pickerel frog (*Rana palustris*) or the wood frog (*Rana sylvatica*). It appears that frogs requiring standing water in the warmer months do well in urban areas where ponds almost never dry up. Frogs that leave the ponds during part of the summer are more vulnerable in densely populated areas.

In rural areas, bullfrogs and green frogs often coexist in the same ponds. But bullfrogs seem to win out in most urban ponds. I am not suggesting that this has anything to do with competition between the two. It may be that green frog tadpoles are less tolerant of rich, murky water. In the summer, when the water warms up and visibility through it is severely restricted, it is common to observe bullfrog tadpoles surfacing for what appear to be gulps of air, probably in response to the oxygen deficit on the bottom of the pond. Perhaps some green frog tadpoles cannot survive these stressful conditions.

Nevertheless, green frogs are widespread in urban environments, though they seem to choose habitats that differ slightly from the areas where bullfrogs do best.

→→ **7** ←←

REPTILES

The fact that any reptiles at all can live in cities is remarkable. Like birds, most reptiles lay large, conspicuous, shelled eggs. That works out all right for many urban bird species because most are able to nest up off the ground, where their eggs are far less vunerable to predation. But a city is a terrible place to live if, like the reptiles, you have to lay your eggs on the ground. Certain birds have been able to do this with some success—the pheasant may be the best example—but most ground-nesting urban birds now lay their eggs on flat roofs. Unfortunately, reptiles have to bury their eggs, so they don't have the luxury of laying them on roofs, and most reptiles couldn't climb a building anyway. As a result, we have a relatively depauperate urban reptile fauna.

Reptiles found in cities fall into several categories. One is composed of pet turtles that have been released in ponds and lakes. Though these turtles may do well, most species cannot reproduce themselves. Some have been released in the wrong part of the country, others can't find a mate, and still others can't find a suitable place to lay their eggs. The eggs or the young might not survive very long anyway, given the many rodents and other obstacles they have to overcome. Yet, as it turns out, turtles actually do survive and even reproduce in many city ponds, and they are discussed in this chapter.

The second group of urban reptiles is the lizards. Because most lizards live in warm climates, we don't find many species in the urban areas of the north, but the exceptions are discussed. Urban lizards are found in the most southern portions of this country. There are many lizards living in the Miami area, and information about each of them is offered, along with facts about lizards in other cities around the country.

Snakes make up the third group of urban reptiles. Snakes aren't the most beloved of animals, of course, so it stands to reason that there aren't many of them in most cities. Even those snakes that have been able to survive in cities and suburbs are not doing well, for the most part. Generally, these populations are relictual and probably won't survive much longer. But there are some exceptions, and these species are discussed.

SEA TURTLES

Seven species of sea turtles live in the coastal waters of the United States. Four of them—the leatherback (*Dermochelys coriacea*), the loggerhead (*Caretta caretta*), the green turtle (*Chelonia mydas*), and the hawksbill (*Eretmochelys imbricata*)—live in both the Atlantic and the Pacific. Recently the Pacific subspecies of green turtle (*Chelonia mydas agassazi*) was elevated to its own specific status, *Chelonia depressa*, the flatback turtle. The names of the other two species—the Atlantic ridley (*Lepidochelys kempi*) and the Pacific ridley (*Lepidochelys olivacea*)—will tell you where they live.

Usually sea turtles are thought to inhabit remote, tropical regions, far from human disturbance. In part, this perception is true, but largely it is a reflection of how poorly we understand these animals, all of which are endangered. Over 99 percent of sea turtle research focuses on nesting behavior, egg incubation, and hatchling emergence, even though this represents less than 1 percent of their life history. We know little else because it is difficult to study these turtles during their extended migrations, often more than 1,250 miles (2,000 km), to remote feeding areas and nesting beaches. The only time most researchers find it feasible to study them is when the turtles congregate at their nesting beaches. As a result, we are left with a very lopsided understanding of sea turtle biology. This may explain why it comes as such a surprise to learn that although sea turtles tend to return to the same tropical beaches to lay their eggs, they travel far and wide at other times, sometimes feeding in the waters near major coastal cities.

For years the Atlantic leatherback (*Dermochelys coriacea coriacea*) was thought to be rare off the East Coast. However, an artifact of our times has revealed the presence of more leatherbacks than we suspected. Dead leatherbacks weighing from 700 to 1,000 pounds (318 to 455 kg) now regularly wash ashore along the New York and New Jersey coastlines. A leading cause of these deaths seems to be an important component of their diet: they eat jellyfish—or what they think are jellyfish. The garbage being flushed and dumped into our coastal waters includes many plastic bags. In the water these bags look much like jellyfish, and they are being consumed by unsuspecting leatherbacks. The plastic then clogs the turtles' alimentary canal and eventually kills them. Boat propeller damage also takes a large toll. It is difficult to tell if the turtles get hit by boat propellers because they are not wary of fishermen, or if the turtles, already dying, are spotted, then run over by curious boaters.

The leatherback turtle is easily distinguished from all other sea turtles by the twelve ridges on its leathery shell, five above, five below, and one on each side. The older leatherbacks can grow up to 8 feet (2.5 m) long, and can weigh as much as 1,600 pounds (726 kg).

Recently loggerhead sea turtles have been turning up in unlikely places, leading some people to believe that they are regular visitors to urban marine waters. For years it has been occasionally reported in the Northeast that a loggerhead has been hooked by anglers from the shore. This sea turtle was known to be a regular summer visitor as far north as Cape Cod and Long Island, frequently entering inlets. I have substantial reason to believe that loggerheads have always frequented these coasts. Dead specimens have washed ashore in Queens and Brooklyn, and Don Riepe, who works at the Jamaica Bay Wildlife Refuge, reports having seen turtles fitting the description of loggerheads in Jamaica Bay, New York City. Despite the considerable pollution in these waters, horseshoe crabs (*Limulus polyphemus*) are still doing quite well; each year they come into shallow water to mate and lay their eggs. It could be that these breeding aggregations lure in the loggerheads, which are known to eat a wide range of foods, including such hard-shelled animals as horseshoe crabs. One of the dead loggerheads that washed ashore in New York City during the summer of 1979 was opened up by Matthew Lerman, a high school teacher in Rockaway Park, Queens. He found remains of horseshoe crabs in the digestive tract.

Loggerheads are identified by their five or more lateral laminae, the plates on each side of their carapace, which is the shell on their back. Also, they have two pairs of scutes, thin, horny, shields, in contact with each other on the top of their head between their eyes. The old ones can get as large as 7 feet (2.13 m) and weigh as much as 1,200 pounds (544 kg).

Another sea turtle, the Kemp's ridley, also known as the Atlantic ridley, has three ridges running down the top of the shell, and five lateral laminae on each side of the carapace. They only grow 2½ feet (76 cm) long, weighing about 100 pounds (45 kg). This species has also been found to frequent the waters of some unlikely urban areas. It is the most endangered of all the sea turtles. Like the loggerhead, the ridley lives in shallow coastal waters where it feeds on crustaceans, gastropods, echinoderms, and some marine plants. Both species, along with some hawksbills, are being drowned in fishing nets and shrimp trawls in the waters off the southeast coast. The sea turtles get caught in the nets and, unable to surface for air, expire. It would help the turtles considerably if fishermen were forced to trawl farther offshore where they will catch fewer turtles and, in the process, preserve a greater portion of the shrimp spawning grounds. Nets have been redesigned to avoid drowning of turtles, but of the more than 6,000 vessels towing more than 20,000 shrimp nets in southeastern U.S. waters, no more than 300 vessels are using the new turtle-excluder device.

Sea turtles occasionally become stranded in urban or suburban waters. The New York Marine Mammal and Sea Turtle Stranding Network, operated by the Okeanos Ocean Research Foundation, began recording data on sea turtle strandings in 1977. From 1977 to 1984 they averaged 24 turtles a year. The most numerous were leatherbacks; only a fraction were loggerheads, Kemp's ridleys, and green turtles. Then in late 1985 and early 1986, 52 stranded sea turtles were recovered from the New York shores of Long Island Sound. Most of the turtles were found washed ashore or floating in the surf along the north shore of Long Island. Among the 52 turtles recovered were three different species: Kemp's ridleys, green turtles, and loggerheads. It was thought that all were stunned by severely cold temperatures. Thirty-nine of the turtles were positively identified as ridleys, and two more were probably ridleys. All of them were nearly the same length, between 9 and 13 inches (23 to 33 cm) measured from notch to notch along the carapace. Ridleys this size are all immatures. These cold-stunned turtles have led researchers to question whether Long Island Sound has always been part of their normal, but previously unrecognized, habitat during this stage of their life. It has also been suggested that this was an anomalous event caused by a change in the Gulf Stream, the major northward flowing current in the western Atlantic, and that the turtles may have followed eddies of warm water that led into Long Island Sound. However, Sam Sadove, program coordinator for the Stranding Network and research director for the Okeanos Foundation, suggests that the waters of Long Island Sound may serve as an important habitat for developing juvenile Kemp's ridleys.

Green turtles, though found in our coastal waters from Massachusetts to Mexico, and from southern California to Chile, are uncommon almost everywhere throughout their range except in the Caribbean and around the Galapagos Islands. The adults tend to be extremely rare in the more northern waters, but the juveniles appear to tolerate cooler temperatures, and they range farther north. This species, like the hawksbill, has four lateral laminae. Unlike the loggerhead and the hawksbill turtles, the green turtle does not have two pairs of scutes touching each other on the top of the head between the eyes.

Green turtles are uncommon in most of their range, and they are seldom seen near urban areas, but where conditions are right and where there are beds of turtle grass (*Thalassia testudinum*) to graze on, they will come in near shore, even near people and constant motorboat traffic, and feed at their leisure in large groups. I have seen this during summers in Bermuda, where hundreds of juvenile green turtles feed. They readily graze on stands of turtle grass in Castle Harbor, which is near the island's busy airport, some of its largest hotels, and considerable boat traffic.

I know of no true urban areas where hawksbills are common. These turtles, which grow only about 3 feet (91 cm) long and 280 pounds (127 kg) in weight, range in the western Atlantic from Brazil to Massachusetts, and in the eastern Pacific from the California coast to Peru; they seem to be rare throughout. At one time they were relatively common in the waters along the southeastern United States, but now they are found only on occasion off North Carolina, South Carolina, and Georgia. There may be more hawksbills farther off the coast than is currently recognized, because from time to time they are seen in the waters off most tropical islands. This turtle has the best shell for "tortoise shell," causing severe pressure on them throughout their range. In the tropics, especially, the natives supply a bountiful trade, kept lively by droves of tourists. Even though real tortoise shell is an illegal import, as long as there's a market, and insufficient numbers of people hired to enforce the laws, hawksbills will risk paying the supreme price, extinction.

PAINTED TURTLES

The painted turtle is probably one of the most numerous turtles in North America. This turtle thrives in conditions where few other animals survive. Four subspecies in the United States have an aggregate range extending over the East, Midwest, and Northwest. Painted turtles have stripes of uniform width along the neck, beginning red and becoming yellow farther out on the head. The length of the shell rarely exceeds 6 inches (15 cm). The background color of the carapace is quite dark, while the scutes along the margins are black, red, and yellow, and the scutes along the sides and back are bordered with yellow. The bottom shell, the plastron, is usually yellow.

The eastern painted turtle (*Chrysemys picta picta*) is distributed from Nova Scotia to Alabama, overlapping considerably from Maine to Pennsylvania with the midland painted turtle (*Chrysemys picta marginata*), which has some dark markings in the middle of the plastron. The midland subspecies appears to be better adapted to the cooler temperatures of the upland, while the eastern painted turtles, which are distinguished by their pure yellow plastrons, are better adapted to the warm coastal plain of the

Painted turtle

Atlantic Coast. Some populations of midland turtles colonized coastal land masses when the last glaciation ended and the glacier receded northward. As the glacier melted, the sea level rose, isolating many areas, which became islands. When the climate warmed, eastern painted turtles moved north and mixed with the midland stock, but they couldn't mix with the stock that had become established on the coastal islands because painted turtles avoid salt water.

The southern painted turtle (*Chrysemys picta dorsalis*) has the most restricted range of the four subspecies. It is found in a strip of territory extending from southern Illinois and Missouri south along the east and west banks of the Mississippi to the Gulf Coast of Louisiana. Their range also includes an eastward extension through northern Mississippi and Alabama. There is also a relictual population in southeastern Oklahoma. This subspecies is distinguished from the others by a prominent red or yellow stripe that runs right down the middle of its back.

The western painted turtle is the only painted turtle with a reticulate carapacial pattern, that is, a netlike design on its top shell that is not part of the sutures, or seams, between the scutes, or plates, that cover the shell. It ranges from western Ontario through southern Canada to British Columbia, south to Missouri, and west through most of Kansas, then diagonally northwest to northern Oregon. There are other isolated populations in Colorado, New Mexico, and Chihuahua, Mexico. In the North-west, where reptiles are less common than in warmer regions, this is one of the most common turtle species after the western pond turtle, or Pacific pond turtle (*Clemmys marmorata*). The latter ranges west of the Cascade-Sierra crest from southwestern British Columbia to northwestern Baja California.

The western pond turtle doesn't have the red and yellow stripes along the neck and head that the painted turtles have, and the western pond turtle's carapace is a uniform, dark color without any bright red or yellow markings. Because the western pond turtle is aquatic, and is commonly found in ponds, marshes, streams, rivers, and irrigation ditches, even in brackish coastal waters, it is far more numerous in densely populated areas than are its eastern relatives, the wood turtle (*Clemmys insculpta*), the spotted turtle (*Clemmys guttata*), and the bog turtle (*Clemmys muhlenbergi*). The bog turtle is often called the rarest turtle in North America. Each of the eastern species in this genus is shrinking in numbers and range, perhaps because much of their critical habitat has been destroyed. The wood turtle, characterized by the super-imposed concentric growth rings on its dorsal laminae, has several spe-cific habitat requirements; if one is not met, the turtles are unable to maintain their numbers in the area. The spotted turtle, which rarely exceeds 5 inches (12.7 cm) in length, is recognized by the bright yellow spots on the almost black shell. And the bog turtle, a small brown turtle with yellowish orange blotches on each side of the neck, cannot live long without adequate acreage of wetlands and with an adjacent upland area in which to lay its eggs.

The painted turtle and western pond turtle thrive because they do well in the ponds that are distributed in areas where people live. But without well-targeted conservation efforts, all three of the other species related to the western pond turtle could continue their decline until only a few, protected, isolated populations survive.

SNAPPING TURTLES

The common snapping turtle (*Chelydra serpentina serpentina*) has a range that extends from southern Canada to northern Florida and west to the Rocky Mountains. Some people regard the Florida snapping turtle (*Chelydra serpentina osceola*) as a subspecies of the snapping turtle. Others have elevated it to a species (*Chelydra osceola*). This turtle, at any rate, ranges from northern to southern Florida. These snapping turtles spend most of their time in aquatic habitats, including streams, marshes,

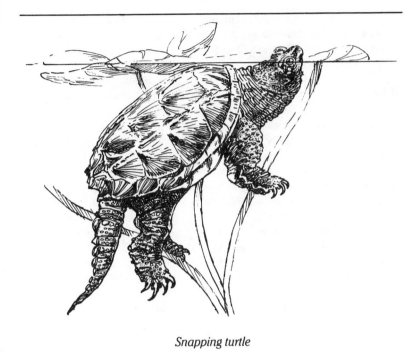

Snapping turtle

and ponds. In many coastal areas they live in brackish habitats, and on occasion are found in pure saltwater. Their capacity to thrive in a variety of aquatic habitats may have some bearing on their ability to survive where most other amphibians and reptiles were extirpated long ago, including urban and suburban ponds. This is a turtle with endurance. Seldom seen by most people, the snapping turtle spends much of its adult life resting on or moving along muddy and weedy water bottoms, eating whatever animal matter is available.

For a freshwater turtle, this species is rather large. The shell (carapace) of older adults often reaches a length of a foot (30 cm) or more. The carapace is dark brown to black and becomes quite smooth with age. The head is large and pointed, and when the mouth is opened, the turtle looks fierce, which it is. The yellowish plastron is small and cruciform in shape, leaving much soft skin exposed. The skin along the neck has dark tubercles on it, and the especially long tail is equipped with a considerable amount of armor.

Many people are afraid of snapping turtles. They think the turtles pose a significant threat to bathers. Actually, these people have little to worry about. It is true that snappers can leave a nasty wound, but they bite only when they are out of the water being bothered. As far as I know, no one has ever claimed to have been bitten underwater. The turtles mind their own business and are very willing to leave people alone. People should take the hint.

Unlike most turtles that have a problem finding safe places to lay their eggs in urban settings, snapping turtles often locate suitable nesting sites quite close to the urban ponds in which they thrive. Since people are often afraid to enter city parks at night, the turtles have many hours to accomplish their egg-laying tasks after dark without being noticed or disturbed, except perhaps by raccoons and other animals. Urban turtles usually lay their eggs during overcast, cloudy, or rainy weather, or at dusk, dawn, or during the night. Nocturnal egg laying appears to be the norm with snapping turtles, which are sometimes caught in the act by joggers out for an early morning run around the city pond. Even in Manhattan, snappers have occasionally been found methodically completing their time-honored egg-laying ritual just before or just after the sun comes up.

MUSK TURTLES

Four species of musk turtles in the genus *Sternotherus* can be found in the United States, some of them in city and suburban parks. The group gets its name from the foul-smelling secretion emitted by their musk glands. All are limited to the eastern part of the country. These are small, inconspicuous turtles with carapacial lengths ranging from about 3½ to 5½ inches (9 to 14 cm). The most common musk turtle, known as the stinkpot (*Sternotherus odoratus*), inhabits clear, shallow ponds and lakes as well as rivers in most eastern states. Indigenous to a large area, this species ranges from Maine's coastal region to the southern tip of Florida, west to Wisconsin, and south to the Gulf Coast. The carapace may be light to dark brown, with or without spots, and is often covered with a green algal growth. The plastron is a light cream or yellow color, while the head and soft parts are all quite dark. Small, narrow, and roughly cruciform, the plastron is more like that of the snapping turtle than most of the other freshwater turtles. Unlike the snapping turtle, the shell is domed, the size is always small, and the tail is short.

The stinkpot has been eliminated from many of its former localities. During the decades when DDT and other pesticides and herbicides were being used widely, many detrimental effects were set in motion. It took years before people noticed that animals at the top of the food chain, such as ospreys (*Pandion haliaetus*), peregrine falcons (*Falco peregrinus*), and

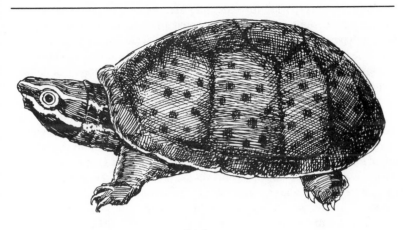

Stinkpot

bald eagles (*Haliaeetus leucocephalus*), were decreasing in numbers. And it was even longer before the government finally got around to banning the use of the worst of these chemicals. In the meantime, the poisons accumulated in the groundwater and sediments, as well as in the tissues of organisms throughout the ecosystem, and their effects continued to ripple through the environment. Substantially less conspicuous animals, such as amphibians and reptiles, tended to be overlooked by the press and the government, not to mention the scientific community, but their numbers, too, decreased dramatically. Evidence that I have gathered from a region in Long Island, New York, indicates that many of the species of lower vertebrates that lived in agricultural areas treated with DDT were killed off, and few have ever returned.

The absence of amphibians and reptiles at many sites reveals how poorly we understand the disappearance and lack of recolonization of salamanders, toads, frogs, snakes, and turtles. Being extremely vulnerable to human disturbance, many of these species are among the first to disappear from altered areas, though they are rarely the first to be noticed. When pollutants break down or are flushed out of the environment, plants, invertebrates, birds, and mammals may readily reinhabit previously disturbed areas, largely because of their relatively rapid dispersal rates. Amphibians and reptiles, however, are at a disadvantage when it comes to repopulating areas where they have been eliminated.

Those animals that live in urban areas where the few remaining ponds and woodlots are widely dispersed have been reduced to small, isolated, vulnerable populations. Once extirpated, they have little chance of being reestablished.

Ponds in city parks, for example, are isolated within large urban buffers where they have been protected from agricultural chemicals. Although pesticides, herbicides, and fungicides were widely used in cities in the past, their usage is in decline because of costs and environmental sensitivity. Some cities still use these chemicals, of course, but urban amphibians and reptiles that are able to survive just about anything have managed to survive.

Few species of turtles do well under these conditions, however, and it has come as a surprise to find adult stinkpots and hatchlings in Belvedere Lake in Manhattan's Central Park. This is the first indication that there might be an urban stinkpot population in the Northeast. One reason musk turtles were always absent from Manhattan is that the island is surrounded by deep water on all sides. They couldn't get to Manhattan Island because it would have taken far too much energy for these little-legged turtles to continually paddle all the way to the surface for a breath of air. During such a long swim they would have tired and drowned. In some areas, musk turtles will take to deeper water in cold weather, and they will remain on the bottom for months without ever surfacing for air—but not in the Hudson, Harlem, and East rivers. Manhattan's waterways are largely brackish, and they flow with powerful currents. The turtles couldn't cross such formidable barriers.

The salt tolerance of local populations of eastern mud turtles (*Kinosternon subrubrum*) explains their presence in some salt marshes along the East Coast. There are even some in Staten Island, but most urban and suburban populations are doing very poorly.

The stinkpot, like most urban species, is brought into cities such as Manhattan by humans, and then they either escape or are eventually released. Most of the animals that are released in an urban environment do the best they can under the circumstances, but they don't last long. Few attain their natural life expectancy, and even fewer find others of the same species, mate, and establish a population. In Belvedere Lake, however, the stinkpots seem to have beaten the odds.

The New York City Department of Parks and Recreation has been considering dredging and expanding Belvedere Lake. Such a move could have a major impact on the musk turtles. Urban ponds are prone to silting in much more rapidly than most ponds and lakes because of the runoff caused by nearby erosion. In this case, the common reed (*Phragmites australis*) has been invading the shallow waters along the shore and is shading out the new plantings on the bank. By draining the lake and bulldozing the bottom sediments, the park workers would make the lake deeper, temporarily solving the *Phragmites* problem. In my opinion, it would make more sense to leave the *Phragmites* alone. The plant is attractive, it provides cover for nesting birds, including red-winged blackbirds (*Agelaius phoeniceus*), and it isn't bothering anyone. Should the time come when the reed really needs to be controlled, it would be less destructive and possibly more cost-effective to cut it by hand.

In other regions, especially in the South, related species of musk and mud turtles have been maintaining relatively stable populations in man-made bodies of water. In southern Florida the stinkpot, the eastern mud turtle (*Kinosternon subrubrum*), and the striped mud turtle (*Kinosternon baurii*) are doing quite well in a number of urban ponds.

URBAN LIZARDS

Few of the urban lizards in this country are native. The ruin lizard (*Podarcis sicula*), native to southern Italy, Sicily, and the Lipari Islands, escaped in the 1960s in West Hempstead, Long Island, New York, and is now breeding and established in several Nassau County suburbs, most notably Garden City South, West Hempstead, and Franklin Square. The ruin lizard's range appears to be restricted to a square kilometer sur-rounding its initial point of release. The length from the tip of the snout to the end of the tail is almost 10 inches (25 cm). This oviparous (egg-laying) insect-eater is narrow, elongate, and greenish on top.

No one is predicting a rapid increase in numbers of this lizard. Similar cases have not led to rapid range extensions when only a small number of lizards have been released or have escaped. A small population of *Podarcis sicula* lasted at least 28 years in Philadelphia, though. And in Topeka, Kansas, a small population of green lizards (*Lacerta viridis*) is still surviving in a busy suburban part of town near a shopping center. These individuals are descendants of lizards that escaped over 30 years ago. The larger specimens get as long as 15 inches (38 cm). The adults are greenish above and whitish below, while the juveniles are brownish with two to four light longitudinal stripes.

Each of these lacertid populations was established by a small number of escaped individuals, but other lizards have been purposely introduced. In 1942, for example, Carl Kauffeld, who was the Curator of Reptiles at the Staten Island Zoo, released 29 fence lizards (*Sceloporus undulatus hyacinthus*) on Staten Island, in New York City. The lizards had been caught in the Rossville area of the New Jersey pine barrens. By 1960 their numbers had increased, and their range had expanded. This population is now common in several areas of Staten Island, especially where pines are growing on sandy soil. I have heard that additional fence lizards were added later by other collectors; this may have contributed to the overall diversity of the population's gene pool and increased their chances of survival.

The eastern fence lizard is a member of the largest genus of lizards in North America. There are sixteen species of *Sceloporus* north of Mexico. This oviparous spiny lizard rarely gets much larger than 8 inches (20 cm) from the snout to the end of the tail. The back is a brownish gray, and each side of the male's belly has a large patch of blue.

The genus *Anolis* has more than 300 species living in North America, Central America, the Caribbean, and South America. This is an exceedingly complex assemblage of lizards, and the taxonomy is far from settled. Several different genera have been proposed, but since things are still in flux, I will proceed, using *Anolis* when referring to species in this group. Only one member, the green anole (*Anolis carolinensis*), is definitely native to the United States, inhabiting much of the Southeast. Several other species in this "genus" have been introduced to southern Florida where they are now well established and where many of them live in urban areas. The green anole is about 8 inches (20 cm) long, can change colors with its physiological state from green to brown and back again, and has small, almost granular scales. It has a dewlap, or throat fan, which can be extended to reveal the pink color, although some are gray or bluish.

The South American ground lizard (*Ameiva ameiva*)—a member of the family, Teiidae, which includes 225 species that all live in the Americas—has been introduced to the Miami area, where it is doing well. Ameivas thrive in urban and suburban areas in warmer climates because they are amazingly brazen, quick, and adept at finding and eating just about anything that looks or smells like food. Unlike most other lizards, ameivas readily take foods as wide-ranging as insects, dead fish and mammals, dog food, cat food, and scraps put out for the chickens. The backyards of many homes offer endless opportunities to a small scavenger that comes out in the heat of the day, so the ameiva may have a future in southern Florida where at least two subspecies have been introduced. Both are native to South America.

Southern Florida seems to be one of the major hot spots for introduced lizards in North America. During the past several decades many lizards have become established in Florida's suburban and urban areas, and some are moving into the more rural areas. For the most part, however, the lizards that are doing well there are those that are more or less confined to human-related habitats. One is the bark anole (*Anolis distichus*), which was probably introduced from the Bahamas. This anole has a yellow dewlap.

A native lizard that is doing well in some urban areas in southern Florida is the reef gecko (*Sphaerodactylus notatus*). Like the anoles, geckos have very small, granular scales, but they don't have a dewlap. The reef gecko grows only 2½ inches (6.4 cm) long. They are brownish to reddish brown, with darker spots that sometimes align in rows.

Living with these species are many others that have been introduced in different ways. The Jamaican giant anole (*Anolis garmani*), the Puerto Rican lizard (*Anolis cristatellus*), and the curly-tailed lizard (*Leiocephalus carinatus*) probably arrived in Florida as stowaways. The Mexican spiny-tailed iguana (*Ctenosaura pectinata*) probably came in with the animal trade. Lizards that arrived on ships with produce or plants include the green bark anole (*Anolis distichus*), the brown anole (*Anolis sagrei*), the yellow-headed gecko (*Gonatodes albogularis*), the Indo-Pacific gecko (*Sphaerodactylus argus*), and the ashy gecko (*Sphaerodactylus elegans*). Lizards that were released by animal dealers or pet owners include the South American ground lizards in both the Hialeah and Suniland populations, the brown basilisk (*Basiliscus vittatus*), the rainbow lizard (*Cnemidophorus lemniscatus*), the tokay gecko (*Gekko gecko*), the green iguana (*Iguana iguana*) in the airport population, and the Hispaniolan curly-tailed lizard (*Leiocephalus schreibersi*). Species that were introduced by people not associated with the animal trade are the large-headed anole (*Anolis cybotes*), the knight anole (*Anolis equestris*), the curly-tailed lizards (*Leiocephalus carinatus*) in the Palm Beach population, and the Indo-Pacific gecko (*Hemidactylus garnoti*) in the South Miami and Coconut Grove populations. The Key Biscayne populations of both the South American ground lizard and the green iguana escaped from the zoo exhibits there, and the Virginia Key population of curly-tailed lizards originated from the exhibits in that city's zoo.

Native populations of some lizards have been severely reduced in urban areas in southern Florida, although these species are still doing fine in undisturbed areas. These lizards include the six-lined racerunner (*Cnemidophorus sexlineatus*) and the ground skink (*Scincella lateralis*). Native species that are widespread in both natural and urban-agricultural areas in southern Florida include the southeastern five-lined skink (*Eumeces inexpectatus*) and the island glass lizard (*Ophisaurus compressus*). Exotic species that are doing well in urban and agricultural areas in southern Florida include the knight anole, the Indo-Pacific gecko, the Mediterranean gecko (*Hemidactylus turcicus*), and the ashy gecko.

The Mediterranean gecko has moved from town to town as a stowaway and is now established in the Gulf states, Texas, Oklahoma, Arizona, and parts of Mexico, as well as on many islands in the Caribbean. These geckos are most often seen on buildings. Another gecko, *Mabuya mabouya*, which has been very adept at establishing new populations throughout the Caribbean, apparently made the jump to the mainland United States recently. Gregory Pregill, curator of herpetology at the San Diego Natural History Museum, told me that some have been found in trash piles in southern San Diego. There is still no evidence that they are breeding there.

Since most lizards do better in warmer climates, most of the species that have been introduced to the United States are in the southernmost part of the country. It is interesting that southern Florida has a disproportionate number of introduced species. This is probably attributable to several factors. First of all, much of the trade between South America, the Caribbean, and the United States uses ships that pull into ports in southern Florida. Also, Florida has a large Hispanic population. These people travel back and forth between their homes in America and the homes of their friends and family in South America and the Caribbean. And third, because the state is so close to the Bahamas and the Caribbean islands, it is common for vacationers in Florida to take quick trips to the islands. Often people bring "souvenirs" back to Florida, many of which eventually escape or are released. Almost anywhere else in the country these animals' chances wouldn't be very good, but southern Florida has a very hospitable climate, and many of the lizards survive. Those that have established populations farther north are all species that live in cooler environments around the world, but these are the exceptions.

Now that so many populations of lizards are found in southern Florida, it may be just a matter of time before some of the lizards travel as stowaways, or by some other means, to additional cities and towns in the South, where they will again escape, or be released, and establish satellite populations. They won't necessarily spread as rapidly as some introduced species of birds or fish, but in several more decades we may find added diversity in this country's urban herpetofauna.

GARTER SNAKE AND BROWN SNAKE

Garter snakes (*Thamnophis* spp.) range through the northern United States and southern Canada from coast to coast. They comprise some of the most common and numerous snakes in North America. There are thirteen species in this genus in the United States. All have keeled scales, that is, the scales along the back have a ridge down the middle. Most garter snakes have stripes and are variations on shades of brown, yellow, and orange. Populations occupy a wide range of habitats including arid areas, fields, woods, marshes, and stream and river banks. Their ecological versatility is probably related to their widespread occurrence. However, this accounts for only part of the reason that they persist in many densely populated regions where other snakes have not been able to survive. Life history streamlining also appears to account for this persistence. Most reptile populations decline when they are surrounded on all sides by an environment that is difficult to move about in—parking lots, buildings, roads, sidewalks, and other inhospitable structures. For

Garter snake

aquatic animals, a body of water can provide a refuge that filters out cars and people. As long as the aquatic species can accomplish all or almost all that is necessary in that body of water, possibly utilizing some adjacent property some of the time as well, they may be able to survive. But terrestrial animals don't have any barrier between them and us. As a result, they are extremely vulnerable in cities. Most snakes are terrestrial, and few have been able to do well in densely populated regions. Some species have proved to be exceptions, however, the garter snakes among them.

The single most significant preadaptation that appears to account for garter snakes' ability to survive in urban environments is viviparity: garter snakes do not lay eggs; rather, they bear their young live. This eliminates many complications. Just eliminating the need to find a place to lay their eggs is significant. Cities present formidable obstacles to egg-laying animals, especially those laying eggs on the ground; due to trampling, much urban soil has been compacted over the years so that its bulk density is often greater than that of concrete; the layer of humus is reduced in depth by erosion; and large numbers of rodents patrol the parklands, scavenging anything edible. But viviparity allows the garter snakes to live in such a habitat. If the population can survive on a relatively small plot of land—just large enough for them to feed, mate, overwinter, and bear their young—there is a chance that the snakes will survive.

Young garter snake

More secretive snakes, those that live under things and those that are small, also seem to have a better chance of surviving in urban environments. One species that fits this description is the brown snake, or DeKay snake (*Storeria dekayi*), which is small, secretive, doesn't move much, can maintain a population in a relatively small area, and is viviparous. This is one of the few species that actually does well in some suburbs and even in some cities. Believe it or not, the brown snake is alive and well in New York City. There are enough parks and vacant lots with the right habitat requirements to allow brown snakes to thrive. The food they eat is small and abundant, and they seem to survive being moved around by

Brown snake

dump trucks that remove earth and debris—which often contains these small, inconspicuous snakes—from one part of the city, dumping it in another.

Brown snakes are much smaller than garter snakes. The largest brown snake is in the neighborhood of 20 inches (51 cm), though most are considerably smaller. The largest garter snakes can reach a length of 50 inches (127 cm), but most are less that 3 feet (91 cm). The brown snake is usually light brown; some have dots or stripes; and the young have a light ring around the neck. They are sometimes called DeKay snakes because they were named for James DeKay, a 19th-century zoologist.

WATER SNAKE

The northern water snake (*Nerodia sipedon*) ranges throughout much of the eastern portion of the United States, all the way to the eastern slope of the Rocky Mountains in Colorado and south through Kansas to the Gulf of Mexico. Along the East Coast, it is distributed south to North Carolina, where its range continues south, but only inland, through western South Carolina, Georgia, Alabama, and Mississippi. Along the coastal plain from central North Carolina south, this species is replaced by other species of water snakes.

The genus is *Nerodia* rather than *Natrix* now, in the more recent parlance of herpetologists (those who study reptiles and amphibians). Depending on the northern water snake subspecies, some have alternating light and dark brown lateral bars along the dorsal surface; others have an indistinct pattern. In many coastal areas the water snake will go into brackish and saltwater, at least temporarily, and will eat any number of different food items, such as fish, frogs, and salamanders. But this snake lives almost exclusively in freshwater habitats in most of its range.

Like the garter snake, this species is widespread and has persisted longer than most other species of snakes in suburbs and some smaller cities; unlike the garter snake, this species seems to have narrower habitat requirements. This may explain why it is not more common in larger cities. It seems that the more urban an area gets, the fewer opportunities exist for species other than a few preadapted, opportunistic animals. Among snakes, this continues to hold true. The water snake, too, is viviparous, which probably is not mere coincidence. Any factor that complicates the life history of an animal will be a strike against its chances for survival in the urban habitats that are available and otherwise suitable.

BRAHMINY BLIND SNAKE

Unlike lizards, which have many established non-native species living throughout the country, only one introduced species of snake is now well established. This is a small worm snake, the Brahminy blind snake (*Ramphotyphlops bramina*). As a stowaway it has moved to and become established in Australia, Japan, Southeast Asia, Hawaii, and other islands in the Pacific. It is now doing well in suburban Miami.

Because it has moved from port to port with such ease, probably in dirt and packing material, it is difficult to establish its original range, but the Brahminy blind snake is definitely an Old World species. Julian Lee, a professor at the University of Miami, told me that there has been speculation that some of these snakes in Miami may be parthenogenetic, which means that the females do not need males in order to reproduce, and their offspring are all females. If this is so, establishing new populations will be facilitated, since only one individual is needed. Each snake can reproduce on its own, greatly increasing its reproductive capacity. Should it turn out that this species is in fact parthenogenetic, that will be a first for snakes. We know about many invertebrates that can reproduce in such a manner, as well as some fish, amphibians, and lizards; but until now, no snakes are known to have this ability.

Often living submerged in the ground or under things, these small snakes have some of the qualities of the brown snake that preadapt them to survive in urban areas. They eat small amounts of small food items, do not require large spaces, are easily transported unintentionally in earth and debris, and may well expand their range throughout more southern cities and suburbs in this country.

8

BIRDS

Birds are quite common and even diverse in cities and suburbs. Their flight accounts for much of the diversity: during their spring and fall migrations, birds move through densely populated regions, often stopping to rest or to feed in parks and backyards, in trees, along the shore, and in marshes. The number of resident species, those that remain to breed, is smaller, but there are many species that do well in metropolitan areas. Bird feeders help sustain some birds, but generally, each of these species would do all right on their own anyway.

In the most restrictive habitats, those that are paved over and built up, the house sparrows, starlings, and pigeons are consummately successful urban dwellers. Each of these species was introduced from Europe to North America. When were they brought over? Why? How did they become established in this country? Why are they doing so well, often at the expense of or instead of native species? The answers to all these questions are discussed in this chapter.

Other city species such as grackles, red-winged blackbirds, cowbirds, house finches, and mourning doves are also presented. Ground nesters such as pheasants are mentioned, as are killdeer plovers and common nighthawks, which often nest on flat roofs. Crows, gulls, and mallards are also briefly discussed, as are some recently introduced doves, partridges, and parrots.

Some herons have been adapting to ponds and marshes in cities, and these are described, as are species of swifts, swallows, and martins that nest in buildings and boxes, under bridges, in pipes sticking out of walls, and in chimneys. Other species that have taken to nesting in bird houses, such as the house wren and screech owl, are discussed, along with barn owls and some hawks, eagles, and falcons that have been occurring in what might seem like unlikely places.

HOUSE SPARROW

It is hard to imagine an American city without house sparrows (*Passer domesticus*), yet they weren't always a part of our urban scene. During the first half of the 19th century, the human population of New York City surged to three million, which caused major changes to the environment. Trees were cleared, habitats were destroyed, and many of the native species were pushed out. Because most of the native insectivorous birds had been driven out, it wasn't long before plants began to suffer severe insect damage. Out of control cankerworms, moth larvae from the family Geometridae, some of which are called inchworms, stripped the leaves from the trees. This led to the widespread sentiment that something had to be done. So New Yorkers set out to rectify the problem.

Remembering the house sparrows that fed on insects in European cities, people decided to introduce this species to New York. In 1850 a group of New Yorkers ordered eight pairs of house sparrows from England. When the sparrows were released, they did all right for a while, but without breeding, they eventually died. Disappointed by this failure, Nicholas Pike, director of the Brooklyn Institute, traveled to Liverpool,

House sparrow

England, where he collected 100 house sparrows, which he then shipped back to New York. Half of them were released when they arrived, and the other half were held in Greenwood Cemetery in Brooklyn. There they built nests and their young fledged. New Yorkers were pleased to hear that the adult birds were feeding their young with insects.

Because of the excitement stimulated by this effort, the initial shipment from Liverpool was followed by another 22 shipments from Europe, primarily from England and Germany. Portland, Maine, received a shipment in 1854, and a town in Rhode Island brought in some house sparrows in 1858. Between 1860 and 1866, three more shipments arrived in New York, where the sparrows were released. A shipment arrived in Quebec City in 1866. The following year New Haven, Connecticut, ordered some, and 20 birds were released on Boston Common the year after that. In 1869, Philadelphia went all out, releasing a thousand house sparrows. By that time, New Yorkers had released sparrows in Greenwood Cemetery, Central Park, and Union and Madison squares. The imported pairs had so many descendants that other cities started ordering house sparrows from New York. The people of Cincinnati ordered 66 pairs to control their insect problems and to fill the void left by the birds that had fled their downtown region. San Francisco, too, placed an order. In time, the sparrow populations in Philadelphia and Boston grew to such proportions that these cities also began supplying birds to other regions.

House sparrows do particularly well in cities, but don't compete well with native species in the more rural areas, except around farms. Few native bird species had adapted to city life before the house sparrows were brought over. The situation was like a recently plowed field. The seeds planted first have a major impact on all the plants that follow. If a few American bird species had been nursed along and been given the opportunity to adapt and take hold in our cities before we brought European species over, the house sparrow introductions might have failed. As it is the sparrows are firmly entrenched in all our cities and are making determined inroads into the suburbs.

House sparrows are members of the family Passeridae, which used to be known as Ploceidae. The Old World sparrows, or weaver finches, are a large family represented by only two species in North America. The house sparrow is little more than 5 inches (12.7 cm) long. Females and young have a rather uniform tannish brown color with a darker eyestripe. Mature males have a black bill and a black throat, sometimes referred to as a black bib, and their cheeks are white. The other member of this family in North America is the Eurasian tree sparrow (*Passer montanus*), similar to the house sparrow, except that it is slightly smaller. Both sexes look alike, having a chestnut crown, small black bib, and a black spot on the white cheek. Introduced to St. Louis, Missouri, in 1870, they have remained confined to the St. Louis area.

These species are similar in that they are urban birds. They eat insects, seeds, and the bread and other grain products that are readily available on the streets and sidewalks of most cities. Although house sparrows consume many of the same foods that people feed to pigeons, they differ by eating insects, and their nesting habits are different. The house sparrows nest in small holes found around the city, in pipes, buildings, or trees.

HOUSE FINCH

The house finch (*Carpodacus mexicanus*), a native of the western United States, was introduced in the East and has been doing well. Released in New York City in 1940, the house finch has expanded its range to beyond the Mississippi. They are about 5½ inches (14 cm) long, and are commonly misidentified as either the purple finch (*Carpodacus purpureus*) or as a Cassin's finch (*Carpodacus cassinii*). They can be distinguished from both of these look-alikes by the more restricted areas of red on the male. The male Cassin's finch has a brilliant red crown contrasting with the browner back of the neck. Unlike the Cassin's or purple finch, the sides and belly of the male house finch are striped. The female house finch has a drab, brown body, similar to that of the Cassin's and purple finches. The head of the female house finch is distinguished by her lack of a dark eye-line, dark cheek patch, or dark mustache. And for those who have the opportunity to take the time to compare the different species, their distinctive calls make which is which readily apparent. That of the house finch is less varied than both the Cassin's and purple finch's, and it has some harsher notes, slightly reminiscent of a house sparrow's call.

Of the three *Carpodacus* species described above, the house finch is by far the most common in urban areas, and it is also successful in suburbs and farmland. The Cassin's finch is more restricted to western conifers, and the purple finch is common in woodlands and suburbs, in both the East and the West

In the West, house finches have done well on their own in cities and towns. If the European species, such as the house sparrow and starling, had not been introduced, house finches probably would be much more common in most American cities. Before there were any cities in the West, house finches nested in cactus thickets, or in cottonwoods along stream beds. Now they are one of the most conspicuous birds in many western cities.

EUROPEAN STARLING

Starling is a popular bird name, used for many different bird species all over the world. The one starling that is now found in North America is the European starling (*Sturnus vulgaris*), which is a dark bird, ranging from about 7½ to 8½ inches (19 to 22 cm) long. Adults are dark and iridescent, while the young are brown with the coloring of a cowbird (*Molothrus ater*). The winter plumage is dark with characteristic white speckles at the tips of the feathers that wear off by the spring. Also diagnostic is their yellow bill during spring and summer, which is black during fall and winter. Unlike other generic blackbirds, such as the red-winged blackbird (*Agelaius phoeniceus*), common grackle (*Quiscalus quiscula*), and cowbird, the starling's tail is quite short. In flight the wings look brown and are pointed.

The starling's song is long, varied, and often squeaky, although whistles, chuckles, clicks, and rattles are typical. It is common for starlings to imitate the calls of other birds. There is even a chance that some can be taught to talk. From late summer until early spring, starlings

European starling

congregate at night in large communal roosts. Should you be so unfortunate as to park under one of these roosts, the next morning you may find your car needing a wash.

It is Eugene Schieffelin, a wealthy New York drug manufacturer, who has the dubious honor of being responsible for introducing the European starling to North America. He lived during the 19th century when it was fashionable among the well-to-do to plant gardens containing all the species of plants mentioned in Shakespeare's works. Mr. Schieffelin, inspired by his love of Shakespeare and his fondness for birds, decided to take things one step further; his contribution would be to introduce all the birds mentioned in Shakespeare's works into the United States. In retrospect, it's unfortunate that Shakespeare wrote of the starling.

Shakespeare only mentioned the starling in one of his prodigious lifetime's works (*Henry IV, Part 1:* I.3.224). And Mr. Schieffelin caught it. After already having unsuccessfully attempted to introduce chaffinches (*Fringilla coelebs*), song thrushes (*Turdus philomelos*), nightingales (*Luscinia megarhynchos*), and skylarks (*Alauda arvensis*) to New York City, in 1880 Schieffelin imported 80 European starlings, which he released in Central Park. Many survived, built nests, mated, and reared young. The following year he brought over another 40, and the rest is history. The original individuals are the ancestors of the millions of starlings that now inhabit North America, ranging all the way from Mexico to Canada and Bermuda.

During the first several years, the starlings remained in Central Park, but gradually they began to expand their range to other parts of the city. By 1904 they were already reported in Connecticut, New Jersey, and upstate New York. They were in Massachusetts by 1912; Vermont and Rhode Island reported them in 1913; Washington, D.C., in 1916; Maryland and New Hampshire in 1917; Virginia in 1920; and Delaware and Ohio in 1922. By 1930 they had reached southern Ontario, the Midwest, and the Gulf states, and by 1950 starlings were well established in all 48 states and all of the Canadian provinces.

Most introductions aren't as successful as this one. It seems that starlings were behaviorally and physiologically well adapted, or if you prefer, preadapted, to take advantage of the opportunities in this country, despite the fact that the first several attempts by other individuals to introduce the starling had been unsuccessful. It also appears that Schieffelin's starling introductions were well executed. Rarely are 80 individuals of a species introduced at one time and followed closely by another 40. In just sheer numbers, the starlings were off to a good start. Then, too, Schieffelin released them in a huge city park where there were few competitors and predators. The starlings spent a couple of years settling in, becoming acclimated to the local conditions, and raising several clutches of American-born and -bred individuals. This gave them a secure foothold before they began expanding their range.

From the city the starlings moved to the suburbs, and then to the agricultural and rural regions of the country. Being hole-nesting birds, they readily took advantage of cavities in trees, cliffs, and walls, as well as in boxes set out for other birds. They aggressively pushed other hole-nesters from their nests, in some cases having a severely detrimental effect on native populations. It's thought that through competition for nesting sites, starlings have been responsible for the marked decrease in numbers of eastern bluebirds (*Sialia sialis*).

When starlings first became established in North America, few anticipated the negative effect they could have on native bird populations. What wasn't foreseen was that starlings and other introduced cavity nesters would move into many of the suitable nesting sites that other native species had used previously.

It's interesting that some of the introduced birds that have come to dominate urban birdlife are cavity nesters. The reason for this may be that there are a lot of suitable cavities in cities: holes in trees, abandoned buildings, rotted eaves, holes leading to cavities in attics, and all the protected areas in the many man-made structures everywhere you look. These urban opportunities are often occupied by cavity-nesting species.

Cities can provide a sanctuary for some of these species to nest, raise their young, and then spread out to the suburbs and agricultural areas during other times of the year. Starlings have become the ultimate reverse commuters. Nesting is probably the most vulnerable time for any bird species, when the eggs and the young are easily preyed upon. Nesting in cities, where there are few predators to contend with, allows an unnaturally high fledging survival rate. Cities have provided a tremendous nursery for birds, such as the starling, that have been able to capitalize on the urban opportunities.

The starling's success in agricultural regions is known only too well to the farmers who each fall and winter encounter flocks comprising hundreds or even thousands of blackbirds, which include starlings, grackles (*Quiscalus quiscula*), red-winged blackbirds (*Agelaius phoeniceus*), and cowbirds (*Molothrus ater*). These flocks swarm in huge hordes and descend on crops, often with devastating effects. Elaborate methods have been devised to kill the plagues of blackbirds, but the attempts are futile in that they represent only short-term solutions.

Millions of overwintering blackbirds descend on Tupelo, Mississippi, each winter, arriving from the north around mid-November and leaving around the beginning of March. During the 1986 to 1987 winter, about three million blackbirds created quite a problem for the Tupelo Municipal Airport.

GRACKLES

The common grackle is a dark, medium-sized bird with an iridescent head and a long, keel-shaped tail that broadens toward the end. The young have brown eyes until the fall when the iris becomes yellow. Common grackles (*Quiscalus quiscula*) are often seen flocking with other blackbirds such as red-winged blackbirds and starlings. In cities grackles are seen scavenging along the shores of ponds and lakes, looking for insects or carrion. Since they are adept at finding seeds and insects on mowed lawns, they do well in suburban areas, too, as well as in farm regions throughout the East and Midwest. Grackles winter in the southern portion of their range from the mid-Atlantic states westward. They are most obvious during the spring and fall migrations when their flocks are distinguished from other generic blackbirds by the racket they make.

Boat-tailed grackles (*Quiscalus major*) are considerably larger and even noisier than common grackles. They are found from central Texas east to the Gulf states and along the Atlantic as far north as New Jersey. In recent years they have been breeding as far north as Staten Island, in New York City. Boat-tailed grackles are primarily restricted to coastal marshes and nearby habitat. They are very tolerant of densely populated surroundings.

In addition to the boat-tailed grackles, many other species of birds have been expanding their ranges northward. No one is absolutely certain what accounts for this trend, but it could have something to do with the sprawl of cities and suburbs. This sprawl means new food sources for birds: rich effluents being dumped into the marshes, periodic fish kills from algal blooms and red tides, and pollutants that hurt some species but create better feeding opportunities for others. Also, there are often fewer predators in urban areas, and the warmer temperatures radiated from cities may have some effect.

BLACKBIRDS

Male red-winged blackbirds (*Agelaius phoeniceus*) are distinguished by their red shoulders. This marking is so distinctive that these birds could be confused with only one other species, the tricolored blackbird (*Agelaius tricolor*). The tricolor also has red shoulder patches, but the red is darker and more brilliant. Also, in the red-winged blackbird, the red patches are bordered below with yellow, but in the tricolored blackbird they are bordered with white.

Red-winged blackbird

Red-winged blackbirds move north in early spring. The males leave before the females, being the first to return to the areas where they fledged and to which they may have returned in previous years. Once the flocks arrive in the general region, the male birds disperse and stake out territories. Then they lure in the females, which soon follow. It appears the males that get mates are the ones that claim the best territories, which are usually located in the marshes with the most abundant food sources nearby. The inferior nesting sites are upland, where less food and more predator pressure infringe on nesting success. Often these are the territories that are defended by the first-year males or by older males that have passed their prime.

Since good wetlands are in short supply, freshwater and coastal wetlands, even those in busy cities, tend to have redwing populations everywhere. In the West, the yellow-headed blackbirds (*Xanthocephalus xanthocephalus*) are found in cattail (*Typha* spp.) or bulrush (*Scirpus* spp.) marshes, nesting right alongside redwings, even in cities such as Denver. The tricolored blackbird is more of a West Coast species. The Brewer's blackbird (*Euphagus cyanocephalus*) is another species that tolerates urban areas. In the West, Brewer's blackbirds have become another urban success story. Though commonly associated with farmlands, fields, lawns, and roadsides, they seem to be as much at home as the house sparrow in downtown areas of major cities. In the middle of San Francisco, Brewer's blackbirds are so common that if you didn't know better, you might think they were an out-of-control introduced exotic. It's good to see a native species thriving in our cities.

In the United Kingdom, the blackbird (*Turdus merula*), which is actually a relative of the American robin (*Turdus migratorius*), breeds in urban areas and has been found to fledge its young a full three weeks earlier in cities than in rural areas. This difference is attributed to the increased heat generated by the urban environment. The warmer conditions probably increase the effective time the young have to feed and grow before leaving their homes in the fall. The added weeks of growth may give many urban-reared birds an advantage over their rural counterparts. Our robin, too, is a very successful inhabitant of suburbs and cities, where it is commonly seen searching for insects and earthworms on lawns, in backyards, and in parks.

COMMON CROW AND FISH CROW

We have the crow to thank for a fascinating genre of American folk art—the scarecrow. These effigies sometimes worked in the days when farmers were more inclined to shoot crows, but the scarecrows were never very effective. Crows quickly learned to differentiate between real people and stuffed facsimiles. Now scarecrows have become part of the rustic landscape, rather like snowmen, jack-o'-lanterns, and Indian corn.

The fish crow (*Corvus ossifragus*) is found in the East along the Atlantic Coast from Rhode Island, Connecticut, and New York south to Key West, and west to southeastern Texas. Like the common crow (*Corvus brachyrhynchos*), it is a large, all-black bird. The fish crow is slightly smaller, however, and has a slimmer bill. Its call is shorter and more nasal than the distinctive caw of the adult common crow. The voice of the adult fish crow is similar to that of the young common crow. Fish crows primarily feed on the ground, but are also seen in trees from time to time. They are most commonly found feeding along the shoreline, where they take crustaceans, like small crabs and shrimp, as well as fish, insects, and other small invertebrates. They will also take some berries, fruits, and grain.

The bluejay (*Cyanocitta cristata*) is another member of the crow family, the corvids, which in addition to the crows, includes the jays, magpies, and ravens. Bluejays are also common throughout urban and

Common crow

especially suburban environments in the East and Midwest. Crows and their allies have been prominent urban dwellers for years, particularly in Europe, Asia, and parts of Africa. Finding large numbers of crows in North American cities, however, is a new phenomenon.

The common crow ranges across the country from southern Canada to southern California and along the East Coast all the way to the southern tip of Florida. Like the gulls, the common crow is a large urban scavenger. The behavior and diet of these species overlap to some extent; both are generally very successful opportunists. Crows aren't nearly as numerous as gulls, but they manage to maintain stable populations in most major cities. They nest early, in tall trees. Although crows are raucous and draw considerable attention much of the time, they become extremely secretive when they are near their nests, drawing little attention to themselves and their young. In the fall, after the young have fledged, it is commonplace to see large groups of crows wheeling overhead above the city. Many of these groups stay together during the winter, but the flocks break up the following spring, and the individuals go off to find places to breed.

Whenever there is a roadkill in the suburbs, we find common crows out bright and early, cleaning up the carcass. No doubt the increase in automobile traffic has had a positive effect on the crow's diet. Agriculture has also proved a big plus. Crows will work over a newly turned field, consuming any invertebrates that become available.

Derek Goodwin wrote in *Crows of the World* that crows surpass most birds in versatility and initiative when seeking food, though house sparrows and common grackles may equal them. Crows are omnivorous and are constantly on the lookout for an easy meal, but, if necessary, they will work long and hard to find their food. More and more crows are now seen near homes, walking around on the lawn, gleaning whatever looks interesting. These days, fewer people are eager to shoot anything that moves, and the result is the boldness seen in some birds, such as many suburban crows.

However, to some extent, the tendency not to shoot may be changing in a few parts of the country. The Danville, Illinois, police force was just empowered to shoot the crows that recently moved into their city. The reason cited for killing the crows was that Health Commissioner Jerry Brown felt the crows were a health hazard. Clearly, the health hazard explanation is a pretense. Crows do not constitute a health hazard, and considerable quantities of their droppings aren't dangerous either. New York City has as many as seven million pigeons, probably thousands of times the number of crows in Danville, and it's rare for anyone to contract a disease from them.

It has been suggested that the crows stayed in Danville during the winter of 1986–87 because the weather was relatively mild. Normally they might have moved farther south. But these crows probably represent a trend that is occurring in the region. During the past several years, Centralia, Illinois, has had crows roosting in the town despite repeated efforts to eradicate the birds. There are many other species that have begun to stay north during the winter because of the opportunities that humans provide. Mockingbirds and cardinals are two examples.

If these crows are just roosting in certain areas each night, and that appears to be the case, and if the real problem faced by the community is the hazard encountered by those walking or parking under the trees that the birds are roosting in, then there's every reason to believe that the local human residents will learn to avoid the danger zones.

Should humans continually interfere with the native species that attempt to move in and become established in urban environments, cities may never achieve their natural potential. Until cities harbor a diverse number of species with stable populations that interact somewhat predictably, we are going to have to learn to tolerate and appreciate the many inevitable surprises. Otherwise, our cities will remain considerably more humdrum than is necessary or desirable.

Crows are among the most intelligent species of birds in the world. Some estimates rank them with cats and monkeys for conscious, problem-solving capabilities. They should be tolerated because they represent an incremental step among hundreds, even thousands, of species that, given the proper set of circumstances, will eventually colonize our cities.

PIGEON

It may not be a coincidence that all of the major domesticated birds are seed-eaters. Domestication probably did not always occur as a result of conscious human effort. Rather, it is likely that the animals attracted to populated areas were among the first to be domesticated. This might lead one to believe that pigeons (*Columba livia*) were initially attracted to towns when agriculture was developed, or, more specifically, when certain plants—like the grasses with large seeds such as barley, oats, rice, and wheat—were cultivated. However, there is some evidence that pigeon domestication began as early as the Neolithic era. If this is so, then the weeds that grew around human dwelling could have been sufficient to attract certain species. This is the reason mourning doves (*Zenaidura macroura*) are attracted to the suburbs, though they've never been

Pigeon

domesticated. It is thought that once pigeons moved into and around towns, they began nesting in the area. Unlike mourning doves, which build stick nests in trees, pigeons, which are also known as rock doves, naturally nest on rock ledges, along cliffs, under overhangs, and just inside small rock caves. In towns, window ledges, barns, and vacant buildings provided a host of new nesting opportunities.

Once the pigeons were well established in urban areas, people responded to their cooing and constant courting, thinking that these birds were great lovers. They were elevated as symbols of love and fertility in western Asia. From 4500 B.C. on, we find many references to pigeons in the literature of most Old World cultures. Although some city dwellers are not fond of pigeons now, the birds were tolerated thousands of years ago, perhaps because they were associated with love or because they are very good to eat. The Romans had towers where pigeons lived. Their wings were clipped and the legs were broken so the birds could be fed and fattened up. In England some pigeon houses have survived that were constructed during Norman times. Pigeon houses and towers were also constructed in the East for centuries. The Chinese have been raising pigeons for food for more than 2,000 years. In Hong Kong alone, 800,000 pigeons are still consumed annually.

Although pigeons don't migrate, it was discovered early that they could home. Carrier pigeons were used to transmit messages during the time of Antony and Cleopatra. Nero also used carrier pigeons, as did the Crusaders. Enthusiasts race carrier pigeons in many places in the United States. While they are usually raced over relatively short distances, some have raced over hundreds of miles; records document that the best homing pigeons can return over distances in excess of 1,000 miles (1,600 km).

During the past twenty years scientists at many prominent universities have been attempting to understand how birds home and migrate. Researchers have found that they use their sight, smell, the wind direction, the sound of air currents that are inaudible to humans, memory, the earth's rotation in relation to the movement of the sun, the earth's magnetic field, and even the stars. Like most birds that migrate, pigeons do not rely on one specific type of information. Rather, as in many other complex behaviors, they integrate cues from different sources to determine where they are going.

The American colonists who brought their domesticated animals, such as chickens, ducks, pigs, cows, and horses, to this country also brought pigeons. The pigeons were quite independent, foraging on their own. Many of the pigeons nested in barns, providing their young, or squabs, that were gathered and cooked. From these original pigeons descended all the others now found in this country.

Pigeons are not nearly as common in the country or in small towns as they are around cities. It has been estimated that there are seven million of them in New York City, almost as many pigeons as people. While this figure may be high, these birds are amazingly successful in cities, due, in part, to their opportunism. They will, of course, eat bread, as well as just about any kind of grain, and they love nuts. They don't chew things, so they don't get the sensations that we get from eating, but they may get sensations from partially broken-down foods in their crop, or they may taste just the outside of an item and know whether it is good to eat. Since peanuts have considerably more fat and protein than most grains, it might seem that pigeons aren't as dumb as people think. Of course, appropriate food preferences shouldn't be thought of as intelligence; all the same, if you ever want to think you are making a lot of friends instantly, feed the local pigeons a bag of peanuts, shelled of course.

Besides nuts and seeds, in the wild pigeons will eat berries, worms, and insects. This probably accounts for their willingness to eat discarded urban staples such as hot dogs, shish kebab, and Chinese food. I once saw pigeons eat the contents of a smashed bag of frozen broccoli. Cars had run over it, so the broccoli was totally pulverized; the pigeons were only too happy to take advantage of such an opportunity. You don't often see birds eating leafy vegetables, but in New York's Chinatown, it is common to see canaries in bird cages stocked with birdseed and bok choy. The birds peck at the leaves of this Chinese vegetable, which is thought to serve as a nutritional dietary supplement. Leafy material may be more common in bird diets than is usually acknowledged.

Although pigeons eat a wide range of material found on the streets and sidewalks, many people provide them with birdseed or bread handouts. What percentage of their diet consists of handouts has never been determined. Pigeons and house sparrows were far less reliant on handouts when horses were still the primary mode of transportation. During those years there was always a ready supply of oats and other grains around the city.

A law was recently passed in Connecticut making it illegal to throw uncooked rice at weddings. It was feared that some of the birds cleaning up the churchyard were getting sick and dying. Small birds eating Minute Rice® can be damaged because this specially prepared grain is designed for rapid water absorption. But larger birds are not adversely affected, and ordinary rice never appears to be a problem.

Water may be a limiting factor for pigeons in the winter when food is available, but the water is frozen. I doubt that pigeons can go long without any water, so there must be some way for them to get around this problem. It's never been reported that thousands of dead pigeons turned up anywhere after a long cold spell so there may be considerably more available water than is apparent. During recent frigid temperatures, I watched several pigeons and house sparrows pecking at the snow where there didn't seem to be anything to peck at; it looked as if they were eating the snow. Perhaps the available liquid water was contaminated with the salt used to melt the snow and ice, so eating the clean, uncontaminated snow was a functional alternative. Many animals in the North eat snow when all available freshwater is frozen. It's remotely possible that pigeons simply don't need much water. After all, some species of doves do incredibly well in arid regions. Since pigeons are doves—at least, pigeons and doves are all in the order Columbiformes and in the family Columbidae—it stands to reason that pigeons may be able to tolerate arid conditions. Considering the extremes of water conditions in most urban environments, cities are characteristically more arid than the surrounding regions.

While some doves migrate, pigeons don't. Since pigeons are not found in the more northern parts of Canada, the temperatures there may be too cold for even pigeons to tolerate.

A recent occurrence in Boston forced people to reassess the safety of their urban birds. During the summer of 1986, a red-tailed hawk (*Buteo jamaicensis*) caught a pigeon on Boston Common. Could it be only a matter of time before other opportunistic raptors catch on to the vast reservoir of untapped pigeon meat available in our metropolitan areas? Although hawks are not generally keen on city life, there's no reason they couldn't eventually change. Once they catch on to the fact that they can hunt with impunity in our cities, they'll probably start doing it. Such a behavioral shift would certainly happen very slowly though. Since hawks aren't very social, it would take a long time for a new behavior pattern to be passed through an entire population. Still, an opportunity as good as the one presented by urban birds that have virtually no predators seems too good to be passed up forever. It's only a matter of time before some predator moves in for the kill. Peregrine falcons (*Falco peregrinus*) are another potential predator; they are discussed in detail later in this chapter.

When I noticed that pigeons aren't as abundant in Boston as they are in other major cities, I started asking for opinions on the subject. I was told, straight-facedly, that it's common practice for the proprietors of Boston's Chinese restaurants to trap pigeons on their roofs and fire escapes, then to serve the pigeons in chicken dishes. I can't swear that this never happens, of course, but the story sounds like a fine example of another urban legend. This time, instead of alligators in the New York sewers, Boston's Chinese restaurants are getting nailed.

In some parts of the country, people have taken action against the burgeoning pigeon populations. Recently, residents of the Manhattan neighborhood known as Clinton, or Hell's Kitchen, which is just west of midtown, have seen several plastic owls placed on the tops of buildings. It appears that pigeons have an innate fear of owls, although it's not known whether owls prey on urban pigeons. The owl pellets that I've pulled apart in cities contained only mouse, rat, and rabbit bones and fur. It would be interesting to find pigeon bones in some of these pellets. Gardeners have used plastic owls to scare off birds for years, as have boaters who want to keep gulls away. As many as 30 plastic owls have been placed on the arch at the American Telephone and Telegraph Building at Madison Avenue and East 56th Street. They are also used on the rafters of the Long Island Railroad stations and on the roof of the New Jersey State House in Trenton. These artificial owls have some effect, but if they aren't moved around, the pigeons start to ignore them.

Most zoos have pigeon problems because all the grain put out for the animals attracts them, along with mice, rats, and sparrows. To keep these animals in check, zoo administrators sometimes use poison in conjunction with trapping. At the Bronx Zoo, many of the pigeons that are trapped are later gassed, plucked, and fed to the alligators and crocodiles. Feeding time in the Reptile House is one of the zoo's popular attractions. The reason the pigeons are plucked before being fed to the alligators is to keep the feathers from clogging the drains.

Even the American Museum of Natural History in New York has pigeon problems that have to be dealt with discreetly. Pigeons roosting on the eaves, overhangs, and window ledges tend to make quite a mess. Museum administrators say that the feathers, nesting materials, and droppings interfere with the air conditioning units, so they have hired pigeon removers. They don't like to call them exterminators, because the pigeons are trapped and supposedly released somewhere else. I find it odd that an institution that employs such fine scientists actually believes that releasing pigeons in the outer boroughs will be the end of their problem. Given the homing abilities of many pigeons, it seems likely that they'll just keep flying right back. So either they are flying back, or maybe they really don't return once released, or perhaps they aren't released at all.

DOVES AND PARROTS

The ringed turtledove (*Streptopelia risoria*), once known in this country as a cage bird, is now breeding in downtown Los Angeles and in other urban areas, including Baltimore and Miami. It is recognized by its sandy plumage and the black crescent on the back of its neck. The spotted dove (*Streptopelia chinensis*) has been introduced and is now locally common in Los Angeles County, occurring from Santa Barbara to San Diego. This dove is heavier bodied than the mourning dove (*Zenaidura macroura*), which is our most common native dove, found in suburbs, farmlands, and cities in the United States. The spotted dove is the only dove in North

America with the black and white "lace-neck" pattern, and the pattern occurs only in the adults. Spotted doves are primarily found in city parks, suburbs, and agricultural areas.

In addition to these doves, other cage birds have escaped and made some progress toward becoming established in local breeding populations. Most of them are parrots and parakeets, which have been among the most popular cage birds in this country for years. The budgerigar, or parakeet (*Melopsittacus undulatus*) is common in the St. Petersburg, Florida, area and is locally common in other parts of southern Florida and southern California. These parakeets are native to Australia. The green parakeet (*Aratinga holochlora*), a native of Mexico, can be distinguished by its gold underwings. It is rare in southern Texas and Florida. The Hispaniolan parakeet (*Aratinga chloroptera*) has been reported in the Miami area. It is native to the West Indies, and it looks similar to the green parakeet, except that it has red underwing coverts (stripes). The orange-fronted parakeet (*Aratinga canicularis*), also a native of Mexico, occurs locally in areas from southeastern Florida to New York.

From South America, the black-hooded conure (*Nandayus nenday*), recognized by its black head and red pant legs, has been recorded in the Northeast and in Loma Linda, California. The monk parakeet (*Myiopsitta monachus*), from temperate regions of South America, came close to becoming well established in the eastern United States. Monk parakeets were building large colonial stick nests on telephone lines, but when the nests were removed, most of the birds seemed to die off. There are still occasional reports of breeding pairs in the Northeast.

The canary-winged parakeet (*Brotogeris versicolurus*), from South America, is now well established in southeastern Florida and San Pedro, California, and occurs locally in the Northeast. The wings are characteristically white, yellow, green, and blue. The orange-chinned parakeet (*Brotogeris jugularis*) is also locally common in southeastern Florida. Native to Central and South America, this species is recognized by its orange chin, small wedge-shaped tail, and brown shoulders.

Two species in the genus *Amazona*, both native to Mexico, are found locally in a few areas. The yellow-headed parrot (*Amazona ochrocephala*) is found in the South, particularly in Florida and California. It is recognized by its yellow head, red patches on its shoulders, a large red wing patch, and a little bit of red at the base of its tail. The red-crowned parrot (*Amazona viridigenalis*) has a red cap and a red wing patch. It is now established in southeastern Florida, and has been seen occasionally in the Los Angeles area and in parts of Texas.

Two species in the genus *Psittacula* are now breeding locally in a few parts of the country. The rose-ringed parakeet (*Psittacula krameri*) has a green head, red bill, and light green tail. Populations have been reported in parts of the Northeast and in some areas in southern California and

Florida, notably Miami. The blossom-headed parakeet (*Psittacula roseata*) is recognized by its rose head, orange bill, and in the males, a black neck band. The juveniles are all green except for a yellow bill. This species has also been reported in some areas in the Northeast. Both psittaculas were originally from Asia.

RING-NECKED PHEASANT

The ring-necked pheasant (*Phasianus colchicus*) is a spectacularly colored bird. The male's flamboyant plumage sharply contrasts with the dull, drab, camouflaged female's. The cock's dark green head has touches of iridescent greens and purple, with bright red patches around the eyes. The dark colors of the head are separated from the reddish and yellowish browns of the chest by the characteristic white ring around the neck. This bird is a member of the order Galliformes, as are quails, grouse, turkeys, and chickens. The true pheasants, those in the genus *Phasianus*, are native to portions of the Middle East, central Asia, China, and Japan. At least three species and twenty-nine subspecies occur in their native range.

Ring-necked pheasant

Pheasants were well established in England during colonial days. The first attempt to introduce them into North America was made by Thomas Jefferson's nephew around 1790 in New Jersey, with a second attempt in 1800. Pheasants imported from China in 1881 were stocked in Willamette Valley, Oregon. After that, more stock was brought in from England. Prized as game birds, these pheasants were propagated on farms and introduced all over the United States. They are now locally abundant in open grasslands from coast to coast, and are doing suprisingly well in some urban areas. Pheasants are often seen in the larger parks in New York City, such as Pelham Bay in the Bronx, Kissena Park in Queens, and Marine Park in Brooklyn. These parks have extensive stands of the common reed (*Phragmites australis*) that thrives on the sanitation fill that characterizes much of the city's parkland. Although for many years it was thought that the *Phragmites* was worthless groundcover, we continually find more species that have adapted to it. Among these species is the ring-necked pheasant. While pheasants don't only live in the reeds and no-where else, *Phragmites* does provide a significant portion of their habitat requirements in many locations.

It has been observed that pheasants have substantial calcium requirements. The pheasant diet includes weeds, seeds, and insects, which probably reflect the lime concentration in the soil. Because those pheasants reared on calcareous soils grow more rapidly and appear to do better than those on limeless soils, it has been suggested that the calcium may be important for the growth of these birds' bones. They are large, heavy-bodied animals with considerably more substantial bones than most of the smaller and lighter species. This may be one of the reasons that they fare well in the larger, wilder city parks. These parks, more often than not, are built on sanitation landfill, which is composed of vast quantities of demolished buildings, roads, and bridges. The cement contains calcium carbonate that slowly leaches into the soil. The plants and animals growing on these soils may, in turn, be high in calcium.

It's not uncommon to find pheasants out on park lawns, under trees, along the forest edge, or roaming around in woods. They appear to be tolerant of a much wider range of habitats than was previously thought. Not many ground nesters have been able to breed and thrive in city parks. One would think the pheasants wouldn't have a prayer, given the feral cats, the dogs allowed to run without a leash, the raccoons, and all the rats that will attack the young birds given the chance. But these birds appear to be secretive, wily, and fast enough to survive.

Another gallinaceous bird introduced to this country is the gray partridge (*Perdix perdix*), which is found in agricultural areas in the northern United States and southern Canada. The chukar (*Alectoris chukar*), a large European partridge, is now well established in the Northwest, and the black francolin (*Francolinus francolinus*) has become established in Calcasieu Parish, Louisiana.

GULLS

In terms of sheer numbers, there may be at least five to seven times as many pigeons as herring gulls within the New York City limits. Herring gulls weigh about 2½ pounds (1.2 kg), however, so their total weight could be greater than that of all the pigeons; it's almost certainly greater than that of all the city's starlings as well.

The herring gull (*Larus argentatus*) and the ring-billed gull (*Larus delawarensis*) are two of the most common and widely found gulls in the United States. The herring gull has a length of 20 inches (51 cm) and a wingspan of 55 inches (140 cm). It is larger than both the California gull (*Larus californicus*), which is found only in the West, and the ring-billed gull, which ranges across the country. Unlike the herring gull, the adult ring-billed gull has a complete black ring on its yellow bill; the herring

Herring gull

gull has a red spot on its yellow mandible. The California gull has a black and red spot on its yellow mandible. The adult herring gull is a large, gray-mantled gull with black wing tips, spotted with white at the very ends. Its legs are flesh-colored. The immatures are uniformly dark and dusky. After the first winter, the tail and underparts become whiter; the gray mantle grows in as the birds mature more fully the following year or two.

Herring gulls are normally found near harbors and wharves along the coastlines. They are also common on lakes and rivers, where they are commonly seen with ring-billed gulls. Many more gulls move to these inland areas during the winter. Recently, herring gulls have begun to breed along the East Coast as far south as Virginia and North Carolina.

Primarily a scavenger, the herring gull will pick up mollusks and break them open by dropping them on rocks or pavement. Large numbers of gulls feed at garbage dumps. (If sanitation landfill sites are ever phased out, the effect on gull populations could be dramatic.) Herring gulls will also come near people to take scraps, including those thrown from docks and boats. Herring gulls are often seen soaring like hawks above most northeastern cities. They may be riding the rising hot air coming off the streets and buildings before moving farther along the coastline toward a garbage dump, or back to their nesting grounds. Nests are usually on offshore islands protected from much disturbance. The gulls rarely venture close to the ground in midtown areas. Perhaps the winds down among the buildings are too unpredictable for these birds. Their wings are suited to a slower, more leisurely flight pattern, and if the birds are caught in rapidly shifting, high-velocity winds, the wings might get twisted and snap. Gulls will congregate inland and land in open fields in city parks when a storm is brewing, however.

During the summer of 1986, a group of New York City officials went to North Brother Island to investigate the real-estate prospects there. Until twenty years ago, the island, which lies in the East River between Manhattan and Queens, was inhabited, but in the 1960s all the buildings were abandoned. Over the years, birds moved to this island and are now using it as a nesting colony. Herring gulls (*Larus argentatus*), which normally nest on the ground, were found nesting on the flat roofs of the island's derelict buildings. This could be the beginning of something new. We've seen that killdeers and nighthawks nest on roofs, but no one has ever documented when or where this addition to their behavioral repertoire began. If this nesting colony on North Brother Island is left alone, we may find that some of the birds reared there will nest on roofs elsewhere. If so, this addition to the gulls' North American nesting behavior will be well worth documenting. Landlords are unlikely to appreciate the gull rookeries on the roofs of their structures, but the abandoned buildings found in most urban areas could provide a valuable habitat for the gulls.

For years some herring gulls have been nesting on roofs in England, where permitted.

The gull most often seen around city ponds is the ring-billed. As mentioned earlier, it is slightly smaller than the herring gulls; the adult has yellow-green legs and a black ring around its yellow bill. Along the southeast coast is the laughing gull (*Larus atricilla*), which breeds as far north as the islands in Jamaica Bay, New York City. Like many other gulls, it takes to fields from time to time, where it will feed on earthworms after a plow has turned the soil over. During the summer laughing gull adults have a dark head and solid, dark wing tips. In the winter the adult's head is mottled and the bill is darker.

During the winter, the rare gulls from the North sometimes join the herring and ring-billed gulls at the garbage dumps, where the gulls appear to gather much of their food. Among these flocks it isn't rare to see a glaucous gull (*Larus hyperboreus*) or an Iceland gull (*Larus glaucoides*). These are the only gulls with pure white wings. The glaucous gull is slightly larger than the herring gull, while the Iceland gull is the same size as a herring gull, or slightly smaller.

The great black-backed gull (*Larus marinus*) is another common species generally found along the East Coast. This gull has been increasing its numbers, range, and types of preferred habitats, and is now sometimes found near inland lakes.

The California gull and the western gull (*Larus occidentalis*) are common along the West Coast and are regularly seen in all the major urban and suburban areas along the Pacific Ocean.

The increased numbers of gulls around many American cities have caused problems at nearby airports. Flocks of gulls and other birds endanger jetliners, causing from $25 to $40 million in damage to commercial aircraft each year. The most serious accidents occur when the birds get sucked into a jet's turbine engines, choking the turbine and ruining the engine. The problem is so serious that at about 25 airports full-time bird-control units have been hired to harass the birds on the runway and nearby to reduce the number of bird-plane collisions.

KILLDEER PLOVER

Like the pheasant, the killdeer plover (*Charadrius vociferus*) is a ground nester. Few such birds actually nest on the ground in urban areas, however, having moved to flat roofs. The killdeer goes both ways. It is common to find them nesting on the ground along the edge of a meadow, but they will just as readily nest on a flat roof.

Killdeer plover

This is probably the most successful shorebird, order Charadriiformes, in terms of feeding as well as breeding in urban areas. Killdeers live and nest in places that most other shorebirds would shy away from—golf courses, ballfields, the edges of parking lots, disturbed sites overgrown with weeds, landfill areas, you name it. Killdeers are not unusually numerous, but they continue to make their presence known in areas where most other ground nesters wouldn't have a chance.

Another plover, the piping plover (*Charadrius melodus*), used to nest on sandy beaches along the East Coast, but due to the increasing numbers of sunbathers on those shores, fewer and fewer good piping plover nesting sites survive, and the birds have become quite rare.

The least tern (*Sterna antillarum*) nests in habitats similar to those of the piping plover. If the vegetation along the beach is managed with carefully timed burns, so that it doesn't become too overgrown, the tern colonies will persist and grow in numbers, rather than decline and move elsewhere.

The few remaining beach nesting grounds need to be protected and properly managed if the birds that utilize these habitats are going to survive. In urban areas, where the beaches are used intensely, it is very important that people obey the signs stating that a bird-nesting area is off limits.

HERONS

Several species of herons have been doing increasingly well in suitable habitats around and within urban regions. Originally, herons seemed quite skittish and wary, avoiding areas where people went. The herons were thought of as species inhabiting the more wild, remote, pristine habitats. But more and more we are finding that some of these species are feeding in areas where previously only the boldest of the bird species dared venture. Though most of the herons require rather quiet areas to nest—quiet insofar as the birds are concerned, meaning away from people—some species will nest in neglected areas not far from considerable human activity. Even so, herons are not what one would consider daring when it comes to where they nest.

One of the most common species in many urban and suburban areas is the green heron (*Butorides striatus*), which is identified by its small size. In North America, of the ciconiforms, the herons and their allies, only the least bittern (*Ixobrychus exilis*) is smaller. The green heron is about 14 inches (36 cm) long, with a wingspan of 25 inches (64 cm). They are

Black-crowned night heron

distinguished by their dark underparts, bluish or greenish back, and bright orange or yellow legs. These small herons are often seen during the summer, wading in the shallow backwaters of many urban ponds.

Another of the more common urban ciconiforms is the black-crowned night heron (*Nycticorax nycticorax*), which is a large-bodied bird with a short neck; compared to most other herons, it has relatively short legs. Its usual stance appears hunched over, rather than with the neck extended, a look that typifies many other species in the order Ciconiformes. About the same size as the yellow-crowned night heron (*Nycticorax violaceus*) and the American bittern (*Botaurus lentiginosus*), having a length of 20 inches (51 cm) and a wingspan of 44 inches (112 cm), the black-crowned night heron is commonly seen standing at the water's edge, in shallow water, or perched on a snag, or up in a tree.

The adult has a black back and white underparts, while the immature birds are streaked with varying shades of brown, much like the American bittern. Black-crowned night herons are difficult to distinguish from juvenile yellow-crowned night herons. Herons are more skittish than gulls and less inclined to tolerate human disturbance. This has been changing in recent years, however.

The black-crowned night heron has taken to feeding along the edges of ponds in some of the busiest city parks in major American cities. In the larger parks, such as Central Park in New York and Fairmount Park in Philadelphia, relatively large numbers of black-crowned night herons can be seen almost any day of the week. Initially more of a night feeder, in urban parks the black-crowned night heron is now commonly seen feeding almost any time of the day. At night both this species and the yellow-crowned night heron, which is much less common, will sometimes take advantage of strategically situated lights that illuminate worthwhile hunting areas.

Rich urban pond water containing nutrients from fertilizers, erosion, and bird excrement support large algal blooms and dense populations of microorganisms, which are fed upon by small fish and tadpoles. These become larger fish and frogs, providing a bountiful supply of food for black-crowned night herons. When stalking prey, these birds often draw a crowd; this forces the birds to keep an eye on the people, which distracts them from their fishing.

In many areas, particularly in the South, the cattle egret (*Bubulcus ibis*) is seen in agricultural areas, in fields, along roadsides, and even on the grass in cities. During recent years the cattle egret has expanded northward in a rather explosive manner. Another ciconiform that is found around people is the snowy egret (*Egretta thula*), which is all white except for its black bill, long black legs, and yellow feet. Like the black-crowned night heron, the snowy egret feeds in fresh, brackish, and saltwater marshes, even in some amazingly polluted areas.

SWALLOWS AND SWIFTS

The barn swallow (*Hirundo rustica*), the only swallow with a deeply forked tail, is probably the most ubiquitous of the swifts and swallows, being found all over the world except in the hottest and coldest regions. This is the only swallow with white spots in the tail. Its back is bluish black and the breast is cinnamon brown, with a darker brown throat. Unlike the cliff swallow (*Petrochelidon pyrrhonota*), the barn swallow doesn't have a light-colored rump.

The flight pattern of the barn swallow is quite similar to that of the northern rough-winged swallow (*Stelgidopteryx serripennis*), being directed rather than irregular like that of the bank swallow (*Riparia riparia*), which is likely to dart about in what appears to be a haphazard fashion.

Over the years, the barn swallow has shifted its nesting sites. It used to nest under natural overhangs, but now it is found under eaves and inside barns, garages, and abandoned buildings that have accompanied human settlements. Barn swallows do very well in agricultural and suburban areas, and now they are even nesting in the Riverdale section of the Bronx. They have not yet begun to nest in the many other available

Barn swallow at nest, feeding young

Cliff swallow

communities in major cities, however. Perhaps there is too little insect food, or these cities have more noise and pollution than barn swallows can tolerate.

The northern rough-winged swallow, like the bank swallow, has a brown back and lighter underparts, but the northern rough-winged swallow has a brownish throat while the bank swallow has a dark breastband. Like the barn swallow, the northern rough-winged swallow nests in farm areas, suburbs, and outlying sections of major cities. These birds nest most frequently in burrows in banks, in pipes, and in holes in concrete walls. Their summer range does not extend into northern New England, but they are found in most of the rest of the United States.

The adult tree swallow (*Tachycineta bicolor*) is the only swallow with a bluish green back and white underparts. The immature swallow has a brownish back that makes it easy to confuse with the northern rough-winged swallow, which has a darker throat, and also with the bank swallow, which has a complete breastband. The tree swallow arrives in the northern half of the country in early spring before the other swallows. The insects these birds feed on seem to be the first to come out, allowing the tree swallows to move in early. During migration they are often seen feeding above ponds and lakes where early insects are more concentrated. And unlike the other swallows, if it's too cold and there aren't any insects, they'll eat berries. Like barn swallows and northern rough-winged swallows, the tree swallows have adapted to nesting in man-made structures. Originally they nested in tree holes, but more and more they are choosing nesting boxes.

Other bird species that use nesting boxes include the wood duck (*Aix sponsa*), American kestrel (*Falco sparverius*), eastern screech owl (*Otus asio*), western screech owl (*Otus kennicottii*), barn own (*Tyto alba*), purple martin (*Progne subis*), house wren (*Troglodytes aedon*), European starling (*Sturnus vulgaris*), eastern bluebird (*Sialia sialis*), western bluebird (*Sialia mexicana*), and mountain bluebird (*Sialia currucoides*). The tree swallow takes particularly well to areas where nesting boxes have been put up, and sometimes establishes large colonies there.

The largest North American swallow is the purple martin. The male is bluish black above and below, while the female has lighter underparts. This swallow does well in urban and suburban areas. Purple martin boxes have attracted them, and over the years the martins have established huge colonies in these man-made structures.

Another bird, though not related, that is often associated with the swallows and the purple martin is the chimney swift (*Chaetura pelagica*),

House wren

Purple martin

which is actually closely related to the hummingbird. Chimney swifts also nest in colonies, as well as singly, throughout the Great Plains and in the East. This bird, dark both above and below, has a straight, stiff tail that never forks or fans out. The long, slightly curved wings flutter in a distinctive manner. Their loud, rapid, chipping vocalizations reveal their presence when they are flying over cities, towns, and suburbs.

Chimney swifts used to nest in hollow trees before they began to take advantage of whatever benefits might be associated with nesting in urban, man-made structures. Chimneys may provide a similar nesting environment to hollow trees, but they also harbor considerably fewer mammalian predators, such as opossums and raccoons, that, being quite opportunistic, probably fed on whatever chimney swift eggs, nestlings, and adults they could capture.

Few large mammals can climb up and down a chimney, but chimney swifts can nest in those with a rough interior; they need an irregular surface for their feet to grip onto. It's also important that the diameter of the chimney be wide enough to allow the birds to fly in and out. Since their wingspan is 12 inches (30 cm), clearly the chimney has to be wider than that. Some of the larger industrial chimneys from old factories that were either shut down or have their furnaces cold during the summer can become the home for a sizable colony.

Chimney swifts have little feet that are not built for perching in quite the same way as most other birds. Their small claws allow them to hang onto the vertical surface of the inside of a chimney, propped up by their short, spine-tipped tail feathers. They spend much of the rest of the time on their nest or on the wing, where their acrobatics speak for themselves. Anyone who has watched chimney swifts overhead as they dip and dive and swivel about has some appreciation of their capabilities.

Because of their restricted perching capacity, they have a peculiar method of gathering twigs to build their nests. In flight, they grab a dead twig with their feet; if it breaks off, they transfer the twig to their mouth. The twig is then coated with their gooey saliva, enabling them to attach it to the chimney wall.

Many species of swifts are well-known for their saliva. Some species, particularly those in Southeast Asia, have become quite rare because for centuries their saliva has been the base for bird's-nest soup. The Chinese believe this delicacy keeps people young and healthy. Unlike our local swift species, some Asian swifts construct their nests almost entirely of fast-drying saliva, creating a sturdy matrix by connecting the more incidental quantity of feathers and droppings.

When cooked, these nests don't taste like much, but when prepared with crab, shrimp, or pork, the gelatinous soup is said to be quite good.

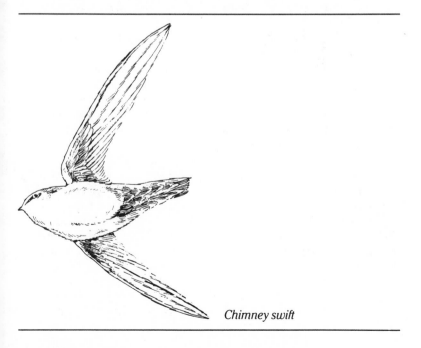

Chimney swift

Because of human encroachment on the bird's habitat as well as over-collecting, most of the nests being brought to market are now coming from remote cliffs in China, Thailand, Vietnam, Malaysia, and Indonesia. As the birds have become increasingly rare, the price paid for their nests has increased accordingly. In Hong Kong the best nests are currently bringing more than $1,000 a pound. One might think such an outrageous price would stem all demand for the product, allowing the birds to make a comeback, but the reverse seems to be true. The high price has made the bird's-nest soup seem even more precious, so the nests are still collected, and the price continues to rise.

BARN OWL AND SCREECH OWLS

Of all the owls, the barn owl (*Tyto alba*) is probably the most cosmopolitan, being found in North America, South America, Europe, Africa, Asia, and Australia. This light buffy, brown-and-tan bird has a distinctive heart-shaped outline around its face. Unlike most other owls, which have long feathers covering much of their breast and legs, the barn owl has short breast feathers that reveal their legs, which are long relative to their body size. Their eyes are small and dark. The barn owl's diet consists mainly of small nocturnal rodents, though occasionally it takes rats and even rabbits.

The nest sites most frequently used in remote areas are tree cavities, but the owls seem to prefer being around human habitation, where they will nest in barns and abandoned buildings, on eaves, in holes in old buildings, and in many other suitable sites. Several pairs nest in Brooklyn in the otherwise unoccupied airplane hangars left behind by the U.S. military. The National Park Service has proposed renting or selling these structures to the highest bidder, without giving any thought to the owls. To encourage the few pairs still nesting in the Bronx, there are plans to erect some nest boxes in Pelham Bay Park.

The eastern (*Otus asio*) and western screech owls (*Otus kennicottii*) are quite similar in size and habits, except that the eastern screech owl occurs in two color phases, one a bright rust and the other gray; the western screech owl is brown. All the other eared owls, or those with small tufts of feathers on their head that look like, but actually aren't, ears, are considerably larger than these small birds, which stand only about 8 inches (20 cm) high and have a wingspan of 22 inches (56 cm).

They do well in cities and suburbs across the country, but because most owls are nocturnal, few people are aware of their presence. Having studied the eastern screech owl for twenty years, Frederick Gehlbach, a

Barn owl

professor at Baylor University in Waco, Texas, has found that the avail-ability of food is several times more concentrated in the suburbs than in more rural environments. This enables the owls to establish smaller hunting ranges, where they catch moths, katydids, beetles, crickets, earthworms, and other small prey that they find on foliage and on the ground. Screech owls even thrive in people's yards, where they will take the insects attracted to the lights.

Screech owls naturally nest in holes in trees, such as those previously made by woodpeckers, but they respond well to nest boxes, too.

NIGHTHAWK

The common nighthawk (*Chordeiles minor*) is one of the few birds that flies around our cities at night. In the order Caprimulgiformes, family Caprimulgidae, this relative of the whip-poor-will (*Caprimulgus vociferus*) has soft feathers like an owl, which increase its ability to fly silently without alerting its prey. Caprimulgidae literally means goatsucker, a name they were given when it was thought that their large mouths were

Common nighthawk

used to suck goat teats rather than to catch insects. The common nighthawk has large eyes and a mottled brown "dead leaf" pattern, which gives it camouflage when roosting and nesting on the ground. The common nighthawk is about 9 inches (23 cm) long and has a wingspan of approximately 23 inches (58 cm).

Many caprimulgids are named for their calls, such as the whip-poor-will, common pauraque (*Nyctidromus albicollis*), and chuck-will's widow (*Caprimulgus carolinensis*). However, this isn't true of the nighthawk which has a nasal "peent" that can be heard at dusk and through the night over cities all over the United States during the summer months. The call is not much different from the sound made by the American woodcock (*Scolopax minor*), which is primarily heard in the East during the spring when it is courting. It may not be accidental that these two species utter such similar sounds. Both species make their calls at night, and the brief nasal bursts may have a maximum effect in the dark. Because nighthawks commonly call while flying high, apparently while feeding, the sound may inform other nighthawks about territory or about a location where the feeding is good. Or perhaps the sounds let nearby nighthawks know each other's whereabouts to avoid flying into one another. It's also possible that the "peent" has an echolocation function—that is, the sound bounces off objects informing the nighthawk about what lies ahead.

Presumably, for most of the caprimulgids, the larger the mouth, the better. To increase the effectiveness of the gape, they also have whiskers similar to those of cats, and the whiskers probably serve a very similar function for both groups: they are sensory organs that make it easier for the animal to find prey. Anything near the mouth that touches a whisker instantly alerts the predator to realign its mouth and snap it shut.

The nighthawks are probably the most common goatsuckers in urban areas. Urban-dwelling nighthawks seem to do best in medium-sized cities where human populations range from 25,000 to several hundred thousand. Often seen flying past lights to catch insects, nighthawks may benefit from the extended dusk made possible by city lights. It could be that the illuminated skies over smaller cities have more aerial plankton—the small creatures flying around—than the skies over larger cities.

Although normally ground nesters, most urban nighthawks nest on the gravelly surface of flat roofs. A population of nighthawks may need just so many flat-roofed buildings; anything more is unnecessary. As the cities grow larger, the availability of insects and of overall good insect-producing habitat drops proportionately. Those birds that take up life in relatively small cities, where the risks of predators are diminished and where nesting on roofs eliminates most of the inconveniences encountered by other urban ground nesters, probably do quite well. Some nighthawks continue to inhabit parts of a city even when it grows too large, such as those still living in New York. But they tend to live in the more outlying areas in Brooklyn where there are flat roofs, the skies are lit, and there is sufficient insect-producing habitat to support the local nighthawk population.

PEREGRINE FALCON

Although endangered, the peregrine falcon (*Falco peregrinus*) is thought to be slowly making a recovery. This species has captured the imagination of the American people. Few other endangered species affect us quite as deeply as the peregrine. These birds are not as numerous in cities as are some other species, and few Americans have ever actually seen one, but the sight of a peregrine falcon is an unsurpassed thrill. From the roof of my apartment building in midtown Manhattan during the summer, I often watch the local peregrine working the neighborhood over in search of pigeons. This falcon's power and speed are nothing short of magnificent. And during the late winter of 1987 I watched a peregrine hunting from the tops of buildings, right in the middle of Times Square.

Like other falcons, the peregrine has pointed wings and a long narrow tail. Strong directed flight, powerful wingbeats, and occasional fluttering while hovering overhead are typical. From time to time they

Peregrine falcon

can also be seen soaring with their tail feathers spread apart, but this is uncommon. The peregrine is quite large, about the size of a crow. Only the prairie falcon (*Falco mexicanus*) and the gyrfalcon (*Falco rusticolus*) are in the same approximate size class. They are differentiated from one another by a few specific characteristics. The prairie falcon has the coloration of the young, lighter, immature peregrine. Like the peregrine, the prairie falcon has a dark cap and mustache, though the prairie falcon's mustache is considerably thinner than the peregrine's. The gyrfalcon, which is larger than the peregrine and has noticeably slower wingbeats, doesn't have the peregrine's contrasting light and dark coloration on the head. In the arctic there are black, gray, and white gyrfalcon color morphs, though only the darker morphs are seen south of the Canadian border.

Through the 1940s, peregrines bred from the southern United States to Hudson Bay, but new generations of pesticides put an end to that. DDT and related toxic polychlorinated chemicals accumulated in fatty tissues of many animals. Each time an animal consumed another animal, the body of the predator absorbed these dangerous, long-lived chemicals. Animals at the top of the food chain, such as the peregrine, consumed large amounts of poison that had been biomagnified in their prey. As a result, they were the first to show the detrimental effects of DDT. Peregrines were among those hit hardest. They were entirely eliminated from their range east of the Rockies. Since DDT was banned in the early 1970s, peregrine sightings have been increasing, but they are still rare. Along the Atlantic Coast, most sightings are made during migration.

For almost twenty years, peregrines have been part of a captive breeding program at Cornell University's Hawk Barn, directed by Tom Cade who has led an effort to restock areas where peregrines had been extirpated. One of the sites chosen for reintroductions was New York City. It was well known that peregrines used to nest along the Palisades, the columnar basaltic cliffs on the New Jersey bank of the Hudson River, but those birds died out decades ago. There were also nesting attempts in New York City as recently as the 1940s. One was on the Hotel St. Regis on Fifth Avenue; another was on an abandoned building at West End Avenue and West 72nd Street. These early efforts to nest in New York City were unsuccessful because of human interference. Today, however, landlords, corporations, and the city government are happy to collaborate when given the opportunity to help reintroduce peregrines to the city. Many young peregrines from Cornell were brought to New York City and raised with the hope that they would regard the city as their home and return each succeeding year ultimately to pair off and breed in the area. Cornell's long-term effort is beginning to pay off. Several pairs of peregrines have been nesting successfully in New York during the past few years.

On the West Coast, only two pairs of peregrines were known to have survived into the 1970s when DDT was banned. These birds were living on the Monterey County coast. Since 1977, owing to efforts of the Predatory Bird Research Group at the University of California at Santa Cruz, about 300 peregrines have been introduced to the rugged coastal areas and to sites in the Sierra Nevada Mountains. These birds were incubated from eggs laid in captivity.

From 1984 to 1986, a dozen peregrines were released just north of San Francisco, on the headlands south of Muir Beach in Marin County. Since then, peregrines have been sighted in the San Francisco Civic Center Plaza, on the Golden Gate Bridge, and on the Bay Bridge. During the summer of 1986 two peregrine falcons were often seen hunting in the canyons of San Francisco's financial district. They regularly perched on a sign at the top of the 31-story Mutual Benefit Life Building. Each day they were seen there from 8:30 until 10:00 A.M., and would return in the afternoon and remain, looking for prey from 3:30 till about 5:00 P.M.. The mature male always perched on the *M*, the immature female perched on the *L*. It was thought that they were eating pigeons, but none was ever seen being taken or consumed. Though people usually assume that the larger urban-dwelling hawks and falcons are hunting for pigeons, there are several other common bird species that would constitute reasonable

Mallard

prey. They include the mallards (*Anas platyrhynchos*), which commonly occur in large numbers in urban waters. Other common potential prey species include house sparrows, starlings, grackles, and Brewer's blackbirds. Los Angeles also has released peregrines, which are living and breeding in the downtown area. Peregrines have been seen in Salt Lake City, Utah, as well.

The peregrines don't seem to mind whether the cliff face they hunt from, or perch and nest on, is natural or man-made. They readily take to urban cliffs where they hunt city species that may be safer to eat than the rural quarries because fewer herbicides and pesticides are used in cities. Urban areas may also be safer in that few human city dwellers feel a need to shoot every wild thing that flies by.

The number of peregrines that are breeding in the United States has been steadily increasing during the past fourteen years. In 1986, the estimate published by the Audubon Society was placed at 1,200.

AMERICAN KESTREL

The most common falcon, as well as the smallest in North America, is the American kestrel (*Falco sparverius*). About the size of a blue jay

(*Cyanocitta cristata*), this falcon has a rusty back; on each side of the face are two dark stripes, which some people think look like whiskers. The American kestrel, also known as the sparrow hawk, nests in tree holes, bird boxes, and building crevices, and has adapted quite well to urban conditions.

Its cousin, the kestrel (*Falco tinnunculus*), which lives in Europe and parts of Asia, nests on cliffs and buildings and commonly makes its home right in the center of town. The American kestrel doesn't seem to do quite as well in urban areas, usually requiring open spaces in which to feed, but it is found in many of our largest cities. Marya Dalrymple and her coworkers at Rebus, Inc., a book packaging firm, recently watched and photographed an American kestrel perched on top of a building just south of midtown Manhattan as it leisurely ate a house sparrow. In densely populated areas American kestrels will look for prey in any field, park, or along the roadsides; in rural areas they contain most of their hunting to meadows and agricultural fields.

The sparrow hawk's name is somewhat deceptive, since they don't take very many sparrows. During the summer, grasshoppers and other large insects account for most of their diet, but when insects aren't available, such as in most urban areas or during the winter, then sparrow hawks will rely more heavily on small birds and rodents.

American kestrel

RED-TAILED HAWK

Peregrines may not have a corner on the pigeon market forever. During the summer of 1986, a red-tailed hawk (*Buteo jamaicensis*) swooped down on Boston Common, caught a pigeon, and ate it while about 200 people watched in disbelief. Red-tails have been seen elsewhere in the Boston area, including the Back Bay and Fenway sections of the city and at the Arnold Arboretum in Jamaica Plain. Red-tailed hawks are now seen regularly perched in trees along roads and highways across the country, looking for any unsuspecting prey that may be foraging out in the open.

Times have changed since house sparrows were initially introduced to Boston and shrikes moved right in and started capturing them. The city's response back then was to hire a few people to go out and shoot the shrikes. Now people have a completely different attitude toward birds of prey. Instead of thinking of them as butcher birds, a more reasonable perspective has been adopted. With millions of pigeons and house sparrows and comparatively few hawks and owls, we tend to favor the rarer species.

Red-tailed hawk

Part of this more positive response toward birds of prey may result from our having been responsible for their decline. Many recent efforts to stem the decline of birds of prey have been well publicized. We now no longer believe that hawks are out there devouring all our lambs and heifers. In addition, only about 5 percent of the American population lives on farms, compared to about 95 percent of the population 100 years ago. Far fewer people are attempting to protect their chickens from what was perceived to be a mortal danger.

The red-tailed hawk preys primarily on rodents and slow-moving birds, making urban areas good hunting grounds. The only thing that seems to hold them back is their well-founded fear of people. Hawks don't naturally fear people, but have learned to keep their distance after being shot at through the years. During the past couple of human generations, this pressure has been easing slightly. Many of the people who once would have shot at hawks for target practice are now inclined to think twice.

When seen perched along the highways, hawks are almost invariably high in a dead tree. Even during the winter they seem to prefer the dead trees, possibly because so many rodents live in and among the roots. If you look underneath a big old dead tree in the winter, when there's snow on the ground, you'll usually see mouse tracks all around. If it's the mice that are pulling the hawks in, then city parks probably provide many additional attractive feeding opportunities. In addition to the mice, cities harbor large populations of rats, but these are generally too large to be taken regularly. All winter long, red-tailed hawks hunt for rodents at the old sanitation landfill sites near Newark, New Jersey.

Readily nesting in relatively small woodlots, red-tailed hawks have been able to withstand many of the changes that humans have caused across the country. While most other large hawks still nest only in the more protected, older, more expansive forests, red-tails have not been so restricted. They are now one of the most numerous and widespread of the North American buteos. These include the other thick-set hawks with broad, rounded wings and rounded tails that are seen circling overhead, then dropping on their prey by pulling into a steep dive.

Red-tails are slightly larger than most crows, being about 20 inches (51 cm) long with a wingspan of 50 inches (127 cm). In the East the color of the adult's tail is characteristic: reddish brown above and pinkish below. The immature birds have dark gray tails that may or may not show distinct horizontal bands. The adults have a band of dark streaks across the belly, although the presence or absence, as well as the degree, of this streaking is more variable in the West, where there are populations with significantly darker breasts.

9

MAMMALS

M ost people think that few mammals besides rats live in cities, but that is far from true. Mice and rats are among the more successful urban species, however, so reasons for their success will be discussed. Since most of the dominant mice and rats are from Europe and Asia, I will talk about how and when they were introduced and why they are doing so well. I'll also discuss other successful urban rodents—squirrels, chipmunks, and woodchucks—where they live, how they have survived, and why they are absent from some seemingly suitable urban habitats.

Rabbits, skunks, and bats are other mammals that do well in many densely populated regions around the country. I will explain which species do best, where they live, what they eat, how they are able to survive, and why they are doing better than other species. Cats and dogs are presented because their histories are less well known. When were they domesticated? What led to their domestication? What effects might they have on wild populations of urban species? All of these topics are dealt with.

I've also included some marine mammals in this chapter. Not many of them live in cities, but some migrate nearby, and for that reason they are discussed. Humphrey the Whale made headlines in 1985, as did a beluga whale that returned to Long Island Sound a couple of years in a row. Because there is widespread interest in marine mammals, they are discussed in their relation to urban areas.

COMMON HOUSE MOUSE

Many rats and mice that live in close association with people around the world are members of the same family that includes the house mouse (*Mus musculus*). This group has been lumped with the indigeneous New World rats and mice. Rats and mice belong to the largest mammalian order, Rodentia, which includes about 1,685 species, depending on who's doing the counting. Many Old World murids have been introduced to other parts of the world. Some have become cosmopolitan in their distribution, living in wild areas, sparsely populated places, rural agricultural regions, and large cities.

The house mouse, originally from southern Asia, is now common throughout the world. Wooded habitats represent unlikely areas for them, but they may be found, along with mouse populations that live in field and along fence-rows, where there is enough cover and minimal environmental disturbance. Of these populations, some live outdoors during the summer and move into buildings during the winter. The forms that live with the completely "wild" populations, neither harming nor helping one another, generally have longer tails and are darker than the wild forms. There are also many domesticated varieties of *Mus musculus*, the most common of which is an albino. Some strains carry black-and-white patterns; others are various shades of black and gray.

Wild populations are grayish brown dorsally, with lighter tones underneath. From the tip of their nose to the beginning of their tail they

Common house mouse

measure from 3 to 3½ inches (7.6 to 8.9 cm) long; the thin scaly tail is about 3 to 4 inches (7.6 to 10.2 cm) long. These seemingly high-strung little animals leave their calling cards, tiny cigar-shaped black turds, everywhere they go. Adept climbers, they will crawl about on your shelves, in your cabinets, on tabletops, on top of the refrigerator, and they can even walk upright along the electrical cord.

Wild house mice that live outdoors are generally nocturnal, but it is easy to catch them in traps set during the day. While house mice that live indoors also tend to be nocturnal, they readily adapt and are active when there is the least amount of human activity. These mice are able to eat a wide range of foods, including almost any human food. If the household is exceptionally clean, the mice can subsist on some rather bizarre items, such as soap, glue, and paste. In the wild they eat seeds, roots, leaves, and stems. They will also eat insects and some meat when available.

Their nests are made of soft materials. They often make this material by shredding things with their teeth. They eat through many substances, looking for food or nesting material, and in the process can do quite a bit of damage. Considering the things they eat through, sometimes you'd swear they can smell right through plastic bags. This may well be true, considering that the arrangement of molecules in some plastics allows for the diffusion of certain odors.

House mice breed throughout the year, particularly during the warmer months, and may produce more than five litters annually, with three to twelve young per litter. House mice are hardly ever seen, but occasionally their populations increase dramatically. Such "ecological explosions" occurred in the Central Valley of California in 1926–27 and again in 1941–42. Numbers exceeding 82,000 per acre were estimated during one of the worst explosions; in time the numbers decreased to normal levels. Mice can be the hosts of typhus, spotted fever, salmonellosis, and rickettsial pox, and if food is contaminated with their urine or feces, diseases may be spread to humans. However, in most American cities where the majority of diseases carried by house mice are not a major problem, these animals are relatively harmless.

NORWAY RAT AND BLACK RAT

The Norway rat (*Rattus norvegicus*) and the black rat (*Rattus rattus*), like the house mouse, are murids, members of the group of Old World rats and mice that has been lumped with the New World rats and mice. The genus *Rattus* contains approximately 78 species. Most live in Southeast Asia and Africa, but many have been introduced elsewhere around

Norway rat

the world. Both Norway rats and black rats are quite common in urban areas throughout North America.

The Norway and black rats eat virtually anything they can get their teeth through, but when given a choice, they consume food that gives them a well-balanced diet. Because they eat through things looking for food, they cause considerable damage. Their gnawing doesn't stop at paper and plastic bags; they will also eat through the insulation around wire and have been known to chew on lead pipes and even concrete dams. The total amount of damage these two species cause each year is estimated to amount to billions of dollars worldwide.

The black rat originally was restricted to Asia Minor and the Orient. It is thought to have been introduced into Europe during the Crusades, although there is reason to believe it may have been in Ireland as early as the 9th century. It then made the vogage to North America on ships of early settlers; one account puts the date at about 1650.

The Norway rat is probably native to eastern Asia and Japan, where it lived along stream banks, and later spread to the rice fields and canals. Unlike the black rat, the Norway rat is more or less confined to areas where the habitat is right for it to build its burrows. It wasn't until 1553 that Norway rats were first reported in Europe, probably having arrived there on ships. They were first reported in North America around 1775.

Why have these Old World murids been so successful in urban

settings? They may have had a jump on American species at adapting to living with humans. Since the house mouse, the black rat, and the Norway rat were living in towns and cities all over the Old World before America had any cities, it stands to reason that when America's cities began to be built, they would have been the first to become well established in the new environment. They may even have been able to outcompete otherwise well-suited native species. They may also have been firmly established before any Old World rat and mouse diseases made it to America. Their omnivorous habits could account for part of their success. We've repeatedly found that omnivory is one of the better strategies for success in cities and suburbs. The capacity to eat and to digest many different types of available food gives these species a considerable edge when foraging on the streets of a major city, in large apartment buildings, or in city parks.

Washington, D.C., has been fighting a war on rats since 1968 when about half of the city was infested. Today, however, James Murphy, the local government official in charge of rodent elimination, estimates only about 4 percent of the city is plagued by rats. Murphy's staff wages a constant war on the rodent populations. They search the city's monuments, buildings, and neighborhoods looking for signs of rats, then leave poison pellets in the infested areas. They also educate the public about rat prevention, explaining the importance of storing trash in sealed containers, properly disposing of debris that rats could nest in, and cleaning up dog feces that would otherwise attract rats. The key to avoiding rats is limiting available food.

Those urban parks that have the greatest number of visitors are also likely to have the greatest density of rats. In response, parks departments often pour poison down the rat holes. After many years of this, it may or may not have dawned on park officials that the rats are still alive and well, but many of the chipmunks and other species are long gone.

Rats in some cities have been fed so much rodenticide that the survivors appear to have developed a resistance to chemicals. In New York there is evidence that the effects of some of the newer rodenticides are not altogether unpleasant to the rats. It has, in fact, been suggested that the rats now experience an agreeable high. Robert Angelone, who serves as Central Park's unofficial rat-reduction strategist, has said it is almost like giving the rats cocaine.

Angelone started testing different rodenticides when New Yorkers complained about the strange daytime behavior of the rats. Rats normally are rather secretive and come out only at night, or when people aren't around. But some of the chemicals intended to kill the rats were just changing their behavior. Instead of dying, the rats began calmly walking around during the day as if they owned the park. To deal with this new problem, Angelone has begun rotating different poisons; he believes this is killing many of the rats. But no matter what Angelone believes, anyone who goes for a walk in Central Park will see rats brazenly strolling around in the middle of the day.

I'm not entirely sure what all the rat-related hysteria is about. The fear of rats seems to be a learned phobia. Rats are basically just another rodent, without a bushy tail. If we could get over our fear of rats, we might not have to pour so much poison down their holes and endanger so many other animals. Keeping our parks clean would be a less expensive, more effective, and far more attractive method of rodent control.

EASTERN GRAY SQUIRREL

The eastern gray squirrel (*Sciurus carolinensis*) is one of the tree squirrels, a group of about 55 species that ranges over most of Europe, much of Asia, Japan, and the New World from southern Canada to northern Argentina. These animals live in deciduous, coniferous, and tropical forests. The gray squirrel, native to eastern North America, is one

Eastern gray squirrel

of the best-known squirrels in the world. It has been successfully introduced in some cities on the Pacific Coast as well as into Great Britain and
South Africa. In certain areas, introduced populations have become pests,
damaging crops and trees.

Although gray squirrels are forest dwellers, they often do better in
suburbs and cities than in rural forests. There is much food available to
them in city parks because people like to feed them and also because
people leave edible trash behind. As a result, squirrel populations often
expand to densities considerably greater than would be possible in the
wild. This sometimes leads to problems, as in Washington, D.C., where
some people wanted large numbers of squirrels to be trapped and moved
to alleviate the crowded conditions.

Certain species of tree squirrels occur in distinctly different color
forms—or morphs—within the same population. A dark morph has been
reported in several urban gray squirrel populations in the East, including
Rochester, and Albany, New York; Princeton, New Jersey; and New York
City. It is hard to understand why these melanistic squirrels have been
turning up in cities in the Northeast. If the melanistic squirrel represents a
new mutation, how could it have traveled so rapidly between all these
cities? And why isn't it expressed in the intervening regions? It may be
that the melanistic gene was always part of the gray squirrel's genetic
repertoire in the Northeast; when it was expressed, those individuals
were selected against. Now, with few predators preying on urban squirrels, the dark individuals are not culled from the population. As a result,
melanistic squirrels have been increasing in numbers in several urban
areas.

Because squirrels come out during the day, much of their behavior
includes visual cues. Their long, bushy tails move around in ways that are
significant to other squirrels in the area. Being agile and arboreal, they
can avoid being run down by dogs and other animals. Squirrels in city
parks will search the grass under trees for food while people walk all
around them. But when a dog appears in the distance, the squirrels all
move to within several feet of the nearest tree trunk, in case they have to
make a run for it.

Squirrels collect nuts and bury them in caches within their well-
defended territory. When you see squirrels digging through the snow,
they may be trying to find the place where they stashed away some nuts
during the fall. It is thought that they find these caches by smelling them.
Memory may also help, but many of the nuts are never retrieved and
appear to have been forgotten. This is why squirrels in the wild are
credited with a significant role in reforestation: if the nuts had been left
on the forest floor, they might have been consumed by other animals.

During the summer, gray squirrels build large nests of leaves and
branches and nestle them into the crotches of trees. In addition to these

nests they also enlarge and pad holes in the larger trees. During the winter, even though they don't hibernate, several squirrels will often hole up together to keep one another warm, and the leaves used to pad the summer nests act as insulation. On warm sunny days during the winter the squirrels often leave their nests to eat, drink, urinate, and defecate. This overwintering behavior is not true hibernation. Animals that hibernate shut their digestive systems down for the winter because their metabolisms slow down so much and their body temperatures become so low that food would only sit inside them and possibly rot. Hibernating animals go into a very deep sleep that is actually physiologically distinct from sleeping.

Squirrels are occasionally seen vigorously chasing other squirrels. Much of this behavior is related to establishing and maintaining their social hierachy. Sometimes they leave scent markings, odors that mark the territory within which they hide their nuts. Any unwanted squirrel within that marked territory may be chased out. Sometimes the chasing is part of their behavior during mating season, which is usually during the middle of winter. It is common to see males chasing females in trees and on the ground, and the males are often seen fighting among themselves over which gets priority in male-female interactions. Winter may not seem like the most appropriate time for such behavior, but, for squirrels, it beats sleeping.

CHIPMUNK

There is only one species of chipmunk in eastern North America. It is the eastern chipmunk (*Tamias striatus*), which lives in southeastern Canada and in most of the eastern half of the United States, except the extreme South.

There are about sixteen species of chipmunk in the West, all of them in the genus *Eutamias*. They are all difficult to differentiate from one another in the field as well as in the hand. The eastern chipmunk is only about 5 or 6 inches (12.7 to 15.2 cm) long; the tail adds an additional 3 to 4 inches (7.6 to 10.2 cm). They look something like a small, striped squirrel. The tail is bushy and stands straight up when they run about. They always seem slightly high-strung. Their facial stripes, as well as the stripes running the length of their body and ending at the reddish rump, distinguish them from most other species that live within their range.

Chipmunks are commonly found in deciduous forests with some shrubs in the understory, a few stone walls, and some dead trees. They

Eastern chipmunk

are largely confined to the ground, but they will climb some trees in search of food. They build burrows that may be as long as 15 feet (4.6 m), extending about 3 feet (91 cm) deep, that contain storage chambers for food to be eaten during the winter when the chipmunks awaken from hibernation. In colder regions, chipmunks may store as many as three gallons of seeds and nuts for the winter. They choose items with a long shelf life. Chipmunks collect other more perishable items, such as fruits, berries, and mushrooms, but they eat them right away.

Although common in most suburbs with some woodlots, chipmunks are rarely as common as squirrels in urban areas, perhaps because they

Least chipmunk

need more undergrowth than is generally available in city parks. Since most dead trees and old stone walls have also been removed, many of the important aspects of their preferred habitats are unavailable. Despite these drawbacks, populations of eastern chipmunks have persisted and even thrive in most eastern cities, but they are vulnerable to certain changes. Environmental changes may be important, as well as other factors that could bring chipmunks into direct competition with the Norway rats. In such cases, the rats may win. Another critical factor could be the extensive use of rodenticides to control rats. Pouring poisoned pellets down rodent holes may temporarily decrease the rat population while inadvertently eliminating other non-targeted species such as chipmunks; the result being that those parks with the greatest number of human visitors usually have the worst rat problems, and are now devoid of most other native rodents. One exception is Rocky Mountain National Park, where many people visit each year and leave as much of a mess as people leave anywhere. Yet the chipmunk and ground squirrel (*Spermophilus* spp.) populations are as healthy as ever. Perhaps the winters there are too harsh for the rats. Without the rats, the National Park Service personnel don't lay down rodenticides, so the chipmunks around the cabins and the Park Service headquarters are safe. In most suburbs, where rat control measures are not necessary, one finds healthy chipmunk populations.

WOODCHUCK

The woodchuck (*Marmota monax*), also known as the groundhog, is a member of the genus *Marmota*, which contains about sixteen species that live in the northern hemisphere, through part of Alaska, most of Canada and the United States, western Europe, and much of Asia. This is the largest-bodied group in the squirrel family, Sciuridae. Six species live in North America; of these the woodchuck probably comes closest to being an urban dweller. It has been included here because it has done well in many areas where people have modified the landscape.

The marmots of North America tend to be western in their distribution, living on talus slopes, often at high elevations, and in valleys. The woodchuck is the only *Marmota* that lives in the eastern half of the United States. Its range extends into the West, but primarily through Canada. The length from the tip of its nose to the end of its body, excluding its tail, is about 16 to 20 inches (41 to 51 cm); the tail is an additional 4 to 7 inches (10 to 18 cm) long. The body is quite stocky, and the legs are short. On their back the fur is a frosted yellowish brown, the belly is slightly lighter, and the feet are dark brown or black.

Woodchuck

These animals live on the ground, where they dig tunnels that provide a refuge from predators, shelter at night, and a place to rear their young. Since woodchucks and marmots hibernate, the den is where they overwinter. In some areas hibernation can last as long as eight months. After having put on about a half-inch (1.3 cm) of fat under the fur on their backs and shoulders during the summer and fall, they retreat into their burrows, which may be as long as 45 feet (almost 14 m), extending to a depth of 3 to 6 feet (91 to 183 cm). While hibernating, they become torpid, which for woodchucks means their body temperature drops from the normal 99°F (37°C) to somewhere between 37°F and 57°F (3°C to 14°C), and their heartbeat decreases from more than 100 beats a minute to approximately 4 beats per minute. Breathing also slows down to as little as one breath every six minutes.

Woodchucks do best in meadows that have a forest nearby. They used to be found most often in the country living near farms, but now woodchucks are seen on the mowed roadsides along highways, eating the tender plants. It is this preference for young plants that often attracts them to vegetable gardens. In spite of the enmity farmers feel for woodchucks, these animals can be quite beneficial to the animal community.

They provide holes and burrows that many other animals use, and their turning of the earth improves the soil structure.

There are at least four woodchucks still surviving right in the middle of Manhattan, in Central Park. The adult, known as Phyllis, raised three young during the spring of 1987. No one knows whether Phyllis is the last descendant of the woodchucks that lived there when the Europeans first arrived or if it is an old animal that escaped from the Children's Zoo some years ago. But that shouldn't be the real question; people should wonder where all the other woodchucks went. Considering that Central Park comprises more than 800 acres of suitable woodchuck terrain, several colonies should still be there. Were they deliberately eliminated, or have the years of rat poisons, pesticides, herbicides, and fungicides, as well as the many dogs that are allowed to run loose, all taken their toll? The current park management is quite sane with regard to the use of such toxic chemicals, and they would tolerate a few holes being dug and a little munching here and there—all of which makes me wonder if a reintroduction effort might not make sense.

An American rendition of an older European event has become what we call Groundhog Day. Each year it falls on February 2, when the earth is midway in orbit between its location during the Winter Solstice in December, the shortest day of the year, and the Spring Equinox in March, one of the two days of the year when both day and night last twelve hours. The ancient Celts called February 2 Imbolog, which meant sheep's milk. To them it was the start of the lambing season. The Celtic tribes thought that if it was sunny, the winter was going to be long; if the day was cloudy, there would be an early spring. The Romans brought Imbolog to the rest of Europe, where the medieval church already celebrated Candlemas on the same day, the Feast of the Purification. When both merged, it used to be said:

> *If Candlemas be bright and clear*
> *There'll be two winters in the year.*

The original groundhog of Groundhog Day was actually a hedgehog (*Erinaceus* sp.). Medieval Europeans thought the hedgehog awakened from its winter sleep, walked out of its burrow, and looked for its shadow. Then, knowing how much longer the winter was going to last, it went back to sleep. The concept was carried to North America and adapted to our groundhog. But our groundhogs usually don't emerge from hibernation until the end of February or early March; they don't awaken to predict the weather, and its not their shadow they're looking for. After all those months underground, they want only two things—a meal and a mate.

VIRGINIA OPOSSUM

The Virginia opossum (*Didelphis marsupialis*) is doing remarkably well around cities, living in the parks and more residential sections. This species has dramatically extended its range northward during the past 100 years. It has spread through the eastern states all the way to Canada. Following its introduction in the western states in the early 20th century, it rapidly spread north and now occurs from Mexico to Canada. Some of this success is attributable to the opossum's high fecundity, rapid growth, and early maturation. 'Possums are doing so well, they are even found in all five boroughs of New York City.

About the size of a cat, though heavier bodied, this long-haired, gray marsupial has a white face, thin black ears, a pointed snout, short legs, an opposable thumb on its hind feet, and a long, round, ratlike prehensile tail. *Didelphis* means two uteruses, which is a characteristic of these animals. Each uterus has its own cervix, both of which are accommodated by the male's bifurcated penis.

Opossums don't actually hibernate, but they do put on fat in the fall

Virginia opossum

Virginia opossum

and stay in their dens for days in the winter, going out on occasion. When winter temperatures get very low, 'possums can get frostbitten and lose the tips of their ears and the ends of their tails.

Because 'possums are nocturnal, they aren't seen very often unless they happen to be crossing the road when you're driving by. In the suburbs, 'possums are often found dead on the road. That's partly due to their being nocturnal; many are hit before the driver sees them. It also seems that opposums may go out on the roads at night to clean up other roadkills.

These animals will eat corn, eggs, acorns, nuts, fruits, berries, and the contents of garbage cans. At night they even come up on porches to eat out of a dog's dish. Their interest in so many types of food makes them well suited to the city and suburbs, where opportunism proves beneficial to many species.

RACCOON

Raccoons are confined to the New World. Seven species are recognized, all of them found from southern Canada to South America. Five of these species live on islands; the other two range over most of the mainland. The raccoon found in North America is *Procyon lotor*. Like many other mammals that do well in urban and suburban areas, the raccoon is more active at night than during the day.

Holes are important to raccoons. They need places to hole up during the day, and cities have plenty of suitable locations. Many raccoons use sewer pipes, culverts, and drainage pipes. They travel through pipes to get from one area to another. For instance, there may be a marsh on one side of the road and a woodlot on the other, so a culvert becomes their chief route back and forth. This passageway allows them to stay out of sight and to avoid the cars.

Cars are a significant predator. Few people think of them as such because they are inanimate, but cars are among the chief annihilators of wildlife in densely populated regions. Species with low reproductive rates may not be able to survive a rather high level of depredation, and therefore are usually the first to be eliminated from a region when roads are put through. While birds can fly over the cars, most mammals, reptiles, and amphibians are considerably more vulnerable. Therefore, using pipes, culverts, and sewers to get from one side of the road to another has proved extremely advantageous to certain species.

Raccoon

Raccoon

Raccoons tend to do best near a wetland. They like to patrol the water's edge where any number of different feeding opportunities present themselves. Their omnivory allows them to eat seeds, nuts, fruit, grain, fish, frogs, and rodents. The well-known raccoon habit of washing their food before eating it is more common among captive animals than it is in the wild. Apparently they wash their prey to remove grit and to wash off the distasteful or toxic secretions that are released by some species of salamanders, frogs, and toads.

Their winter dormancy is tied to low temperatures and is relatively brief. In the North, this behavior is a valuable adaptation that does not occur among raccoons in the South. This is one of several species that do well around campsites throughout the country. Raccoons seem to be sufficiently opportunistic to seize the advantage of food left out overnight or tossed into trash cans. Their opportunism may account for some of their success in cities and suburbs.

RABBIT

Rabbits, hares, and pikas are all members of the mammalian order Lagomorpha. Rabbits were until recently thought to be rodents, but

Eastern cottontail rabbit

biochemical studies have shown that the two groups have no close relationship. Lagomorphs do have some similarities to various groups of hoofed animals, but the precise relationships need to be worked out. The two North American species of pikas—small, rabbitlike mammals with short ears—are seldom found near people, living only in remote, high elevations. Although pikas live above the timberline in inhospitable environments, they do not hibernate, which shows that some small mammals can get through a harsh winter without going into torpor.

The other six genera of lagomorphs, including the rabbits and hares, are all in the family Leporidae. They live in a wide range of habitats on most major land masses. Members of the family have been introduced to Sumatra, New Zealand, Austrailia, and to many smaller islands around the world.

Of all the species in the rabbit and hare family in North America, the eastern cottontail (*Sylvilagus floridanus*) probably has the widest range and comes in contact with the greatest number of people. These rabbits are found throughout the eastern two-thirds of the United States, with the exception of the northernmost portion of New England. The New England cottontail (*Sylvilagus transitionalis*) also lives in the East, but usually at higher elevations than the eastern cottontail. The two species are virtually impossible to positively distinguish in the field and are difficult to tell apart in the hand. The eastern cottontail is the species most often found in backyards or eating the new sprouts in your vegetable garden. These rabbits do well in suburbia and are found in every borough of New York City, where they live in the parks and some of the more suburban areas. Some cottontails even live in the northern part of Central Park. In more rural areas, birds of prey probably represent their most significant predator, but in cities and suburbs cars and dogs take the largest toll.

Rabbits generally feed during the evening, any time from dusk to dawn. When crossing roads, they can be disoriented by headlights, and many are run over. Although they grow rapidly and breed continuously, producing as many as seven broods a year, with several young per litter, mortality rates are rather high, and the average lifespan is less than a year.

A crate of a western species of hare broke open while being unloaded at Kennedy Airport in New York several years ago, and the escapees have established a successful breeding colony near the runways. To date this is the only location where hares exist in the city, and there is no reason to believe they are spreading. However, because many rabbits are kept in captivity, there have been ample opportunities for others to escape and establish new populations. The main difference is that, compared to a whole crate of rabbits, one escaped individual is rarely enough

Eastern cottontail

to lead to a successful population. A non-native population has become established in the Northwest, where eastern cottontail pets escaped. Their descendants now live wild in western Washington State. Another escaped population lives on San Juan Island, off the Washington coast, where the rabbits have been destructive to the habitat due to their high numbers. This species is the European rabbit (*Oryctolagus cuniculus*). Often such populations of non-native species can prove extremely detrimental, but the San Juan rabbits have been useful as prey for the local bald eagles.

SKUNK

The disagreeable substance that skunks emit from their scent glands is their primary form of protection. It is so effective that people and other animals give skunks a wide berth. As a result, they spray only on rare occasions. When they do spray, it is only after they have given ample warning, and it is never without provocation. Even then, their spray doesn't travel very far, so you'd have to be almost on top of a skunk to get hit. Since they don't do any harm, other than the occasional rabid skunk, and seldom spray anyone, there is little reason to fear them. Most of the skunks we smell are those that have been run over.

Several species live in North America north of Mexico. By some counts there are six, but odds are better that there are only four; a couple of species probably are only geographic variants that don't merit status as separate species. The four distinct species fall into three groups, which are recognized as distinct genera. These are *Spilogale*, which is the spotted skunk (*Spilogale putorius*); *Conepatus*, the hognose skunk (*Conepatus leuconotus*); and *Mephitis*, which includes two species, the striped skunk (*Mephitis mephitis*) and the hooded skunk (*Mephitis macroura*). The spotted skunk is black with a white spot on the forehead, a white spot under each ear, and four broken, irregular white stripes down the neck, back, and sides. The tip of the tail is also white. The spotted skunk is several inches shorter than the other species which range from about 12 to 19 inches (30 to 48 cm) long from the tip of the nose to the end of the body, excluding the tail, which is usually almost as long as the body. The hognose skunk has a naked, elongate snout. Its back and tail are entirely white and the lower sides, legs, and belly are black. The striped skunk has a narrow white stripe right down the middle of the forehead, and a broad white area on the back of the neck that divides into two white stripes, forming a V at the shoulders; each of these stripes goes back along the sides to the tail. The hooded skunk appears as either of two different color morphs, with intermediate variants. One is almost entirely white; the other is nearly all black except for two white stripes along the sides.

The spotted skunk is found through much of the United States from the Pacific Northwest to Pennsylvania and south to the southern tip of Florida. The striped skunk is even more widely distributed; it ranges through most of southern Canada and all of the lower 48 states. The hooded skunk is confined to southern Arizona and New Mexico and south through Mexico; the hognose skunk is also confined to the Southwest, parts of Colorado, Arizona, New Mexico, and Texas.

The striped skunk is most likely the species that comes into contact with the greatest number of people, although sometimes you might see a spotted skunk at night by a campsite. The varied diet of all skunks consists of fruit, berries, green plants, insects, grubs, amphibians, eggs (especially turtle eggs), young birds, small rodents, carrion, and garbage. Skunks can't climb, and their dens are always on the ground, either in other animals' holes or under buildings, which can bring them into contact with people. Also, since their diet is so varied, they are prime candidates for living near people, since the more omnivorous species are among those that do best around humans.

Most dogs, cats, and children know enough to give skunks the right of way, so they rarely have to bite, run, or spray. Some animals make the mistake of getting too close to a skunk, but they seldom make the same mistake a second time. Because nothing wants to bother a skunk, it is not unusual to see them walking about as if they hadn't a worry in the world. Those that get run over may be hit because the headlights are disorienting, or the motorist may not see them until it is too late. Because skunks have such a bad reputation, however, they aren't welcome in most densely populated areas, but many smaller cities and suburbs across the country have relatively large skunk populations.

BIG BROWN BAT

The big brown bat (*Eptesicus fuscus*) is only one of the approximately 900 bat species found throughout the world, representing nearly 25 percent of the 3,800 species of mammals. Mexico, with more than 300, has more species of bats than any other country. North of Mexico there are about 40 species. The big brown bat is probably the most widespread, though possibly not the most numerous. Another common and widespread species is the little brown Myotis (*Myotis lucifugus*). Some cave-dwelling species are so abundant at specific caves that they may outnumber other species found in the rest of the country.

Bats are very difficult to identify on the wing, as well as in the hand, but in flight, the big brown bat can be distinguished from other native species by its relatively large size. They are 4 to 5 inches (10.2 to 12.7 cm) long and have a wingspan of about 12 inches (30 cm). Their steady, directed flight is also distinctive. This is usually the bat seen flying around street lights in cities and suburbs, where they are attracted to insects drawn by the light. Many bats that live in urban areas seek shelter nearby, roosting during the day beneath roof overhangs or in enclosed, protected areas where they are secluded from other species, particularly people.

Some species of bats fly through the woods; others fly out in the open; still others prefer to fly over streams or marshes. Some species eat nectar, fruit, blood, and frogs or fish, in addition to insects. Most of the bats found in North America feed on insects caught in flight. The big brown bat tends to feed while flying fairly high over open areas such as meadows, fields, and water.

For years, bats have been maligned or unappreciated, but a recent push to change their image came about as a result of the detrimental effects of stories about vampires, rabies, and bats getting caught in people's hair, all of which were either blatantly false or greatly exaggerated. The image campaign seems to be helping. People are actually starting to put up bat houses, which are similar to bird houses. Evidently these people know that the number of caves and other good roosting sites

Little brown Myotis

Big brown bat

has declined over the years due to development, so the bats now need man-made habitats. Bats do keep down the numbers of mosquitoes and other insects, actually consuming as many as 3,000 insects a night, so even people who aren't particularly enlightened may feel bats are worth protecting; yet many bat species are declining in numbers to the point of being endangered. It is hoped that the innovative bat houses will take hold and prove helpful. These large wooden structures are closed on the top and the sides, but the bottom is open; the inside has crevices where the bats can hang on. Bat houses are constructed with inner slats that can be moved and arranged to suit the size of the local species. The open bottom allows bats to enter, but it keeps out other species, such as birds, mice, and squirrels, which might otherwise use the bat house as a nest box. Bat Conservation International is now selling bat houses and pushing the profits back into the organization, which has its headquarters at the University of Texas in Austin.

FOX, WOLF, COYOTE, DOG

Foxes, wolves, and coyotes are wild dogs native to North America. Each has suffered markedly from human encroachment, mostly because farms presented opportunities that were too great for the animals to pass up in terms of the relatively easy prey represented by the penned-up chickens, turkeys, ducks, goats, sheep, and other domestic animals. Coming in direct competition with farmers has never been the best way for an animal to earn a living. In most instances, if a farmer so much as suspects an animal of reducing his profits, he kills it. Hundreds of years of such

Coyote

run-ins have pushed some of these animals to the brink of extinction. Most have been extirpated from entire regions.

Both the red fox (*Vulpes vulpes*) and the gray fox (*Urocyon cinereoargenteus*) still persist in many suburbs and even in some remote parts of major cities, though they are seldom seen in New York City anymore. In London, there are areas where foxes are reported to be doing quite well. Foxes are very shy, always two steps ahead of any human in the area, but every once in a while one will be seen. A sighting usually comes as a big surprise to residents, who never dreamed that foxes lived in their area. One reason foxes are seen so infrequently is that they are active primarily at night.

The gray wolf (*Canis lupus*) has been almost entirely eliminated from the southern 48 states, though it is doing well in some parts of Alaska. The red wolf (*Canis niger*) is one of the most endangered mammals in North America. Until recently it was still seen infrequently in a few southern areas, but now the last 75 animals are all being held in captivity where they are being bred. Soon, if all goes according to schedule, breeding pairs of red wolves will be released from their holding pens in North Carolina in a first step to reintroduce this species to the East.

The coyote (*Canis latrans*) was once earmarked by the U.S. government for total elimination, and the results of this policy were disastrous through much of its range. Coyotes once roamed from Alaska through the western states of Mexico, though they were not present in most eastern states. Interestingly, recent accounts of coyotes from many areas in the Northeast show that this species has moved into areas where it has never lived before. Apparently the void left by the extirpation of the gray wolf opened up opportunities that the coyote has been able to exploit. Competition from wolves defending their territory probably excluded coyotes from the East until the wolves were eliminated. However, the coyote that had begun to move into the Northeast is not identical to that of several hundred years ago. All species in the *Canis* genus are closely related and can interbreed without difficulty. That is what has been happening in many areas where coyotes and red wolves occurred together. As a result, the differences between the two, which were slight to begin with, have become even more nebulous. Coyotes have also been mating with domestic dogs, resulting in hybrids referred to as coydogs. Coyotes and gray wolves are not nearly as tolerant of each other, however; where the two overlap, the coyote usually moves on elsewhere.

Coyotes used to be restricted to areas west of the Mississippi, but they may now be in all the eastern states. The same adaptability and opportunistic behavior that brought them into conflict with farmers has proved an asset in non-farm areas. They occur in just about every habitat this country has, from forests to deserts, and from mountains to the shore. Unlike most other North American mammals, this species seems to be able to survive almost anywhere, even in many suburbs. Positive identification is not always easy once they have lived near densely populated areas for a while, because that's where mixing with domestic dogs becomes common. As a result, it's sometimes hard to tell the difference between a pet dog, a feral dog, a coydog, a coyote, a hybrid of a coyote, and a red wolf.

The importance of domestic dogs (*Canis familiaris*) in urban and suburban areas should not be underestimated. While the wild dogs have suffered mercilessly from human brutality, domestic breeds have been the beneficiaries of human kindness, shelter, and companionship. In exchange, dogs give friendship and loyalty. All they require is a meal a day and an occasional romp outside. But during that romp they will, if allowed to run loose, chase down practically anything that moves, or that smells. The result is not just a lot of scared animals, but a lot of dead animals. When unleashed, man's best friend is a powerful predator, probably one of the most destructive predators in suburbs and city parks.

Even though dogs are domesticated, they still have a substantial amount of the wild animal in them. What's worse, unlike wild predators such as bobcats (*Lynx rufus*) and coyotes, unleashed dogs will chase down deer at an alarming rate, killing as many as seven or eight in a day. The problem is especially bad when spring comes to some regions where whitetail deer (*Odocoileus virginianus*) have made it through the winter but are hungry and weak. These deer often fall victim to packs of family pets that are allowed to run loose. In Vermont, game wardens are empowered to shoot dogs seen chasing deer, a powerful incentive for lazy owners to exercise their pets properly—by walking them on a leash.

Dogs haven't always been domesticated. Putting a precise date on when their domestication actually began is difficult because the bones of wolves, jackals, and early domestic dogs are not easy to differentiate. There is some evidence that dogs were already domesticated by the late Paleolithic period. It is believed that domestication began when people took in pups, which were easily raised in captivity. The people soon became fond of these new pets, which were friendly and good natured. Dogs are social animals. When raised with people rather than other dogs, they develop a bond with their captors that is not unlike the bond they might have formed with individuals of their own species.

Canids may have been initially taken in, just as the young of many other species that are brought home from time to time, but given the success of these animals, generations have been raised in close contact with people. In time, the dogs came to depend on their human companions for food, and as the relationship grew, dogs began to perform tasks that made them helpful to their owners—hunting, herding, guarding, and so forth—strengthening the dog-human bond.

Domestic dogs are generally thought of as a distinct species, but it should be kept in mind that they descended from the many species of *Canis* that people came into contact with over a period of thousands of years. With over 55 million pet dogs in the United States, an estimated two-thirds of which are eventually abandoned, problems associated with feral dogs do not appear to be about to decline unless something is done to reduce the amount of pet mismanagement.

CAT

Unlike the dog, which has been living in association with people as a domesticated animal for as much as 12,000 years and has the distinction of being the animal with by far the longest history of domestication, the domestic cat (*Felis catus*) is a relative newcomer to captivity. This could be part of the reason why so many people still believe that cats are independent. Part of that misperception is more closely related to the inherent differences between animals in the dog family and those in the cat family. Social structure and behavior differ markedly.

Domestic cat

With the development of agriculture, fields of grain began to attract granivores, such as rodents. These animals in turn attracted small members of the cat family in the genus *Felis*. Later, grain was stored in vast quantities for use between harvests. These storage areas, too, attracted large, unwelcome rodent populations. The wild cats helped control these rodents, and for this they were valued; in some cultures, notably Egypt, they were revered.

There is evidence from 4,300 years ago that the Egyptians already had a domestic cat, but this date has not been generally agreed on. Some scientists place the date for the earliest domestication of the cat at 3,200 years ago. Cats spread from Egypt to other countries, where domestication continued. In each host country the domestic breed hybridized with the local wild cat. The European wild cat (*Felis silvestris*), which is found through Europe and Asia Minor, hybridized with the domestic breed when the Egyptian variety was brought north. Tame cats bred with the wild cats in each region until the breed became a mixture that appears to have races of many different species. Some breeds have considerably more of one species than another. For instance, the domesticated Persian cat is thought to contain genes from the Pallas or steppe cat (*Felis manul*).

In some parts of the world, cats have reverted to a more wild type after having gone feral. Many of these feral populations have been extremely detrimental to local populations of other species. For instance, many islands in the South Pacific that previously lacked any mammalian predators now have cats that thrive on birds that breed there. Only those birds that can defend their nests have been able to survive; many of the other species are no longer found breeding on any of these islands. Off New Zealand, the Stephen Island wren (*Xenicus lyalli*) was discovered in 1894, and during the same year the lighthouse keeper's cat drove it to extinction.

Suburbs and cities have pet and feral cats that roam at will and play an important role in the current structure of urban ecosystems. New York City alone has approximately 300,000 pet cats. If only a small percentage of those cats escape, are released, or are allowed to come and go as they please, they could have a significant effect on the local species. If we then add in the cats that are already feral, the number of predaceous cats is even more impressive.

WHALES AND PORPOISES

The marine mammals include whales, porpoises, walruses, seals, sea lions, and sea otters. Few of these mammals live in urban areas, but because whales are occasionally seen in densely populated regions, I will briefly mention them here.

In addition to an occasional stranding near a city or town, whales and porpoises regularly pass by many urban centers during their spring and fall migrations. In some areas, small industries have grown up around whale-watching. Boatloads of whale-watchers go out of Cape Cod and Montauk, Long Island. For information, contact the Okeanos Ocean Research Foundation in Hampton Bays, New York. On the West Coast, migrating gray whales (*Eschrichtius robustus*) have been a tourist attraction for years. People go out in boats to watch as approximately 11,000 grays migrate along the coastline between their summer feeding grounds off Alaska and their winter breeding lagoons along the shores of Baja California. During the migrations, boats regularly leave points along the coast. Some of the best towns to leave from are Mission, San Diego, Monterey Bay, San Pedro, and Redondo Beach. A good place to see whales from shore is at Point Reyes Lighthouse north of San Francisco.

Humphrey the Humpback Whale made headlines in October 1985 and drew crowds in California. Humpbacks feed in the Alaskan waters during the summer, then head south for the winter. For some reason, Humphrey left the normal course on the way south. Instead of continuing along the coast, the huge whale swam under the Golden Gate Bridge into San Francisco Bay. Television crews soon appeared, and Humphrey's trip inland made the network news. Almost 70 miles from the ocean, Humphrey finally stopped at the Cache Slough, and stayed there.

Concerned citizens and scientists wanted to get Humphrey back to the Pacific. They organized a flotilla of boats, and they banged pipes trying to get Humphrey back on course. It took some work, but eventually they got the whale to swim back underneath the Cache Slough Bridge, but Humphrey stopped at the Rio Vista Bridge. Thinking the noise from the traffic might have confused the whale, the people stopped traffic, raised the drawbridge, and banged on pipes until Humphrey went under the bridge. But again the whale stopped and refused to go any farther.

Finally, some biologists brought recordings of the sounds that whales make when they are feeding. This ploy worked. The whale followed the sound equipment back to the bay and eventually out into the ocean. Then, in August 1986, Humphrey was seen again, migrating back down the coast, having survived the ordeal without making the same mistake twice. Humpbacks also migrate close to the East Coast each year and can be seen from whale-watching boats.

There was another whale rescue with a similar happy ending not too long before the Humphrey episode. About 3,000 white beluga whales (*Delphinapterus leucas*), representing approximately 10 percent of the entire world population, got trapped in the Senyavina Strait of the Bering Sea when their escape route froze over, making it impossible for them to get out without suffocating. In time their opening in the ice was also going to freeze over, killing the belugas. The Soviet Union sent an icebreaker to cut an escape route, but the whales couldn't be persuaded to take it until the Russians began playing recorded music full-blast from the deck. Jazz didn't work, but classical music is said to have lured the belugas, and they followed the icebreaker to safety.

Another beluga was in the news two years in a row. During the summers of 1985 and 1986, a white beluga stayed near the Connecticut shore where people got to know it and even swam with it. Again in 1986, at the beginning of the summer, it returned along the shore, and people saw it frequently. Then one day the whale washed ashore perforated with bullet holes. Apparently some boaters had used the beluga for target practice.

For several years in a row, a beluga was sighted along Fire Island, a barrier island off the south shore of Long Island that is the home of a summer resort community.

Beluga whales are well adapted to arctic conditions, where they live and breed in great numbers. It is not known why they usually remain in more northern waters, considering that they also appear to do well in warmer waters. It may be partly because of the competition in the more southern waters from established species such as harbor porpoises (*Phocoena phocoena*), harbor seals (*Phoca vitulina*), and gray seals (*Halichoerus grypus*) in the coastal waters, and white-sided dolphins (*Lagenorhyn-*

chus acutus), white-beaked dolphins (*Lagenorhynchus albirostris*), pilot whales (*Globicephala melaena*), and other species in the offshore waters. Sharks, which are more numerous in the warmer waters, could also play a role in limiting the whales' range to northern waters. Or maybe their pinkish color makes them more vulnerable to the stronger solar radiation in the more southern waters.

CONCLUSION

Populations of cities in Third World nations are growing at an average annual rate of 3.5 percent, considerably faster than the rate of growth of most Western cities. By the year 2000, the United Nations estimates that fifteen cities in underdeveloped countries will have grown to between 11 million and 26 million people, larger than all but the five largest cities in the world today. Such growth will greatly increase the burden on the environment, with air and water quality suffering. No one looks forward to the crowded urban conditions, nor the environmental deterioration, but regardless of how bad things get, even these megacities will still harbor an impressive cadre of urban organisms—those species that can tolerate such conditions.

Not all cities, however, are growing uncontrollably. Many cities, such as New York, appear to have reached a plateau, maintained by overcrowding and by market conditions. While developers continue to construct more office space, the number of residents has leveled off. It's encouraging, though possibly premature, to think that there are cities where the quality of life doesn't have to continually diminish until little is left but one huge slum.

European and American cities have shown a degree of stability that the developing nations may eventually emulate, but not until they have suffered considerably during the interim. Although most major Western cities were built as a hodgepodge over hundreds of years, experiencing more than their share of ups and downs, they now exhibit a certain amount of charm and beauty. The net result is distinctive and attractive, and the process involved is worth examining.

The first thing people do when they move to a forested region is clear the trees. If they move to open country, to the plains or a desert, they plant trees. Roads and buildings are then constructed, street trees are planted, and parks are created. Besides changing things for functional and economic reasons, we also attempt to make our surroundings aesthetically pleasing.

Our aesthetic sense is, to some extent, learned, but there may also be a genetic component. Gordon Orians, a professor at the University of Washington, measured the environmental parameters of the African savannah where humans spent much of their evolutionary history. He was attempting to see if there might be similarities between the African savannah and the habitats we continually create for ourselves around the world.

Orians postulated that humans are driven to clear the undergrowth, cut the trees, and then replant some trees because of our genetic background. We evolved in Africa where there were few trees and little undergrowth, in areas where we could see long distances, where we could see the predators before they got too close. When they did get close, there was always a tree nearby that could be climbed. This idea may seem far-fetched, but it's interesting.

Although cities don't have the beauty we would expect in a remote national park, parks like Yosemite and Yellowstone are no longer so remote. Their traffic jams rival ours. It's become so difficult, so expensive, and so inconvenient to leave our urban and suburban environments, the only thing that makes sense is to learn to appreciate our everyday surroundings.

The Urban Naturalist describes the many interesting organisms of our cities and suburbs, fauna and flora that may prove to be as exotic as any to be discovered thousands of miles away; for this, there's no need to wait till your next vacation.

REFERENCES FOR ADDITIONAL READING

GENERAL TOPICS

Barth, Michael C., and Titus, James G. (eds.). 1984. *Greenhouse Effect and Sea Level Rise.* Van Nostrand Reinhold. New York. 325 pp.

Boyle, Robert H., and Boyle, R. Alexander. 1983. *Acid Rain.* Nick Lyons Books. New York. 146 pp.

Clapham, W.B., Jr. 1973. *Natural Ecosystems.* Macmillan. New York. 248 pp.

Claus, George, and Bolander, Karen. 1977. *Ecological Sanity.* McKay. New York. 592 pp.

Coyle, David Cushman. 1957. *Conservation: An American Story of Conflict and Accomplishment.* Rutgers University Press. New Brunswick, N.J. 284 pp.

Cuyvers, Luc. 1984. *Ocean Uses and Their Regulation.* John Wiley & Sons. New York. 179 pp.

Darling, F. Fraser, and Milton, John P. 1966. *Future Environments of North America.* Natural History Press. Garden City, N.Y. 767 pp.

Disch, Robert (ed.). 1970. *The Ecological Conscience.* Prentice-Hall. Englewood Cliffs, N.J. 206 pp.

Ehrenfeld, David W. 1972. *Conserving Life on Earth.* Oxford University Press. New York. 360 pp.

Ehrlich, Paul, and Ehrlich, Anne. 1981. *Extinction.* Random House. New York. 305 pp.

Elton, Charles S. 1958. *The Ecology of Invasions by Animals and Plants.* John Wiley & Sons. New York. 181 pp.

Esposito, John C. 1970. *Vanishing Air.* Grossman. New York. 328 pp.

Frankel, O.H., and Soule, Michael E. 1981. *Conservation and Evolution.* Cambridge University Press. New York. 327 pp.

George, Carl J., and McKinley, Daniel. 1974. *Urban Ecology in Search of an Asphalt Rose*. McGraw-Hill. New York. 181 pp.

Heckscher, August. 1977. *Open Spaces: The Life of American Cities*. Harper & Row. New York. 386 pp.

Hoage, R.J. (ed.). 1985. *Animal Extinctions*. Smithsonian Institution Press. Washington, D.C. 192 pp.

McCurdy, Dwight R. 1985. *Park Management*. Southern Illinois University Press. Carbondale, Ill. 250 pp.

Myers, Norman. 1979. *The Sinking Ark*. Pergamon. Elmsford, N.Y. 307 pp.

Noyes, John H., and Progulske, Donald R. (eds.). 1974. "Wildlife in an urbanizing environment." Symposium, Springfield, Mass. Nov. 27–29, 1973. Planning and Resource Development Series, No. 28. Holdsworth Natural Resources Center, Cooperative Extension Service, University of Massachusetts. U.S. Department of Agriculture and County Extension Services. Springfield, Mass. 182 pp.

Regenstein, Lewis. 1975. *The Politics of Extinction*. Macmillan. New York. 280 pp.

Schelling, Thomas C. 1983. *Incentives for Environmental Protection*. MIT Press. Cambridge, Mass. 355 pp.

Schonewald-Cox, Christine M.; Chambers, Steven M.; MacBryde, Bruce; and Thomas, Larry. (eds.). 1983. *Genetics and Conservation*. Benjamin/Cummings. Menlo Park, Calif. 722 pp.

Seneca, Joseph J., and Taussig, Michael K. 1984. *Environmental Economics*. Prentice-Hall. Englewood Cliffs, N.J. 349 pp.

Stewart, Darryl. 1978. *From the Edge of Extinction*. Frederick Warne Ltd. London. 191 pp.

Wagner, Richard H. 1971. *Environment and Man*. Norton. New York. 491 pp.

GRASSES AND WILDFLOWERS

Angier, Bradford. 1967. *Free for the Eating*. Stackpole. Harrisburg, Pa. 191 pp.

Armstrong, Margaret. 1915. *Field Book of Western Wild Flowers*. Putnam. New York. 644 pp.

Baker, Mary Francis. 1926. *Florida Wild Flowers*. Macmillan. New York. 256 pp.

Berglund, Berndt, and Bolsby, Clare E. 1977. *The Complete Outdoorsman's Guide to Edible Wild Plants*. Scribner. New York. 189 pp.

Bianchini, Francesco, and Corbetta, Francesco. 1976. *The Complete Book of Fruits and Vegetables*. Crown. New York. 303 pp.

_____. 1985. *The Complete Book of Health Plants: Atlas of Medicinal Plants*. Crescent. New York. 242 pp.

Blanchan, Neltje. 1926. *Wild Flowers*. Doubleday, Doran. New York. 270 pp.

Britton, Nathaniel Lord, and Brown, Addison. 1970. *An Illustrated Flora of the Northern United States and Canada*, Vol. 1–3. Dover. New York. 2052 pp.

Coon, Nelson. 1979. *Using Plants for Healing*. Rodale. Emmaus, Pa. 272 pp.

Costello, David F. 1975. *The Prairie World*. Crowell. New York. 242 pp.

Crockett, Lawrence J. 1977. *Wildly Successful Plants: A Handbook of North American Weeds*. Collier. New York. 268 pp.

Culpeper, Nicolas. 1981. *Culpeper's Complete Herbal and English Physician*. Printer Industria Grafica. Barcelona, Spain. 240 pp.

Dana, Mrs. William Starr. 1895. *How to Know the Wild Flowers*. Scribner. New York. 373 pp.

Elias, Thomas S., and Dykeman, Peter A. 1982. *Field Guide to North American Edible Wild Plants*. Outdoor Life Books. New York. 286 pp.

Elliott, Douglass B. 1976. *Roots: An Underground Botany and Forager's Guide*. Chatham Press. Old Greenwich, Conn. 128 pp.

Freeman, Margaret B. 1943. *Herbs for the Mediaeval Household For Cooking, Healing, and Divers Uses*. Metropolitan Museum of Art. New York. 48 pp.

Gibbons, Euell. 1962. *Stalking the Wild Asparagus*. McKay. New York. 303 pp.

———. 1971. *Stalking the Good Life*. McKay. New York. 247 pp.

Gordon, Lesley. 1980. *A Country Herbal*. Gallery Books. New York. 208 pp.

Harris, Ben Charles. 1971. *Eat the Weeds*. Barre Publishers. Barre, Mass. 223 pp.

Hitchcock, A.S. 1971. *Manual of the Grasses of the United States*, Vols. 1, 2. Dover. New York. 1051 pp.

Jepson, Willis Linn. 1911. *A Flora of Western Middle California*. Cunningham, Curtiss, Welch. San Francisco. 515 pp.

Knobel, Edward. 1980. *Field Guide to the Grasses, Sedges, and Rushes of the United States*. Dover. New York. 83 pp.

Mathews, F. Schuyler. 1902. *Fieldbook of American Wild Flowers*. Knickerbocker Press. New York. 552 pp.

Muenscher, Walter Conrad. 1944. *Aquatic Plants of the United States*. Comstock. Ithaca, N.Y. 374 pp.

———. 1951. *Poisonous Plants of the United States*. Macmillan. New York. 277 pp.

———. 1980. *Weeds*. Cornell University Press. Ithaca, N.Y. 586 pp.

Munz, Philip A. 1964. *Shore Wildflowers of California, Oregon, and Washington*. University of California Press. Berkeley, Calif. 122 pp.

Peterson, Lee Allen. 1977. *A Field Guide to Edible Wild Plants of Eastern and Central North America*. Houghton Mifflin. Boston. 330 pp.

Peterson, Roger Tory, and McKenny, Margaret. 1968. *A Field Guide to Wildflowers of Northeastern and Northcentral North America*. Houghton Mifflin. Boston. 420 pp.

Sharsmith, Helen K. 1965. *Spring Wildflowers of the San Francisco Bay Region*. University of California Press. Berkeley, Calif. 192 pp.

Stokes, Donald W., and Stokes, Lillian Q. 1985. *A Guide to Wildflowers*. Little, Brown. Boston. 371 pp.

Stubbendieck, J.; Hatch, Stephan L; and Hirsch, Kathie J. 1986. *North American Range Plants*. University of Nebraska Press. Lincoln, Nebr. 465 pp.

Venning, Frank D. 1984. *Wildflowers of North America*. Golden Press. New York. 340 pp.

TREES

Apgar, Austin C. 1892. *Trees of the Northern United States*. American Book Co. New York. 224 pp.

Berrang, Paul, and Karnosky, David F. 1983. *Street Trees for Metropolitan New York*. New York Botanical Garden Institute of Urban Horticulture. No. 1. Maar Printing Service. Poughkeepsie, N.Y. 179 pp.

Berry, James Berthold. 1966. *Western Forest Trees*. Dover. New York. 238 pp.

Britton, Nathaniel Lord. 1908. *North American Trees*. Holt. New York. 894 pp.

Brockman, C. Frank. 1968. *Trees of North America*. Golden Press. New York. 280 pp.

Constantine, Albert, Jr. 1966. *Know Your Woods*. Constantine. Bronx, N.Y. 384 pp.

Graaf, M.M. 1970. *Tree Trails in Central Park*. Greensward Foundation. New York. 189 pp.

Graves, Arthur Harmount. 1955. *Winter Key to the Woody Plants of the Northeastern United States and Adjacent Canada*. Published by the Author. Wallingford, Conn. 33 pp.

Hepting, George H. 1971. *Diseases of Forest and Shade Trees of the United States*. U.S. Dept. of Agriculture. Agriculture Handbook No. 386. U.S. Government Printing Office. Washington, D.C. 658 pp.

Johnson, Warren T., and Lyon, Howard H. 1976. *Insects that Feed on Trees and Shrubs*. Cornell University Press. Ithaca, N.Y. 464 pp.

Keeler, Harriet L. 1903. *Our Northern Shrubs and How to Identify Them*. Scribner. New York. 521 pp.

Koller, Gary L., and Dirr, Michael A. 1979. "Street trees for home and municipal landscapes." *Arnoldia*, vol. 39. no. 3. May/June 1979. 237 pp.

Little, Elbert L. 1980. *The Audubon Society Field Guide to North American Trees*. Knopf. New York. 714 pp.

Longyear, Burton O. 1927. *Trees and Shrubs of the Rocky Mountain Region*. Putnam. Knickerbocker Press. New York. 244 pp.

Mathews, F. Schuyler. 1915. *Field Book of American Trees and Shrubs*. Putnam. New York. 465 pp.

Montgomery, Frederick Howard. 1977. *Seeds and Fruits of Plants of Eastern Canada and Northeastern United States*. University of Toronto Press. Toronto, Ont., Canada. 232 pp.

Muenscher, Walter Conrad. 1950. *Keys to Woody Plants*. Comstock. Ithaca, N.Y. 108 pp.

Nelson, Peter K., and McGourty, Frederick. 1982. "The hundred finest trees and shrubs for temperate climates." Special Printing, *Plants and Gardens*, vol. 13, no. 3, #25. 80 pp.

Parkhurst, H.E. 1903. *Trees, Shrubs, and Vines of the Northeastern United States*. Scribner. New York. 451 pp.

Peattie, Donald Culross. 1950. *A Natural History of Trees of Eastern and Central North America*. Houghton Mifflin. Boston. 606 pp.

Phillips, George R; Gibbs, Frank J; Mattoon, Wilbur R. 1959. *Forest Trees of Oklahoma*. Forestry Division, Oklahoma State Board of Agriculture. Oklahoma City, Okla. 135 pp.

Platt, Rutherford. 1965. *A Pocket Guide to Trees*. Washington Square Press. New York. 256 pp.

Preston, Richard J., Jr. 1940. *Rocky Mountain Trees*. Iowa State College Press. Ames, Iowa. 285 pp.

Rogers, Julia Ellen. 1914. *The Tree Book*. Doubleday, Page. Garden City, N.Y. 589 pp.

_____. 1926. *Trees*. Doubleday, Doran. New York. 291 pp.

Rogers, Walter E. 1935. *Tree Flowers of Forest, Park, and Street*. Published by the Author. Appleton, Wis. 500 pp.

Spaulding, Perley. 1961. *Foreign Diseases of Forest Trees of the World*. U.S. Dept. of Agriculture. Agriculture Handbook. No. 197. U.S. Government Printing Office. Washington, D.C. 361 pp.

Tattar, Terry A. 1978. *Diseases of Shade Trees*. Academic Press. New York. 361 pp.

Van Der Linden, Peter J., and Farrar, Donald R. 1984. *Forest and Shade Trees of Iowa*. Iowa State University Press. Ames, Iowa. 133 pp.

INSECTS

Borror, Donald J., and DeLong, Dwight, M. 1971. *An Introduction to the Study of Insects*. Holt Rinehart Winston. New York. 812 pp.

_____, and White, Richard E. 1970. *A Field Guide to the Insects of America North of Mexico*. Houghton Mifflin. Boston. 404 pp.

Chapman, R.F. 1982. *The Insects: Structure and Function*. Harvard University Press. Cambridge, Mass. 919 pp.

Cloudsley-Thompson, John. 1978. *Animal Migration*. Putnam. New York. 120 pp.

Comstock, John Henry. 1914. *The Spider Book*. Doubleday, Page. Garden City, N.Y. 721 pp.

_____. 1924. *An Introduction to Entomology*. Comstock. Ithaca, N.Y. 1044 pp.

_____. 1938. *Insect Life: An Introduction to Nature Study*. Appleton. New York. 349 pp.

_____, and Comstock, Anna Botsford. 1904. *How to Know the Butterflies*. Appleton. New York. 311 pp.

Covell, Charles V., Jr. 1984. *A Field Guide to the Moths of Eastern North America*. Houghton Mifflin. Boston. 496 pp.

Dethier, Vincent G. 1962. *To Know A Fly*. Holden-Day. San Francisco. 119 pp.

_____. 1984. *The Ecology of a Summer House*. University of Massachusetts Press. Amherst, Mass. 133 pp.

Dickerson, Mary C. 1901. *Moths and Butterflies*. Ginn and Company, Publishers. Boston. 343 pp.

Doane, Rennie W. 1910. *Insects and Disease*. Holt. New York. 227 pp.

Fabre, J. Henri. 1919. *The Life of the Fly*. Hodder & Stroughton. London. 477 pp.

_____. 1935. *Insect Adventures*. Dodd, Mead. New York. 287 pp.

Fernald, H.T., and Shepard, Harold H. 1955. *Applied Entomology*. McGraw-Hill. New York. 385 pp.

Fichter, George S. 1966. *Insect Pests*. Golden Press. New York. 160 pp.

Fitch, Henry S. 1963. *Spiders of the University of Kansas Natural History Reservation and Rockefeller Experimental Tract*. University of Kansas Museum of Natural History. Miscellaneous Publication no. 33. Lawrence, Kans. 202 pp.

Headstrom, Richard. 1968. *Nature in Miniature*. Knopf. New York. 400 pp.

Herms, William Brodbeck, and Gray, Harold Farnsworth. 1940. *Mosquito Control*. The Commonwealth Fund. Oxford University Press. New York. 315 pp.

Holland, W.J. 1904. *The Moth Book*. Doubleday, Page. Garden City, N.Y. 479 pp.

_____. 1905. *The Butterfly Book*. Doubleday, Page. Garden City, N.Y. 382 pp.

Howard, Leland O. 1904. *The Insect Book*. Doubleday, Page. Garden City, N.Y. 429 pp.

Howe, William H. 1975. *The Butterflies of North America*. Doubleday. Garden City, N.Y. 633 pp.

Jaeger, B. 1859. *The Life of North American Insects*. Harper. New York. 319 pp.

Jaques, H.E. 1941. *How to Know the Insects*. Published by the Author. Mt. Pleasant, Iowa. 140 pp.

Jordan, William H., Jr. 1977. *Windowsill Ecology*. Rodale. Emmaus, Pa. 229 pp.

Lawrence, Gale. 1986. *The Indoor Naturalist: Observing the World of Nature Inside Your Home*. Phalarope Books, Prentice Hall. New York. 210 pp.

Levi, Herbert W., and Levi, Lorna R. 1968. *A Guide to Spiders and Their Kin*. Golden Press. New York 160 pp.

Maeterlinck, Maurice. 1939. *The Life of the White Ant*. Dodd, Mead. New York. 142 pp.

Metcalf, C.L., and Flint, W.P. 1928. *Destructive and Useful Insects*. McGraw-Hill. New York. 918 pp.

Michener, Charles D., and Michener, Mary H. 1951. *American Social Insects*. Van Nostrand. New York. 267 pp.

Milne, Lorus J., and Milne, Margery. 1980. *The Audubon Society Field Guide to North American Insects and Spiders*. Knopf. New York. 989 pp.

Mitchell, John Hanson. 1985. *A Field Guide to Your Own Back Yard*. Norton. New York. 288 pp.

Mitchell, Robert T., and Zim, Herbert S. 1964. *Butterflies and Moths*. Golden Press. New York. 160 pp.

Morse, Roger A. 1974. *The Complete Guide to Beekeeping*. A Sunrise Book. Dutton. New York. 219 pp.

Opler, Paul A., and Krizek, George O. 1984. *Butterflies East of the Great Plains*. Johns Hopkins University Press. Baltimore, Md. 294 pp.

Ordish, George. 1981. *The Living American House: The 350-Year Story of a Home—an Ecological History*. Morrow. New York. 320 pp.

Pennak, Robert W. 1978. *Fresh-Water Invertebrates of the United States*. John Wiley & Sons. New York. 803 pp.

Pyle, Robert Michael. 1981. *The Audubon Society Field Guide to North American Butterflies*. Knopf. New York. 916 pp.

Ricard, Matthieu. 1968. *The Mystery of Animal Migration*. Hill & Wang. New York. 209 pp.

Richards, O.W. 1961. *The Social Insects*. Harper Torchbooks. New York. 219 pp.

Sedgwick, Adam; Sinclair, F.G.; and Sharp, David. 1910. *Peripatus, Myriapods, and Insects*. Macmillan. London. 584 pp.

Stefferud, Alfred (ed.). 1952. *Insects: The Yearbook of Agriculture*. U.S. Dept. of Agriculture. U.S. Government Printing Office. Washington, D.C. 780 pp.

Stokes, Donald W. 1983. *A Guide to Observing Insect Lives*. Little, Brown. Boston. 371 pp.

Tilden, James W., and Smith, Arthur Clayton. 1986. *A Field Guide to Western Butterflies*. Houghton Mifflin. Boston. 370 pp.

von Frisch, Karl. 1950. *Bees: Their Vision, Chemical Senses, and Language*. Cornell University Press. Ithaca, N.Y. 119 pp.

Warren, A., and Goldsmith. F.B. (eds.). 1983. *Conservation in Perspective*. John Wiley & Sons. New York. 474 pp.

White, Richard E. 1983. *A Field Guide to the Beetles of North America*. Houghton Mifflin. Boston. 368 pp.

Wilson, Edward O. 1972. *The Insect Societies*. Belknap Press of Harvard University Press. Cambridge, Mass. 548 pp.

Zim, Herbert S., and Cottam, Clarence. 1956. *Insects*. Golden Press. New York. 160 pp.

FISH

Cacutt, Len. 1979. *British Freshwater Fishes.* Coom Helm Ltd. London, 202 pp.

Cross, Frank B., and Collins, Joseph T. 1975. *Fishes in Kansas.* The University of Kansas Museum of Natural History and State Biological Survey. Public Education Series No. 3. Lawrence, Kans. 189 pp.

Eddy, S. 1957. *How to Know the Freshwater Fishes.* Wm. C. Brown. Dubuque, Iowa. 253 pp.

Fowler, Henry W. 1907. "A supplementary account of the fishes of New Jersey." In the *Annual Report of the New Jersey State Museum.* MacCrellish & Quigley, State Printers. Trenton, N.J. p. 251–408.

Herald, E.S. 1961. *Living Fishes of the World.* Doubleday. Garden City, N.Y. 304 pp.

_____. 1972. *Fishes of North America.* Doubleday. Garden City, N.Y. 255 pp.

Hocutt, Charles H., and Wiley, Edward O. (eds.). 1986. *The Zoogeography of North American Freshwater Fishes.* John Wiley & Sons. New York. 866 pp.

Holcik, Juraj, and Mihalik, Jozef. 1969. *Fresh-Water Fishes.* Spring Books, Hamlyn Publishing Group. New York. 128 pp.

Hubbs, Carl L., and Lagler, Karl F. 1947. *Fishes of the Great Lakes Region.* Cranbrook Institute of Science. Bulletin No. 26. Bloomfield Hills, Mich. 186 pp.

Jordan, David Starr, and Evermann, Barton Warren. 1904. *American Food and Game Fishes.* Doubleday, Page. Garden City, N.Y. 572 pp.

Lagler, Karl F.; Bardach, John E.; and Miller, Robert R. 1962. *Ichthyology.* John Wiley & Sons. New York. 545 pp.

Mackenthun, Kenneth M., and Ingram, William Marcus. 1967. *Biological Associated Problems in Freshwater Environments.* U.S. Dept. of the Interior. Federal Water Pollution Control Administration. U.S. Government Printing Office. Washington, D.C. 287 pp.

Marshall, N.B. 1966. *The Life of Fishes.* World. New York. 402 pp.

Metcalf, Artie L. 1966. "Fishes of the Kansas river system in relation to zoogeography of the Great Plains." University of Kansas Publications. *Museum of Natural History.* Vol 17. No. 3; 23–189. Lawrence, Kans.

Pflieger, William L. 1971. "A distributional study of Missouri fishes." University of Kansas Publications. *Museum of Natural History.* Vol. 20. No. 3: 225–570. Lawrence, Kans.

Schrenkeisen, Ray. 1938. *Field Book of Fresh-Water Fishes of North America North of Mexico.* Putman. New York. 312 pp.

State Board of Fisheries and Game Lake and Pond Survey Unit. 1942. *A Fishery Survey of Important Connecticut Lakes.* State of Connecticut Public Document No. 47. Bulletin No. 63. State Geological and Natural History Survey. Hartford, Conn. 339 pp.

AMPHIBIANS

Bishop, Sherman C. 1943. *Handbook of Salamanders: The Salamanders of the United States, of Canada, and of Lower California.* Comstock. Ithaca, N.Y. 555 pp.

Collins, Joseph T. 1974. *Amphibians and Reptiles in Kansas.* University of Kansas Museum of Natural History. Public Education Series No. 1. Lawrence, Kans. 283 pp.

Cope, Edward Drinker. 1963. *The Batrachia of North America.* Eric Lundberg. Ashton, Md. 525 pp.

DeGraaf, Richard M., and Rudis, Deborah D. 1983. *Amphibians and Reptiles of New England: Habitats and Natural History.* University of Massachusetts Press. Amherst, Mass. 85 pp.

Deuchar, E.M. 1975. *Xenopus: The South African Clawed Frog.* John Wiley & Sons. New York. 246 pp.

Dickerson, Mary C. 1920. *The Frog Book.* Doubleday, Page. Garden City, N.Y. 253 pp.

Goin, Coleman J., and Goin, Olive B. 1971. *Introduction to Herpetology.* W.H. Freeman. San Francisco. 353 pp.

Lazell, James D., Jr. 1976. *This Broken Archipelago: Cape Cod and the Islands, Amphibians and Reptiles.* Quadrangle, New York Times Book Co. New York. 260 pp.

Morris, Percy A. 1974. *An Introduction to the Reptiles and Amphibians of the United States.* Dover. New York. 253 pp.

Mount, Robert H. 1975. *The Reptiles and Amphibians of Alabama.* Agricultural Experiment Station. Auburn University. Auburn, Ala. 345 pp.

Oliver, James A. 1955. *The Natural History of North American Amphibians and Reptiles.* Van Nostrand. Princeton, N.J. 359 pp.

Pickwell, Gayle. 1947. *Amphibians and Reptiles of the Pacific States.* Stanford University Press. Palo Alto, Calif. 236 pp.

Porter, Kenneth R. 1972. *Herpetology.* W.B. Saunders. Philadelphia. 524 pp.

Schwartz, Susan. 1983. *Nature in the Northwest: An Introduction to the Natural History and Ecology of the Northwestern United States from the Rockies to the Pacific.* Prentice-Hall. Englewood Cliffs, N.J. 256 pp.

Smith, Hobart M. 1978. *Amphibians of North America.* Golden Press. New York. 160 pp.

Smith, Philip W. 1961. *The Amphibians and Reptiles of Illinois.* Illinois Natural History Survey Bulletin. Vol 28. Article 1. State of Illinois Dept. of Registration and Education. Natural History Survey Division. Urbana, Ill. 298 pp.

Stebbins, Robert C. 1954. *Amphibians and Reptiles of Western North America.* McGraw-Hill. New York. 536 pp.

_____. 1959. *Reptiles and Amphibians of the San Francisco Bay Region.* University of California Press. Berkeley, Calif. 71 pp.

_____. 1966. *A Field Guide to Western Reptiles and Amphibians.* Houghton Mifflin. Boston. 279 pp.

_____. 1973. *Amphibians and Reptiles of California.* University of California Press. Berkeley, Calif. 152 pp.

Taylor, Douglas H., and Guttman, Sheldon I. (eds.). 1977. *The Reproductive Biology of Amphibians.* Plenum. New York. 475 pp.

Vial, James L. (ed.). 1973. *Evolutionary Biology of the Anurans: Contemporary Research on Major Problems.* University of Missouri Press. Columbia, Mo. 470 pp.

Wilson, Larry David, and Porras, Louis. 1983. *The Ecological Impact of Man on the South Florida Herpetofauna.* The University of Kansas Museum of Natural History. Special Publication No. 9. Lawrence, Kans. 89 pp.

Wright, Albert Hazen, and Wright, Anna Allen. 1949. *Handbook of Frogs and Toads of the United States and Canada.* Cornell University Press. Ithaca, N.Y. 640 pp.

Zim, Herbert S., and Smith, Hobart M. 1956. *Reptiles and Amphibians.* Golden Press. New York. 160 pp.

REPTILES

Anderson, Paul. 1965. *The Reptiles of Missouri.* University of Missouri Press. Columbia, Mo. 330 pp.

Babcock, Harold L. 1971. *Turtles of the Northeastern United States.* Dover. New York. 105 pp.

Bjorndal, Karen A. (ed.). 1982. *Biology and Conservation of Sea Turtles.* Proceedings of the World Conference on Sea Turtle Conservation. Washington, D.C. November 26–30, 1979. Smithsonian Institution Press. Washington, D.C. 583 pp.

Bustard, Robert. 1972. *Sea Turtles: Natural History and Conservation.* Taplinger. New York. 220 pp.

Carr, Archie Fairly, Jr. 1940. *A Contribution to the Herpetology of Florida.* University of Florida Publication. Biological Science Series. Vol. 3. No. 1. Gainesville, Fl. 118 pp.

_____. 1952. *Handbook of Turtles: The Turtles of the United States, Canada, and Baja California.* Cornell University Press. Ithaca, N.Y. 542 pp.

_____. 1973. *So Excellent A Fishe: A Natural History of Sea Turtles.* Anchor. Garden City, N.Y. 266 pp.

Collins, Joseph T. 1974. *Amphibians and Reptiles in Kansas.* University of Kansas Museum of Natural History. Public Education Series No. 1. Lawrence, Kans. 283 pp.

DeGraaf, Richard M., and Rudis, Deborah D. 1983. *Amphibians and Reptiles of New England: Habitats and Natural History.* University of Massachusetts Press. Amherst, Mass. 85 pp.

DeKay, James E. 1842. *Zoology of New York or the New York Fauna; Part 3. Reptiles and Amphibia.* W. and A. White and J. Visscher. Albany, N.Y. 98 pp.

Ditmars, Raymond L. 1908. *The Reptile Book.* Doubleday, Page. Garden City, N.Y. 472 pp.

_____. 1936. *The Reptiles of North America.* Doubleday. Garden City, N.Y. 476 pp.

_____. 1946. *A Field Book of North American Snakes.* Doubleday. Garden City, N.Y. 305 pp.

Ernst, Carl H., and Barbour, Roger W. 1972. *Turtles of the United States.* University of Kentucky Press. Lexington, Ky. 347 pp.

Fitch, Henry S. 1965. "An ecological study of the garter snake, *Thamnophis sirtalis.*" University of Kansas Publications. Museum of Natural History. Vol. 15. No. 10: 493–564. Lawrence, Kans.

Fowler, Henry W. 1907. "The amphibians and reptiles of New Jersey." In the *Annual Report of the New Jersey State Museum.* MacCrellish & Quigley, State Printers. Trenton, N.J. 250 pp.

Heymann, M.M. 1979. *Reptiles and Amphibians of the American Southwest.* Doubleday. Garden City, N.Y. 77 pp.

Lazell, James D., Jr. 1976. *This Broken Archipelago: Cape Cod and the Islands, Amphibians and Reptiles.* Quadrangle, New York Times Book Co. New York. 260 pp.

McCauley, Robert H., Jr. 1945. *The Reptiles of Maryland and the District of Columbia.* Published by the Author. Hagerstown, Md. 194 pp.

Morris, Percy A. 1974. *An Introduction to the Reptiles and Amphibians of the United States.* Dover. New York. 253 pp.

Mount, Robert H. 1975. *The Reptiles and Amphibians of Alabama.* Agricultural Experiment Station. Auburn University. Auburn, Ala. 345 pp.

Oliver, James A. 1955. *The Natural History of North American Amphibians and Reptiles.* Van Nostrand. Princeton, N.J. 359 pp.

Pickwell, Gayle. 1947. *Amphibians and Reptiles of the Pacific States.* Stanford University Press. Palo Alto, Calif. 236 pp.

Pope, Clifford H. 1946. *Turtles of the United States and Canada.* Knopf. New York. 343 pp.

_____. 1955. *The Reptile World: A Natural History of the Snakes, Lizards, Turtles, and Crocodilians.* Knopf. New York. 325 pp.

Pritchard, Peter Charles Howard. 1967. *Living Turtles of the World.* T.F.H. Publications. Neptune City, N.J. 288 pp.

Rudloe, Jack. 1979. *Time of the Turtle.* Penguin. New York. 273 pp.

Ruthven, Alexander G. 1908. *Variations and Genetic Relationships of the Garter Snakes.* Smithsonian Institution United States National Museum. Bulletin 61. U.S. Government Printing Office. Washington, D.C. 201 pp.

Schmidt, Karl P., and Davis, D. Dwight. 1941. *Field Book of Snakes of the United States and Canada*. Putnam. New York. 365 pp.

———, and Inger, Robert F. 1975. *Living Reptiles of the World*. Doubleday. Garden City, N.Y. 287 pp.

Scott, Jack Denton. 1974. *Loggerhead Turtle: Survivor from the Sea*. Putnam. New York. 60 pp.

Smith, Hobart M. 1946. *Handbook of Lizards: Lizards of the United States and of Canada*. Comstock. Ithaca, N.Y. 557 pp.

———. 1982. *Reptiles of North America*. Golden Press. New York. 240 pp.

Smith, Philip W. 1961. "The amphibians and reptiles of Illinois." *Illinois Natural History Survey Bulletin*. Vol. 28. Article 1. State of Illinois Dept. of Registration and Education. Natural History Survey Division. Urbana, Ill. 298 pp.

Stebbins, Robert C. 1954. *Amphibians and Reptiles of Western North America*. McGraw-Hill. New York. 536 pp.

———. 1959. *Reptiles and Amphibians of the San Francisco Bay Region*. University of California Press. Berkeley, Calif. 71 pp.

———. 1966. *A Field Guide to Western Reptiles and Amphibians*. Houghton Mifflin. Boston. 279 pp.

———. 1973. *Amphibians and Reptiles of California*. University of California Press. Berkeley, Calif. 152 pp.

Webb, Robert G. 1970. *Reptiles of Oklahoma*. University of Oklahoma Press. Norman, Okla. 370 pp.

Wilson, Larry David, and Porras, Louis. 1983. *The Ecological Impact of Man on the South Florida Herpetofauna*. University of Kansas, Museum of Natural History. Special Publication No. 9. Lawrence, Kans. 89 pp.

Wright, Albert H., and Wright, Anna A. 1957. *Handbook of Snakes of the United States and Canada*. Vols. 1 and 2. Cornell University Press. Ithaca, N.Y. 1105 pp.

Zappalorti, Robert T. 1976. *The Amateur Zoologist's Guide to Turtles and Crocodilians*. Stackpole. Harrisburg, Pa. 208 pp.

Zim, Herbert S., and Smith, Hobart M. 1956. *Reptiles and Amphibians*. Golden Press. New York. 160 pp.

BIRDS

Arbib, Robert S., Jr.; Pettingill, Olin Sewall, Jr.; and Spofford, Sally Hoyt. 1966. *Enjoying Birds Around New York City*. Houghton Mifflin. Boston. 171 pp.

Bailey, Alfred M., and Niedrach, Robert J. 1965. *Birds of Colorado*, Vols. 1 and 2. Denver Museum of Natural History. Denver, Colo. 895 pp.

Bull, John. 1964. *Birds of the New York Area*. Dover. New York. 540 pp.

_____. 1985. *Birds of New York State*. Cornell University Press. Ithaca, N.Y. 703 pp.

Burton, John A. (ed.). 1973. *Owls of the World: Their Evolution, Structure, and Ecology*. A & W Visual Library. Milan, Italy. 216 pp.

Dubkin, Leonard. 1955. *The Natural History of a Yard*. Henry Regnery. Chicago. 208 pp.

Forbush, Edward Howe. 1907. *Useful Birds and Their Protection*. Massachusetts State Board of Agriculture. Wright & Potter Printing Co. Boston. 437 pp.

_____. 1912. *A History of the Game Birds, Wild-Fowl, and Shore Birds of Massachusetts and Adjacent States*. Massachusetts State Board of Agriculture. Wright & Potter Printing Co. Boston. 622 pp.

Gilbertson and Page Ltd. (eds.). 1933. *Pheasant Rearing and Preservation*. Gilbertson and Page Ltd. Ipswich, England. 206 pp.

Goodwin, Derek. 1976. *Crows of the World*. Cornell University Press. Ithaca, N.Y. 354 pp.

_____. 1978. *Birds of Man's World*. Cornell University Press. Ithaca, N.Y. 183pp.

Kieran, John. 1959. *A Natural History of New York City*. Houghton Mifflin. Boston. 428 pp.

Kinkead, Eugene. 1978. *Wildness Is All Around Us, Notes of an Urban Naturalist*. Dutton. New York. 178 pp.

Knowler, Donald. 1984. *The Falconer of Central Park*. Bantam. New York. 179 pp.

Kress, Stephen W. 1985. *The Audubon Society Guide to Attracting Birds*. Scribner. New York. 377 pp.

Leck, Charles. 1975. *The Birds of New Jersey: Their Habits and Habitats*. Rutgers University Press. New Brunswick, N.J. 190 pp.

Matthews, G.V.T. 1968. *Bird Migration*. Cambridge University Press. Cambridge, England. 197 pp.

McElroy, Thomas P. 1951. *Handbook of Attracting Birds*. Knopf. New York. 163 pp.

Mead, Chris. 1983. *Bird Migration*. Facts On File. New York. 224 pp.

Niedrach, Robert J., and Rockwell, Robert B. 1959. *The Birds of Denver and Mountain Parks*. Denver Museum of Natural History. Popular Series No. 5. Denver, Colo. 203 pp.

Peterson, Roger Tory. 1961. *A Field Guide to Western Birds*. Houghton Mifflin. Boston. 309 pp.

_____. 1980. *A Field Guide to the Birds East of the Rockies*. Houghton Mifflin. Boston. 384 pp.

Proctor, Noble S. 1986. *Garden Birds*. Rodale Press. Emmaus, Penn. 160 pp.

Robbins, Chandler S.; Bruun, Bertel; and Zim, Herbert S. 1983. *Birds of North America*. Golden Press. New York. 360 pp.

Russell, Helen Ross. 1975. *City Critters*. American Nature Society. Wilkins Printers. Cortland, N.Y. 171 pp.

Sage, John Hall; Bishop, Louis Bennett; and Bliss, Walter Parks. 1913. *The Birds of Connecticut*. State of Connecticut State Geological and Natural History Survey Bulletin No. 20. Case, Lockwood, & Brainard Company. Hartford, Conn. 370 pp.

Scanlan-Rohrer, Anne (ed.). 1984. *San Francisco Peninsula Birdwatching*. Sequoia Audubon Society. Burlingame, Calif. 137 pp.

Schmidt-Koenig, Knut, and Keeton, William T. (eds.). 1978. *Animal Migration, Navigation, and Homing*. Symposium held, University of Tubingen, Germany, August 17–20, 1977. Springer-Verlag. New York. 462 pp.

Shriner, Charles A. 1896. *The Birds of New Jersey*. Fish and Game Commission, State of New Jersey. Paterson, N.J. 212 pp.

Stokes, Donald W., and Stokes, Lillian Q. 1979. *Stokes Nature Guides. A Guide to Bird Behavior*. Vol. 1. Little, Brown. Boston. 335 pp.

_____. 1983. *Stokes Nature Guides. A Guide to Bird Behavior*. Vol. 2. Little, Brown. Boston. 334 pp.

Terres, John K. 1953. *Songbirds in Your Garden*. Crowell. New York. 274 pp.

Welty, Joel Carl. 1975. *The Life of Birds*. W. B. Saunders. Philadelphia. 623 pp.

Wheelock, Irene Grosvenor. 1920. *Birds of California*. A. C. McClurg. Chicago. 578 pp.

Wood, Norman A. 1951. *The Birds of Michigan*. Miscellaneous Publications, Museum of Zoology, University of Michigan, Number 75. University of Michigan Press. Ann Arbor, Mich. 559 pp.

MAMMALS

Armstrong, David M. 1972. *Distribution of Mammals in Colorado*. Monograph of the Museum of Natural History, The University of Kansas. Lawrence, Kans. 415 pp.

_____. 1975. *Rocky Mountain Mammals*. Rocky Mountain Nature Association and Rocky Mountain National Park. National Park Service. U.S. Dept. of the Interior. Estes Park, Colo. 174 pp.

Bailey, John Wendell. 1946. *The Mammals of Virginia*. Williams Printing Co. Richmond, Va. 416 pp.

Bennett, Ben. 1983. *The Oceanic Society Field Guide to the Gray Whale*. Legacy. Berkeley, Calif. 50 pp.

Brown, Vinson. 1976. *Sea Mammals and Reptiles of the Pacific Coast*. Collier Macmillan. London. 265 pp.

Burt, William H. 1976. *A Field Guide to the Mammals*. Houghton Mifflin. Boston. 289 pp.

Calhoun, John B. 1962. *The Ecology and Sociology of the Norway Rat*. U.S. Dept. of Health, Education, and Welfare. Public Health Service Publication No.

1008. Bethesda, Md. U.S. Government Printing Office. Washington, D.C. 288 pp.

Cockrum, E. Lendell. 1952. *Mammals of Kansas*. University of Kansas Publications, Museum of Natural History. Vol. 7. No. 1. Lawrence, Kans. 303 pp.

_____. 1962. *Introduction to Mammalogy*. Ronald Press. New York. 455 pp.

Connor, Paul, F. 1971. *The Mammals of Long Island, New York*. Bulletin 416, New York State Museum and Science Service. University of the State of New York. Albany, N.Y. 78 pp.

Davis, P.D.C., and Dent, A.A. 1968. *Animals That Changed the World*. Crowell-Collier. New York. 121 pp.

DeGraaf, Richard M., and Rudis, Deborah D. 1986. *New England Wildlife: Habitat, Natural History, and Distribution*. U.S. Dept. of Agriculture, Forest Service, Northeastern Forest Experiment Station. General Technical Report NE-108. U.S. Government Printing Office. Washington, D.C. 491 pp.

Durrant, Stephen D. 1952. *Mammals of Utah*. University of Kansas, Museum of Natural History. Vol. 6. Lawrence, Kans. 549 pp.

Funkhouser, W.D. 1925. *Wild Life in Kentucky*. Kentucky Geological Survey. Frankfort, Ky. 385 pp.

Godin, Alfred J. 1983. *Wild Mammals of New England*. Globe Pequot. Chester, Conn. 207 pp.

Goodwin, George Gilbert. 1935. *The Mammals of Connecticut*. State of Connecticut State Geological and Natural History Survey. Bulletin No. 53. Hartford, Conn. 221 pp.

Hall, E. Raymond. 1981. *The Mammals of North America*. John Wiley & Sons. New York. 1181 pp.

Hamilton, William J., Jr. 1943. *The Mammals of Eastern United States*. Comstock. Ithaca, N.Y. 432 pp.

Ingles, Lloyd G. 1965. *Mammals of the Pacific States*. Stanford University Press. Stanford, Calif. 506 pp.

Katona, Steven K.; Tough, Valerie; Richardson, David T. 1983. *A Field Guide to the Whales, Porpoises and Seals of the Gulf of Maine and Eastern Canada*. Scribner. New York. 255 pp.

Kieran, John. 1959. *A Natural History of New York City*. Houghton Mifflin. Boston. 428 pp.

Kunz, Thomas H. (ed.). 1982. *Ecology of Bats*. Plenum. New York. 425 pp.

Long, Charles A. 1965. *The Mammals of Wyoming*. University of Kansas, Museum of Natural History. Vol. 14. No. 18: 493–758. Lawrence, Kans.

Nelson, Edward, W. 1918. *Wild Animals of North America*. National Geographic Society. Washington, D.C. 612 pp.

Noyes, John H., and Progulske, Donald R. (eds.). 1974. *Wildlife in an Urbanizing Environment*. Symposium, Springfield, Massachusetts, November 27–29, 1973. Planning and Resource Development, Series no. 28. Holdsworth Natural Resources Center. Cooperative Extension Service, University of Massachusetts. U.S. Dept. of Agriculture and County Extension Services. U.S. Government Printing Office. Washington, D.C. 182 pp.

Palmer, Ralph S. 1954. *The Mammal Guide*. Doubleday. Garden City, N.Y. 384 pp.

Ricciuti, Edward R. 1984. *The New York City Wildlife Guide*. Nick Lyons Books, Schocken. New York. 216 pp.

Schmidly, David J. 1981. *Marine Mammals of the Southeastern United States Coast and the Gulf of Mexico*. U.S. Government Printing Office. Washington, D.C. 165 pp.

South, Frank E.; Hannon, John P.; Willis, John R.; Pengelley, Eric T.; and Alpert, Norman R. (eds.). 1972. *Hibernation and Hypothermia, Perspectives and Challenges*. Symposium, Snowmass-At-Aspen, Colorado, January 3–8, 1971. Elsevier. New York. 743 pp.

Van Gelder, Richard G. 1982. *Mammals of the National Parks*. Johns Hopkins University Press. Baltimore, Md. 310 pp.

Vaughan, Terry A. 1972. *Mammalogy*. W. B. Saunders. Philadelphia. 463 pp.

Walker, Ernest P. 1964. *Mammals of the World*. Johns Hopkins University Press. Baltimore, Md. 1500 pp.

Index

A CATALOG OF SELECTED
DOVER BOOKS
IN ALL FIELDS OF INTEREST

A CATALOG OF SELECTED DOVER
BOOKS IN ALL FIELDS OF INTEREST

CONCERNING THE SPIRITUAL IN ART, Wassily Kandinsky. Pioneering work by father of abstract art. Thoughts on color theory, nature of art. Analysis of earlier masters. 12 illustrations. 80pp. of text. 5⅜ x 8½.   23411-8 Pa. $3.95

ANIMALS: 1,419 Copyright-Free Illustrations of Mammals, Birds, Fish, Insects, etc., Jim Harter (ed.). Clear wood engravings present, in extremely lifelike poses, over 1,000 species of animals. One of the most extensive pictorial sourcebooks of its kind. Captions. Index. 284pp. 9 x 12.   23766-4 Pa. $12.95

CELTIC ART: The Methods of Construction, George Bain. Simple geometric techniques for making Celtic interlacements, spirals, Kells-type initials, animals, humans, etc. Over 500 illustrations. 160pp. 9 x 12. (USO)   22923-8 Pa. $9.95

AN ATLAS OF ANATOMY FOR ARTISTS, Fritz Schider. Most thorough reference work on art anatomy in the world. Hundreds of illustrations, including selections from works by Vesalius, Leonardo, Goya, Ingres, Michelangelo, others. 593 illustrations. 192pp. 7⅛ x 10¼.   20241-0 Pa. $9.95

CELTIC HAND STROKE-BY-STROKE (Irish Half-Uncial from "The Book of Kells"): An Arthur Baker Calligraphy Manual, Arthur Baker. Complete guide to creating each letter of the alphabet in distinctive Celtic manner. Covers hand position, strokes, pens, inks, paper, more. Illustrated. 48pp. 8¼ x 11.   24336-2 Pa. $3.95

EASY ORIGAMI, John Montroll. Charming collection of 32 projects (hat, cup, pelican, piano, swan, many more) specially designed for the novice origami hobbyist. Clearly illustrated easy-to-follow instructions insure that even beginning papercrafters will achieve successful results. 48pp. 8¼ x 11.   27298-2 Pa. $3.50

THE COMPLETE BOOK OF BIRDHOUSE CONSTRUCTION FOR WOODWORKERS, Scott D. Campbell. Detailed instructions, illustrations, tables. Also data on bird habitat and instinct patterns. Bibliography. 3 tables. 63 illustrations in 15 figures. 48pp. 5¼ x 8½.   24407-5 Pa. $2.50

BLOOMINGDALE'S ILLUSTRATED 1886 CATALOG: Fashions, Dry Goods and Housewares, Bloomingdale Brothers. Famed merchants' extremely rare catalog depicting about 1,700 products: clothing, housewares, firearms, dry goods, jewelry, more. Invaluable for dating, identifying vintage items. Also, copyright-free graphics for artists, designers. Co-published with Henry Ford Museum & Greenfield Village. 160pp. 8¼ x 11.   25780-0 Pa. $10.95

HISTORIC COSTUME IN PICTURES, Braun & Schneider. Over 1,450 costumed figures in clearly detailed engravings–from dawn of civilization to end of 19th century. Captions. Many folk costumes. 256pp. 8⅜ x 11¾.   23150-X Pa. $12.95

STICKLEY CRAFTSMAN FURNITURE CATALOGS, Gustav Stickley and L. & J. G. Stickley. Beautiful, functional furniture in two authentic catalogs from 1910. 594 illustrations, including 277 photos, show settles, rockers, armchairs, reclining chairs, bookcases, desks, tables. 183pp. 6½ x 9¼. 23838-5 Pa. $9.95

AMERICAN LOCOMOTIVES IN HISTORIC PHOTOGRAPHS: 1858 to 1949, Ron Ziel (ed.). A rare collection of 126 meticulously detailed official photographs, called "builder portraits," of American locomotives that majestically chronicle the rise of steam locomotive power in America. Introduction. Detailed captions. xi + 129pp. 9 x 12. 27393-8 Pa. $12.95

AMERICA'S LIGHTHOUSES: An Illustrated History, Francis Ross Holland, Jr. Delightfully written, profusely illustrated fact-filled survey of over 200 American lighthouses since 1716. History, anecdotes, technological advances, more. 240pp. 8 x 10¾. 25576-X Pa. $12.95

TOWARDS A NEW ARCHITECTURE, Le Corbusier. Pioneering manifesto by founder of "International School." Technical and aesthetic theories, views of industry, economics, relation of form to function, "mass-production split" and much more. Profusely illustrated. 320pp. 6⅛ x 9¼. (USO) 25023-7 Pa. $9.95

HOW THE OTHER HALF LIVES, Jacob Riis. Famous journalistic record, exposing poverty and degradation of New York slums around 1900, by major social reformer. 100 striking and influential photographs. 233pp. 10 x 7⅞. 22012-5 Pa. $10.95

FRUIT KEY AND TWIG KEY TO TREES AND SHRUBS, William M. Harlow. One of the handiest and most widely used identification aids. Fruit key covers 120 deciduous and evergreen species; twig key 160 deciduous species. Easily used. Over 300 photographs. 126pp. 5⅜ x 8½. 20511-8 Pa. $3.95

COMMON BIRD SONGS, Dr. Donald J. Borror. Songs of 60 most common U.S. birds: robins, sparrows, cardinals, bluejays, finches, more—arranged in order of increasing complexity. Up to 9 variations of songs of each species.
Cassette and manual 99911-4 $8.95

ORCHIDS AS HOUSE PLANTS, Rebecca Tyson Northen. Grow cattleyas and many other kinds of orchids—in a window, in a case, or under artificial light. 63 illustrations. 148pp. 5⅜ x 8½. 23261-1 Pa. $4.95

MONSTER MAZES, Dave Phillips. Masterful mazes at four levels of difficulty. Avoid deadly perils and evil creatures to find magical treasures. Solutions for all 32 exciting illustrated puzzles. 48pp. 8¼ x 11. 26005-4 Pa. $2.95

MOZART'S DON GIOVANNI (DOVER OPERA LIBRETTO SERIES), Wolfgang Amadeus Mozart. Introduced and translated by Ellen H. Bleiler. Standard Italian libretto, with complete English translation. Convenient and thoroughly portable—an ideal companion for reading along with a recording or the performance itself. Introduction. List of characters. Plot summary. 121pp. 5¼ x 8½. 24944-1 Pa. $2.95

TECHNICAL MANUAL AND DICTIONARY OF CLASSICAL BALLET, Gail Grant. Defines, explains, comments on steps, movements, poses and concepts. 15-page pictorial section. Basic book for student, viewer. 127pp. 5⅜ x 8½. 21843-0 Pa. $4.95

BRASS INSTRUMENTS: Their History and Development, Anthony Baines. Authoritative, updated survey of the evolution of trumpets, trombones, bugles, cornets, French horns, tubas and other brass wind instruments. Over 140 illustrations and 48 music examples. Corrected and updated by author. New preface. Bibliography. 320pp. 5⅜ x 8½. 27574-4 Pa. $9.95

HOLLYWOOD GLAMOR PORTRAITS, John Kobal (ed.). 145 photos from 1926-49. Harlow, Gable, Bogart, Bacall; 94 stars in all. Full background on photographers, technical aspects. 160pp. 8⅜ x 11¼. 23352-9 Pa. $12.95

MAX AND MORITZ, Wilhelm Busch. Great humor classic in both German and English. Also 10 other works: "Cat and Mouse," "Plisch and Plumm," etc. 216pp. 5⅜ x 8½. 20181-3 Pa. $6.95

THE RAVEN AND OTHER FAVORITE POEMS, Edgar Allan Poe. Over 40 of the author's most memorable poems: "The Bells," "Ulalume," "Israfel," "To Helen," "The Conqueror Worm," "Eldorado," "Annabel Lee," many more. Alphabetic lists of titles and first lines. 64pp. 5³⁄₁₆ x 8¼. 26685-0 Pa. $1.00

PERSONAL MEMOIRS OF U. S. GRANT, Ulysses Simpson Grant. Intelligent, deeply moving firsthand account of Civil War campaigns, considered by many the finest military memoirs ever written. Includes letters, historic photographs, maps and more. 528pp. 6⅛ x 9¼. 28587-1 Pa. $11.95

AMULETS AND SUPERSTITIONS, E. A. Wallis Budge. Comprehensive discourse on origin, powers of amulets in many ancient cultures: Arab, Persian Babylonian, Assyrian, Egyptian, Gnostic, Hebrew, Phoenician, Syriac, etc. Covers cross, swastika, crucifix, seals, rings, stones, etc. 584pp. 5⅜ x 8½. 23573-4 Pa. $12.95

RUSSIAN STORIES/PYCCKNE PACCKA3bl: A Dual-Language Book, edited by Gleb Struve. Twelve tales by such masters as Chekhov, Tolstoy, Dostoevsky, Pushkin, others. Excellent word-for-word English translations on facing pages, plus teaching and study aids, Russian/English vocabulary, biographical/critical introductions, more. 416pp. 5⅜ x 8½. 26244-8 Pa. $8.95

PHILADELPHIA THEN AND NOW: 60 Sites Photographed in the Past and Present, Kenneth Finkel and Susan Oyama. Rare photographs of City Hall, Logan Square, Independence Hall, Betsy Ross House, other landmarks juxtaposed with contemporary views. Captures changing face of historic city. Introduction. Captions. 128pp. 8¼ x 11. 25790-8 Pa. $9.95

AIA ARCHITECTURAL GUIDE TO NASSAU AND SUFFOLK COUNTIES, LONG ISLAND, The American Institute of Architects, Long Island Chapter, and the Society for the Preservation of Long Island Antiquities. Comprehensive, well-researched and generously illustrated volume brings to life over three centuries of Long Island's great architectural heritage. More than 240 photographs with authoritative, extensively detailed captions. 176pp. 8¼ x 11. 26946-9 Pa. $14.95

NORTH AMERICAN INDIAN LIFE: Customs and Traditions of 23 Tribes, Elsie Clews Parsons (ed.). 27 fictionalized essays by noted anthropologists examine religion, customs, government, additional facets of life among the Winnebago, Crow, Zuni, Eskimo, other tribes. 480pp. 6⅛ x 9¼. 27377-6 Pa. $10.95

FRANK LLOYD WRIGHT'S HOLLYHOCK HOUSE, Donald Hoffmann. Lavishly illustrated, carefully documented study of one of Wright's most controversial residential designs. Over 120 photographs, floor plans, elevations, etc. Detailed perceptive text by noted Wright scholar. Index. 128pp. 9¼ x 10¾. 27133-1 Pa. $11.95

THE MALE AND FEMALE FIGURE IN MOTION: 60 Classic Photographic Sequences, Eadweard Muybridge. 60 true-action photographs of men and women walking, running, climbing, bending, turning, etc., reproduced from rare 19th-century masterpiece. vi + 121pp. 9 x 12.   24745-7 Pa. $10.95

1001 QUESTIONS ANSWERED ABOUT THE SEASHORE, N. J. Berrill and Jacquelyn Berrill. Queries answered about dolphins, sea snails, sponges, starfish, fishes, shore birds, many others. Covers appearance, breeding, growth, feeding, much more. 305pp. 5¼ x 8¼.   23366-9 Pa. $8.95

GUIDE TO OWL WATCHING IN NORTH AMERICA, Donald S. Heintzelman. Superb guide offers complete data and descriptions of 19 species: barn owl, screech owl, snowy owl, many more. Expert coverage of owl-watching equipment, conservation, migrations and invasions, etc. Guide to observing sites. 84 illustrations. xiii + 193pp. 5⅜ x 8½.   27344-X Pa. $8.95

MEDICINAL AND OTHER USES OF NORTH AMERICAN PLANTS: A Historical Survey with Special Reference to the Eastern Indian Tribes, Charlotte Erichsen-Brown. Chronological historical citations document 500 years of usage of plants, trees, shrubs native to eastern Canada, northeastern U.S. Also complete identifying information. 343 illustrations. 544pp. 6½ x 9¼.   25951-X Pa. $12.95

STORYBOOK MAZES, Dave Phillips. 23 stories and mazes on two-page spreads: Wizard of Oz, Treasure Island, Robin Hood, etc. Solutions. 64pp. 8¼ x 11.
23628-5 Pa. $2.95

NEGRO FOLK MUSIC, U.S.A., Harold Courlander. Noted folklorist's scholarly yet readable analysis of rich and varied musical tradition. Includes authentic versions of over 40 folk songs. Valuable bibliography and discography. xi + 324pp. 5⅜ x 8½.
27350-4 Pa. $9.95

MOVIE-STAR PORTRAITS OF THE FORTIES, John Kobal (ed.). 163 glamor, studio photos of 106 stars of the 1940s: Rita Hayworth, Ava Gardner, Marlon Brando, Clark Gable, many more. 176pp. 8⅞ x 11¼.   23546-7 Pa. $12.95

BENCHLEY LOST AND FOUND, Robert Benchley. Finest humor from early 30s, about pet peeves, child psychologists, post office and others. Mostly unavailable elsewhere. 73 illustrations by Peter Arno and others. 183pp. 5⅜ x 8½. 22410-4 Pa. $6.95

YEKL and THE IMPORTED BRIDEGROOM AND OTHER STORIES OF YIDDISH NEW YORK, Abraham Cahan. Film Hester Street based on Yekl (1896). Novel, other stories among first about Jewish immigrants on N.Y.'s East Side. 240pp. 5⅜ x 8½.   22427-9 Pa. $6.95

SELECTED POEMS, Walt Whitman. Generous sampling from *Leaves of Grass*. Twenty-four poems include "I Hear America Singing," "Song of the Open Road," "I Sing the Body Electric," "When Lilacs Last in the Dooryard Bloom'd," "O Captain! My Captain!"—all reprinted from an authoritative edition. Lists of titles and first lines. 128pp. 5³⁄₁₆ x 8¼.   26878-0 Pa. $1.00

THE BEST TALES OF HOFFMANN, E. T. A. Hoffmann. 10 of Hoffmann's most important stories: "Nutcracker and the King of Mice," "The Golden Flowerpot," etc. 458pp. 5⅜ x 8½. 21793-0 Pa. $9.95

FROM FETISH TO GOD IN ANCIENT EGYPT, E. A. Wallis Budge. Rich detailed survey of Egyptian conception of "God" and gods, magic, cult of animals, Osiris, more. Also, superb English translations of hymns and legends. 240 illustrations. 545pp. 5⅜ x 8½. 25803-3 Pa. $13.95

FRENCH STORIES/CONTES FRANÇAIS: A Dual-Language Book, Wallace Fowlie. Ten stories by French masters, Voltaire to Camus: "Micromegas" by Voltaire; "The Atheist's Mass" by Balzac; "Minuet" by de Maupassant; "The Guest" by Camus, six more. Excellent English translations on facing pages. Also French-English vocabulary list, exercises, more. 352pp. 5⅜ x 8½. 26443-2 Pa. $8.95

CHICAGO AT THE TURN OF THE CENTURY IN PHOTOGRAPHS: 122 Historic Views from the Collections of the Chicago Historical Society, Larry A. Viskochil. Rare large-format prints offer detailed views of City Hall, State Street, the Loop, Hull House, Union Station, many other landmarks, circa 1904-1913. Introduction. Captions. Maps. 144pp. 9⅜ x 12¼. 24656-6 Pa. $12.95

OLD BROOKLYN IN EARLY PHOTOGRAPHS, 1865-1929, William Lee Younger. Luna Park, Gravesend race track, construction of Grand Army Plaza, moving of Hotel Brighton, etc. 157 previously unpublished photographs. 165pp. 8⅞ x 11¾. 23587-4 Pa. $13.95

THE MYTHS OF THE NORTH AMERICAN INDIANS, Lewis Spence. Rich anthology of the myths and legends of the Algonquins, Iroquois, Pawnees and Sioux, prefaced by an extensive historical and ethnological commentary. 36 illustrations. 480pp. 5⅜ x 8½. 25967-6 Pa. $8.95

AN ENCYCLOPEDIA OF BATTLES: Accounts of Over 1,560 Battles from 1479 B.C. to the Present, David Eggenberger. Essential details of every major battle in recorded history from the first battle of Megiddo in 1479 B.C. to Grenada in 1984. List of Battle Maps. New Appendix covering the years 1967-1984. Index. 99 illustrations. 544pp. 6½ x 9¼. 24913-1 Pa. $14.95

SAILING ALONE AROUND THE WORLD, Captain Joshua Slocum. First man to sail around the world, alone, in small boat. One of great feats of seamanship told in delightful manner. 67 illustrations. 294pp. 5⅜ x 8½. 20326-3 Pa. $5.95

ANARCHISM AND OTHER ESSAYS, Emma Goldman. Powerful, penetrating, prophetic essays on direct action, role of minorities, prison reform, puritan hypocrisy, violence, etc. 271pp. 5⅜ x 8½. 22484-8 Pa. $6.95

MYTHS OF THE HINDUS AND BUDDHISTS, Ananda K. Coomaraswamy and Sister Nivedita. Great stories of the epics; deeds of Krishna, Shiva, taken from puranas, Vedas, folk tales; etc. 32 illustrations. 400pp. 5⅜ x 8½. 21759-0 Pa. $10.95

BEYOND PSYCHOLOGY, Otto Rank. Fear of death, desire of immortality, nature of sexuality, social organization, creativity, according to Rankian system. 291pp. 5⅜ x 8½. 20485-5 Pa. $8.95

A THEOLOGICO-POLITICAL TREATISE, Benedict Spinoza. Also contains unfinished Political Treatise. Great classic on religious liberty, theory of government on common consent. R. Elwes translation. Total of 421pp. 5⅜ x 8½. 20249-6 Pa. $9.95

MY BONDAGE AND MY FREEDOM, Frederick Douglass. Born a slave, Douglass became outspoken force in antislavery movement. The best of Douglass' autobiographies. Graphic description of slave life. 464pp. 5⅜ x 8½. 22457-0 Pa. $8.95

FOLLOWING THE EQUATOR: A Journey Around the World, Mark Twain. Fascinating humorous account of 1897 voyage to Hawaii, Australia, India, New Zealand, etc. Ironic, bemused reports on peoples, customs, climate, flora and fauna, politics, much more. 197 illustrations. 720pp. 5⅜ x 8½. 26113-1 Pa. $15.95

THE PEOPLE CALLED SHAKERS, Edward D. Andrews. Definitive study of Shakers: origins, beliefs, practices, dances, social organization, furniture and crafts, etc. 33 illustrations. 351pp. 5⅜ x 8½. 21081-2 Pa. $8.95

THE MYTHS OF GREECE AND ROME, H. A. Guerber. A classic of mythology, generously illustrated, long prized for its simple, graphic, accurate retelling of the principal myths of Greece and Rome, and for its commentary on their origins and significance. With 64 illustrations by Michelangelo, Raphael, Titian, Rubens, Canova, Bernini and others. 480pp. 5⅜ x 8½. 27584-1 Pa. $9.95

PSYCHOLOGY OF MUSIC, Carl E. Seashore. Classic work discusses music as a medium from psychological viewpoint. Clear treatment of physical acoustics, auditory apparatus, sound perception, development of musical skills, nature of musical feeling, host of other topics. 88 figures. 408pp. 5⅜ x 8½. 21851-1 Pa. $10.95

THE PHILOSOPHY OF HISTORY, Georg W. Hegel. Great classic of Western thought develops concept that history is not chance but rational process, the evolution of freedom. 457pp. 5⅜ x 8½. 20112-0 Pa. $9.95

THE BOOK OF TEA, Kakuzo Okakura. Minor classic of the Orient: entertaining, charming explanation, interpretation of traditional Japanese culture in terms of tea ceremony. 94pp. 5⅜ x 8½. 20070-1 Pa. $3.95

LIFE IN ANCIENT EGYPT, Adolf Erman. Fullest, most thorough, detailed older account with much not in more recent books, domestic life, religion, magic, medicine, commerce, much more. Many illustrations reproduce tomb paintings, carvings, hieroglyphs, etc. 597pp. 5⅜ x 8½. 22632-8 Pa. $11.95

SUNDIALS, Their Theory and Construction, Albert Waugh. Far and away the best, most thorough coverage of ideas, mathematics concerned, types, construction, adjusting anywhere. Simple, nontechnical treatment allows even children to build several of these dials. Over 100 illustrations. 230pp. 5⅜ x 8½. 22947-5 Pa. $7.95

DYNAMICS OF FLUIDS IN POROUS MEDIA, Jacob Bear. For advanced students of ground water hydrology, soil mechanics and physics, drainage and irrigation engineering, and more. 335 illustrations. Exercises, with answers. 784pp. 6⅛ x 9¼. 65675-6 Pa. $19.95

SONGS OF EXPERIENCE: Facsimile Reproduction with 26 Plates in Full Color, William Blake. 26 full-color plates from a rare 1826 edition. Includes "The Tyger," "London," "Holy Thursday," and other poems. Printed text of poems. 48pp. 5¼ x 7. 24636-1 Pa. $4.95

OLD-TIME VIGNETTES IN FULL COLOR, Carol Belanger Grafton (ed.). Over 390 charming, often sentimental illustrations, selected from archives of Victorian graphics—pretty women posing, children playing, food, flowers, kittens and puppies, smiling cherubs, birds and butterflies, much more. All copyright-free. 48pp. 9¼ x 12¼. 27269-9 Pa. $7.95

PERSPECTIVE FOR ARTISTS, Rex Vicat Cole. Depth, perspective of sky and sea, shadows, much more, not usually covered. 391 diagrams, 81 reproductions of drawings and paintings. 279pp. 5⅜ x 8½. 22487-2 Pa. $7.95

DRAWING THE LIVING FIGURE, Joseph Sheppard. Innovative approach to artistic anatomy focuses on specifics of surface anatomy, rather than muscles and bones. Over 170 drawings of live models in front, back and side views, and in widely varying poses. Accompanying diagrams. 177 illustrations. Introduction. Index. 144pp. 8⅜ x11¼. 26723-7 Pa. $8.95

GOTHIC AND OLD ENGLISH ALPHABETS: 100 Complete Fonts, Dan X. Solo. Add power, elegance to posters, signs, other graphics with 100 stunning copyright-free alphabets: Blackstone, Dolbey, Germania, 97 more–including many lower-case, numerals, punctuation marks. 104pp. 8⅛ x 11. 24695-7 Pa. $8.95

HOW TO DO BEADWORK, Mary White. Fundamental book on craft from simple projects to five-bead chains and woven works. 106 illustrations. 142pp. 5⅜ x 8. 20697-1 Pa. $4.95

THE BOOK OF WOOD CARVING, Charles Marshall Sayers. Finest book for beginners discusses fundamentals and offers 34 designs. "Absolutely first rate . . . well thought out and well executed."–E. J. Tangerman. 118pp. 7¾ x 10⅝. 23654-4 Pa. $6.95

ILLUSTRATED CATALOG OF CIVIL WAR MILITARY GOODS: Union Army Weapons, Insignia, Uniform Accessories, and Other Equipment, Schuyler, Hartley, and Graham. Rare, profusely illustrated 1846 catalog includes Union Army uniform and dress regulations, arms and ammunition, coats, insignia, flags, swords, rifles, etc. 226 illustrations. 160pp. 9 x 12. 24939-5 Pa. $10.95

WOMEN'S FASHIONS OF THE EARLY 1900s: An Unabridged Republication of "New York Fashions, 1909," National Cloak & Suit Co. Rare catalog of mail-order fashions documents women's and children's clothing styles shortly after the turn of the century. Captions offer full descriptions, prices. Invaluable resource for fashion, costume historians. Approximately 725 illustrations. 128pp. 8⅜ x 11¼. 27276-1 Pa. $11.95

THE 1912 AND 1915 GUSTAV STICKLEY FURNITURE CATALOGS, Gustav Stickley. With over 200 detailed illustrations and descriptions, these two catalogs are essential reading and reference materials and identification guides for Stickley furniture. Captions cite materials, dimensions and prices. 112pp. 6½ x 9¼. 26676-1 Pa. $9.95

EARLY AMERICAN LOCOMOTIVES, John H. White, Jr. Finest locomotive engravings from early 19th century: historical (1804–74), main-line (after 1870), special, foreign, etc. 147 plates. 142pp. 11⅜ x 8¼. 22772-3 Pa. $10.95

THE TALL SHIPS OF TODAY IN PHOTOGRAPHS, Frank O. Braynard. Lavishly illustrated tribute to nearly 100 majestic contemporary sailing vessels: Amerigo Vespucci, Clearwater, Constitution, Eagle, Mayflower, Sea Cloud, Victory, many more. Authoritative captions provide statistics, background on each ship. 190 black-and-white photographs and illustrations. Introduction. 128pp. 8⅞ x 11¾. 27163-3 Pa. $13.95

EARLY NINETEENTH-CENTURY CRAFTS AND TRADES, Peter Stockham (ed.). Extremely rare 1807 volume describes to youngsters the crafts and trades of the day: brickmaker, weaver, dressmaker, bookbinder, ropemaker, saddler, many more. Quaint prose, charming illustrations for each craft. 20 black-and-white line illustrations. 192pp. 4⅝ x 6. 27293-1 Pa. $4.95

VICTORIAN FASHIONS AND COSTUMES FROM HARPER'S BAZAR, 1867–1898, Stella Blum (ed.). Day costumes, evening wear, sports clothes, shoes, hats, other accessories in over 1,000 detailed engravings. 320pp. 9⅜ x 12¼. 22990-4 Pa. $14.95

GUSTAV STICKLEY, THE CRAFTSMAN, Mary Ann Smith. Superb study surveys broad scope of Stickley's achievement, especially in architecture. Design philosophy, rise and fall of the Craftsman empire, descriptions and floor plans for many Craftsman houses, more. 86 black-and-white halftones. 31 line illustrations. Introduction 208pp. 6½ x 9¼. 27210-9 Pa. $9.95

THE LONG ISLAND RAIL ROAD IN EARLY PHOTOGRAPHS, Ron Ziel. Over 220 rare photos, informative text document origin (1844) and development of rail service on Long Island. Vintage views of early trains, locomotives, stations, passengers, crews, much more. Captions. 8⅞ x 11¾. 26301-0 Pa. $13.95

THE BOOK OF OLD SHIPS: From Egyptian Galleys to Clipper Ships, Henry B. Culver. Superb, authoritative history of sailing vessels, with 80 magnificent line illustrations. Galley, bark, caravel, longship, whaler, many more. Detailed, informative text on each vessel by noted naval historian. Introduction. 256pp. 5⅜ x 8½. 27332-6 Pa. $7.95

TEN BOOKS ON ARCHITECTURE, Vitruvius. The most important book ever written on architecture. Early Roman aesthetics, technology, classical orders, site selection, all other aspects. Morgan translation. 331pp. 5⅜ x 8½. 20645-9 Pa. $8.95

THE HUMAN FIGURE IN MOTION, Eadweard Muybridge. More than 4,500 stopped-action photos, in action series, showing undraped men, women, children jumping, lying down, throwing, sitting, wrestling, carrying, etc. 390pp. 7⅞ x 10⅝. 20204-6 Clothbd. $25.95

TREES OF THE EASTERN AND CENTRAL UNITED STATES AND CANADA, William M. Harlow. Best one-volume guide to 140 trees. Full descriptions, woodlore, range, etc. Over 600 illustrations. Handy size. 288pp. 4½ x 6⅜. 20395-6 Pa. $6.95

SONGS OF WESTERN BIRDS, Dr. Donald J. Borror. Complete song and call repertoire of 60 western species, including flycatchers, juncoes, cactus wrens, many more–includes fully illustrated booklet. Cassette and manual 99913-0 $8.95

GROWING AND USING HERBS AND SPICES, Milo Miloradovich. Versatile handbook provides all the information needed for cultivation and use of all the herbs and spices available in North America. 4 illustrations. Index. Glossary. 236pp. 5⅜ x 8½. 25058-X Pa. $6.95

BIG BOOK OF MAZES AND LABYRINTHS, Walter Shepherd. 50 mazes and labyrinths in all–classical, solid, ripple, and more–in one great volume. Perfect inexpensive puzzler for clever youngsters. Full solutions. 112pp. 8⅛ x 11. 22951-3 Pa. $4.95

PIANO TUNING, J. Cree Fischer. Clearest, best book for beginner, amateur. Simple repairs, raising dropped notes, tuning by easy method of flattened fifths. No previous skills needed. 4 illustrations. 201pp. 5⅜ x 8½.   23267-0 Pa. $6.95

A SOURCE BOOK IN THEATRICAL HISTORY, A. M. Nagler. Contemporary observers on acting, directing, make-up, costuming, stage props, machinery, scene design, from Ancient Greece to Chekhov. 611pp. 5⅜ x 8½.   20515-0 Pa. $12.95

THE COMPLETE NONSENSE OF EDWARD LEAR, Edward Lear. All nonsense limericks, zany alphabets, Owl and Pussycat, songs, nonsense botany, etc., illustrated by Lear. Total of 320pp. 5⅜ x 8½. (USO)   20167-8 Pa. $6.95

VICTORIAN PARLOUR POETRY: An Annotated Anthology, Michael R. Turner. 117 gems by Longfellow, Tennyson, Browning, many lesser-known poets. "The Village Blacksmith," "Curfew Must Not Ring Tonight," "Only a Baby Small," dozens more, often difficult to find elsewhere. Index of poets, titles, first lines. xxiii + 325pp. 5⅜ x 8¼.   27044-0 Pa. $8.95

DUBLINERS, James Joyce. Fifteen stories offer vivid, tightly focused observations of the lives of Dublin's poorer classes. At least one, "The Dead," is considered a masterpiece. Reprinted complete and unabridged from standard edition. 160pp. 5⅜₆ x 8¼. 26870-5 Pa. $1.00

THE HAUNTED MONASTERY and THE CHINESE MAZE MURDERS, Robert van Gulik. Two full novels by van Gulik, set in 7th-century China, continue adventures of Judge Dee and his companions. An evil Taoist monastery, seemingly supernatural events; overgrown topiary maze hides strange crimes. 27 illustrations. 328pp. 5⅜ x 8½.   23502-5 Pa. $8.95

THE BOOK OF THE SACRED MAGIC OF ABRAMELIN THE MAGE, translated by S. MacGregor Mathers. Medieval manuscript of ceremonial magic. Basic document in Aleister Crowley, Golden Dawn groups. 268pp. 5⅜ x 8½.
23211-5 Pa. $8.95

NEW RUSSIAN-ENGLISH AND ENGLISH-RUSSIAN DICTIONARY, M. A. O'Brien. This is a remarkably handy Russian dictionary, containing a surprising amount of information, including over 70,000 entries. 366pp. 4½ x 6⅛.
20208-9 Pa. $9.95

HISTORIC HOMES OF THE AMERICAN PRESIDENTS, Second, Revised Edition, Irvin Haas. A traveler's guide to American Presidential homes, most open to the public, depicting and describing homes occupied by every American President from George Washington to George Bush. With visiting hours, admission charges, travel routes. 175 photographs. Index. 160pp. 8¼ x 11.   26751-2 Pa. $11.95

NEW YORK IN THE FORTIES, Andreas Feininger. 162 brilliant photographs by the well-known photographer, formerly with *Life* magazine. Commuters, shoppers, Times Square at night, much else from city at its peak. Captions by John von Hartz. 181pp. 9¼ x 10¾.   23585-8 Pa. $12.95

INDIAN SIGN LANGUAGE, William Tomkins. Over 525 signs developed by Sioux and other tribes. Written instructions and diagrams. Also 290 pictographs. 111pp. 6⅛ x 9¼.   22029-X Pa. $3.95

ANATOMY: A Complete Guide for Artists, Joseph Sheppard. A master of figure drawing shows artists how to render human anatomy convincingly. Over 460 illustrations. 224pp. 8⅜ x 11¼. 27279-6 Pa. $10.95

MEDIEVAL CALLIGRAPHY: Its History and Technique, Marc Drogin. Spirited history, comprehensive instruction manual covers 13 styles (ca. 4th century thru 15th). Excellent photographs; directions for duplicating medieval techniques with modern tools. 224pp. 8⅜ x 11¼. 26142-5 Pa. $12.95

DRIED FLOWERS: How to Prepare Them, Sarah Whitlock and Martha Rankin. Complete instructions on how to use silica gel, meal and borax, perlite aggregate, sand and borax, glycerine and water to create attractive permanent flower arrangements. 12 illustrations. 32pp. 5⅜ x 8½. 21802-3 Pa. $1.00

EASY-TO-MAKE BIRD FEEDERS FOR WOODWORKERS, Scott D. Campbell. Detailed, simple-to-use guide for designing, constructing, caring for and using feeders. Text, illustrations for 12 classic and contemporary designs. 96pp. 5⅜ x 8½.
25847-5 Pa. $2.95

SCOTTISH WONDER TALES FROM MYTH AND LEGEND, Donald A. Mackenzie. 16 lively tales tell of giants rumbling down mountainsides, of a magic wand that turns stone pillars into warriors, of gods and goddesses, evil hags, powerful forces and more. 240pp. 5⅜ x 8½. 29677-6 Pa. $6.95

THE HISTORY OF UNDERCLOTHES, C. Willett Cunnington and Phyllis Cunnington. Fascinating, well-documented survey covering six centuries of English undergarments, enhanced with over 100 illustrations: 12th-century laced-up bodice, footed long drawers (1795), 19th-century bustles, l9th-century corsets for men, Victorian "bust improvers," much more. 272pp. 5⅜ x 8¼. 27124-2 Pa. $9.95

ARTS AND CRAFTS FURNITURE: The Complete Brooks Catalog of 1912, Brooks Manufacturing Co. Photos and detailed descriptions of more than 150 now very collectible furniture designs from the Arts and Crafts movement depict davenports, settees, buffets, desks, tables, chairs, bedsteads, dressers and more, all built of solid, quarter-sawed oak. Invaluable for students and enthusiasts of antiques, Americana and the decorative arts. 80pp. 6½ x 9¼. 27471-3 Pa. $8.95

HOW WE INVENTED THE AIRPLANE: An Illustrated History, Orville Wright. Fascinating firsthand account covers early experiments, construction of planes and motors, first flights, much more. Introduction and commentary by Fred C. Kelly. 76 photographs. 96pp. 8¼ x 11. 25662-6 Pa. $8.95

THE ARTS OF THE SAILOR: Knotting, Splicing and Ropework, Hervey Garrett Smith. Indispensable shipboard reference covers tools, basic knots and useful hitches; handsewing and canvas work, more. Over 100 illustrations. Delightful reading for sea lovers. 256pp. 5⅜ x 8½. 26440-8 Pa. $7.95

FRANK LLOYD WRIGHT'S FALLINGWATER: The House and Its History, Second, Revised Edition, Donald Hoffmann. A total revision—both in text and illustrations—of the standard document on Fallingwater, the boldest, most personal architectural statement of Wright's mature years, updated with valuable new material from the recently opened Frank Lloyd Wright Archives. "Fascinating"—*The New York Times*. 116 illustrations. 128pp. 9¼ x 10¾. 27430-6 Pa. $11.95

PHOTOGRAPHIC SKETCHBOOK OF THE CIVIL WAR, Alexander Gardner. 100 photos taken on field during the Civil War. Famous shots of Manassas Harper's Ferry, Lincoln, Richmond, slave pens, etc. 244pp. 10⅝ x 8¼.   22731-6 Pa. $9.95

FIVE ACRES AND INDEPENDENCE, Maurice G. Kains. Great back-to-the-land classic explains basics of self-sufficient farming. The one book to get. 95 illustrations. 397pp. 5⅜ x 8½.   20974-1 Pa. $7.95

SONGS OF EASTERN BIRDS, Dr. Donald J. Borror. Songs and calls of 60 species most common to eastern U.S.: warblers, woodpeckers, flycatchers, thrushes, larks, many more in high-quality recording.   Cassette and manual 99912-2 $9.95

A MODERN HERBAL, Margaret Grieve. Much the fullest, most exact, most useful compilation of herbal material. Gigantic alphabetical encyclopedia, from aconite to zedoary, gives botanical information, medical properties, folklore, economic uses, much else. Indispensable to serious reader. 161 illustrations. 888pp. 6½ x 9¼. 2-vol. set. (USO)   Vol. I: 22798-7 Pa. $9.95
        Vol. II: 22799-5 Pa. $9.95

HIDDEN TREASURE MAZE BOOK, Dave Phillips. Solve 34 challenging mazes accompanied by heroic tales of adventure. Evil dragons, people-eating plants, blood-thirsty giants, many more dangerous adversaries lurk at every twist and turn. 34 mazes, stories, solutions. 48pp. 8¼ x 11.   24566-7 Pa. $2.95

LETTERS OF W. A. MOZART, Wolfgang A. Mozart. Remarkable letters show bawdy wit, humor, imagination, musical insights, contemporary musical world; includes some letters from Leopold Mozart. 276pp. 5⅜ x 8½.   22859-2 Pa. $7.95

BASIC PRINCIPLES OF CLASSICAL BALLET, Agrippina Vaganova. Great Russian theoretician, teacher explains methods for teaching classical ballet. 118 illustrations. 175pp. 5⅜ x 8½.   22036-2 Pa. $5.95

THE JUMPING FROG, Mark Twain. Revenge edition. The original story of The Celebrated Jumping Frog of Calaveras County, a hapless French translation, and Twain's hilarious "retranslation" from the French. 12 illustrations. 66pp. 5⅜ x 8½.
        22686-7 Pa. $3.95

BEST REMEMBERED POEMS, Martin Gardner (ed.). The 126 poems in this superb collection of 19th- and 20th-century British and American verse range from Shelley's "To a Skylark" to the impassioned "Renascence" of Edna St. Vincent Millay and to Edward Lear's whimsical "The Owl and the Pussycat." 224pp. 5⅜ x 8½.
        27165-X Pa. $4.95

COMPLETE SONNETS, William Shakespeare. Over 150 exquisite poems deal with love, friendship, the tyranny of time, beauty's evanescence, death and other themes in language of remarkable power, precision and beauty. Glossary of archaic terms. 80pp. 5³⁄₁₆ x 8¼.   26686-9 Pa. $1.00

BODIES IN A BOOKSHOP, R. T. Campbell. Challenging mystery of blackmail and murder with ingenious plot and superbly drawn characters. In the best tradition of British suspense fiction. 192pp. 5⅜ x 8½.   24720-1 Pa. $6.95

THE WIT AND HUMOR OF OSCAR WILDE, Alvin Redman (ed.). More than 1,000 ripostes, paradoxes, wisecracks: Work is the curse of the drinking classes; I can resist everything except temptation; etc. 258pp. 5⅜ x 8½. 20602-5 Pa. $5.95

SHAKESPEARE LEXICON AND QUOTATION DICTIONARY, Alexander Schmidt. Full definitions, locations, shades of meaning in every word in plays and poems. More than 50,000 exact quotations. 1,485pp. 6½ x 9¼. 2-vol. set.
Vol. 1: 22726-X Pa. $16.95
Vol. 2: 22727-8 Pa. $16.95

SELECTED POEMS, Emily Dickinson. Over 100 best-known, best-loved poems by one of America's foremost poets, reprinted from authoritative early editions. No comparable edition at this price. Index of first lines. 64pp. 5³⁄₁₆ x 8¼.
26466-1 Pa. $1.00

CELEBRATED CASES OF JUDGE DEE (DEE GOONG AN), translated by Robert van Gulik. Authentic 18th-century Chinese detective novel; Dee and associates solve three interlocked cases. Led to van Gulik's own stories with same characters. Extensive introduction. 9 illustrations. 237pp. 5⅜ x 8½. 23337-5 Pa. $6.95

THE MALLEUS MALEFICARUM OF KRAMER AND SPRENGER, translated by Montague Summers. Full text of most important witchhunter's "bible," used by both Catholics and Protestants. 278pp. 6⅝ x 10. 22802-9 Pa. $12.95

SPANISH STORIES/CUENTOS ESPAÑOLES: A Dual-Language Book, Angel Flores (ed.). Unique format offers 13 great stories in Spanish by Cervantes, Borges, others. Faithful English translations on facing pages. 352pp. 5⅜ x 8½.
25399-6 Pa. $8.95

THE CHICAGO WORLD'S FAIR OF 1893: A Photographic Record, Stanley Appelbaum (ed.). 128 rare photos show 200 buildings, Beaux-Arts architecture, Midway, original Ferris Wheel, Edison's kinetoscope, more. Architectural emphasis; full text. 116pp. 8¼ x 11. 23990-X Pa. $9.95

OLD QUEENS, N.Y., IN EARLY PHOTOGRAPHS, Vincent F. Seyfried and William Asadorian. Over 160 rare photographs of Maspeth, Jamaica, Jackson Heights, and other areas. Vintage views of DeWitt Clinton mansion, 1939 World's Fair and more. Captions. 192pp. 8⅞ x 11. 26358-4 Pa. $12.95

CAPTURED BY THE INDIANS: 15 Firsthand Accounts, 1750-1870, Frederick Drimmer. Astounding true historical accounts of grisly torture, bloody conflicts, relentless pursuits, miraculous escapes and more, by people who lived to tell the tale. 384pp. 5⅜ x 8½. 24901-8 Pa. $8.95

THE WORLD'S GREAT SPEECHES, Lewis Copeland and Lawrence W. Lamm (eds.). Vast collection of 278 speeches of Greeks to 1970. Powerful and effective models; unique look at history. 842pp. 5⅜ x 8½. 20468-5 Pa. $14.95

THE BOOK OF THE SWORD, Sir Richard F. Burton. Great Victorian scholar/adventurer's eloquent, erudite history of the "queen of weapons"—from prehistory to early Roman Empire. Evolution and development of early swords, variations (sabre, broadsword, cutlass, scimitar, etc.), much more. 336pp. 6⅛ x 9¼.
25434-8 Pa. $9.95

AUTOBIOGRAPHY: The Story of My Experiments with Truth, Mohandas K. Gandhi. Boyhood, legal studies, purification, the growth of the Satyagraha (nonviolent protest) movement. Critical, inspiring work of the man responsible for the freedom of India. 480pp. 5⅜ x 8½. (USO)   24593-4 Pa. $8.95

CELTIC MYTHS AND LEGENDS, T. W. Rolleston. Masterful retelling of Irish and Welsh stories and tales. Cuchulain, King Arthur, Deirdre, the Grail, many more. First paperback edition. 58 full-page illustrations. 512pp. 5⅜ x 8½.   26507-2 Pa. $9.95

THE PRINCIPLES OF PSYCHOLOGY, William James. Famous long course complete, unabridged. Stream of thought, time perception, memory, experimental methods; great work decades ahead of its time. 94 figures. 1,391pp. 5⅜ x 8½. 2-vol. set.
Vol. I: 20381-6 Pa. $12.95
Vol. II: 20382-4 Pa. $12.95

THE WORLD AS WILL AND REPRESENTATION, Arthur Schopenhauer. Definitive English translation of Schopenhauer's life work, correcting more than 1,000 errors, omissions in earlier translations. Translated by E. F. J. Payne. Total of 1,269pp. 5⅜ x 8½. 2-vol. set.   Vol. 1: 21761-2 Pa. $11.95
Vol. 2: 21762-0 Pa. $12.95

MAGIC AND MYSTERY IN TIBET, Madame Alexandra David-Neel. Experiences among lamas, magicians, sages, sorcerers, Bonpa wizards. A true psychic discovery. 32 illustrations. 321pp. 5⅜ x 8½. (USO)   22682-4 Pa. $8.95

THE EGYPTIAN BOOK OF THE DEAD, E. A. Wallis Budge. Complete reproduction of Ani's papyrus, finest ever found. Full hieroglyphic text, interlinear transliteration, word-for-word translation, smooth translation. 533pp. 6½ x 9¼.
21866-X Pa. $10.95

MATHEMATICS FOR THE NONMATHEMATICIAN, Morris Kline. Detailed, college-level treatment of mathematics in cultural and historical context, with numerous exercises. Recommended Reading Lists. Tables. Numerous figures. 641pp. 5⅜ x 8½.
24823-2 Pa. $11.95

THEORY OF WING SECTIONS: Including a Summary of Airfoil Data, Ira H. Abbott and A. E. von Doenhoff. Concise compilation of subsonic aerodynamic characteristics of NACA wing sections, plus description of theory. 350pp. of tables. 693pp. 5⅜ x 8½.   60586-8 Pa. $14.95

THE RIME OF THE ANCIENT MARINER, Gustave Doré, S. T. Coleridge. Doré's finest work; 34 plates capture moods, subtleties of poem. Flawless full-size reproductions printed on facing pages with authoritative text of poem. "Beautiful. Simply beautiful."—*Publisher's Weekly.* 77pp. 9¼ x 12.   22305-1 Pa. $6.95

NORTH AMERICAN INDIAN DESIGNS FOR ARTISTS AND CRAFTSPEOPLE, Eva Wilson. Over 360 authentic copyright-free designs adapted from Navajo blankets, Hopi pottery, Sioux buffalo hides, more. Geometrics, symbolic figures, plant and animal motifs, etc. 128pp. 8⅜ x 11. (EUK)   25341-4 Pa. $8.95

SCULPTURE: Principles and Practice, Louis Slobodkin. Step-by-step approach to clay, plaster, metals, stone; classical and modern. 253 drawings, photos. 255pp. 8⅛ x 11.
22960-2 Pa. $11.95

THE INFLUENCE OF SEA POWER UPON HISTORY, 1660–1783, A. T. Mahan. Influential classic of naval history and tactics still used as text in war colleges. First paperback edition. 4 maps. 24 battle plans. 640pp. 5⅜ x 8½. 25509-3 Pa. $12.95

THE STORY OF THE TITANIC AS TOLD BY ITS SURVIVORS, Jack Winocour (ed.). What it was really like. Panic, despair, shocking inefficiency, and a little heroism. More thrilling than any fictional account. 26 illustrations. 320pp. 5⅜ x 8½.
20610-6 Pa. $8.95

FAIRY AND FOLK TALES OF THE IRISH PEASANTRY, William Butler Yeats (ed.). Treasury of 64 tales from the twilight world of Celtic myth and legend: "The Soul Cages," "The Kildare Pooka," "King O'Toole and his Goose," many more. Introduction and Notes by W. B. Yeats. 352pp. 5⅜ x 8½. 26941-8 Pa. $8.95

BUDDHIST MAHAYANA TEXTS, E. B. Cowell and Others (eds.). Superb, accurate translations of basic documents in Mahayana Buddhism, highly important in history of religions. The Buddha-karita of Asvaghosha, Larger Sukhavativyuha, more. 448pp. 5⅜ x 8½. 25552-2 Pa. $12.95

ONE TWO THREE . . . INFINITY: Facts and Speculations of Science, George Gamow. Great physicist's fascinating, readable overview of contemporary science: number theory, relativity, fourth dimension, entropy, genes, atomic structure, much more. 128 illustrations. Index. 352pp. 5⅜ x 8½. 25664-2 Pa. $8.95

ENGINEERING IN HISTORY, Richard Shelton Kirby, et al. Broad, nontechnical survey of history's major technological advances: birth of Greek science, industrial revolution, electricity and applied science, 20th-century automation, much more. 181 illustrations. ". . . excellent . . ."–*Isis.* Bibliography. vii + 530pp. 5⅜ x 8¼.
26412-2 Pa. $14.95

DALÍ ON MODERN ART: The Cuckolds of Antiquated Modern Art, Salvador Dalí. Influential painter skewers modern art and its practitioners. Outrageous evaluations of Picasso, Cézanne, Turner, more. 15 renderings of paintings discussed. 44 calligraphic decorations by Dalí. 96pp. 5⅜ x 8½. (USO) 29220-7 Pa. $4.95

ANTIQUE PLAYING CARDS: A Pictorial History, Henry René D'Allemagne. Over 900 elaborate, decorative images from rare playing cards (14th–20th centuries): Bacchus, death, dancing dogs, hunting scenes, royal coats of arms, players cheating, much more. 96pp. 9¼ x 12¼. 29265-7 Pa. $11.95

MAKING FURNITURE MASTERPIECES: 30 Projects with Measured Drawings, Franklin H. Gottshall. Step-by-step instructions, illustrations for constructing handsome, useful pieces, among them a Sheraton desk, Chippendale chair, Spanish desk, Queen Anne table and a William and Mary dressing mirror. 224pp. 8⅛ x 11¼.
29338-6 Pa. $13.95

THE FOSSIL BOOK: A Record of Prehistoric Life, Patricia V. Rich et al. Profusely illustrated definitive guide covers everything from single-celled organisms and dinosaurs to birds and mammals and the interplay between climate and man. Over 1,500 illustrations. 760pp. 7½ x 10⅛. 29371-8 Pa. $29.95

Prices subject to change without notice.

Available at your book dealer or write for free catalog to Dept. GI, Dover Publications, Inc., 31 East 2nd St., Mineola, N.Y. 11501. Dover publishes more than 500 books each year on science, elementary and advanced mathematics, biology, music, art, literary history, social sciences and other areas.